GREAT
WESTERN
HORSE POWER

GREAT WESTERN
HORSE POWER

Janet Russell

OPC

Oxford Publishing Co.

Dedication

To the late Jim Russell, for inspiration, encouragement and assistance.

A catalogue record for this book is available from the British Library.

ISBN 0 86093 425 X

Oxford Publishing Co. is an imprint of Haynes Publishing, Sparkford, near Yeovil, Somerset BA22 7JJ

Printed in Great Britain by Butler & Tanner Ltd, Frome and London
Typeset in Times Roman Medium by MS Filmsetting Limited, Frome, Somerset

Publisher's note: Many of the scale drawings have been reproduced from faded originals. These are included because of their historical interest although some clarity may have been lost. The original scale for most of the GWR drawings was $1\frac{1}{2}$ in to 1 ft.

Contents

Introduction

At first glance a work dealing with the Great Western Railway Company and its association with horses might seem to describe two extremes. On the one hand, the railroad has always been considered to be a system of transportation primarily involving the steam locomotive, eventually eclipsed by the internal combustion engine and finally the modern electric locomotive. A horse, on the other hand, is always regarded as the four-legged animal which laboured on the highways of the United Kingdom in the days of the stage coach and turnpike roads, worked long hours tilling and ploughing the farms of our grandfathers, and was a means of recreation for the landed gentry both for fox hunting and on the racecourse.

It is odd that the many hundreds of writers on the subject of railway history have to a large extent ignored the major part the working horse has played in the development of the railways of Britain. It seems to have been completely forgotten that the very first railways were operated by willing horses in chain harness, dragging wagons and even passenger carriages along the early railways or plateways as they were originally called, long before the introduction of the steam engine. Even after adopting the steam engine for operating passenger and freight traffic, the GWR owned and cared for many thousands of horses which were used for collecting and delivering merchandise in addition to more specialised tasks such as shunting and hauling the company fire engine and other less dramatic vehicles.

The Great Western Railway was one of the first English railway companies to realise the value of the horse as a means of taking both passengers and freight to and from its stations. Horse drawn trams and omnibuses were a common sight at stations, in the same way as buses and taxis are seen now.

In addition to owning many superb horses of their own, the GWR were well aware of the need to convey horses around the country. In the early days, the gentry and even royalty would always expect to undertake any railway journey accompanied by their road carriages and horses. Special rail vehicles were provided for this traffic. Later, apart from the movement of horses from farms, sales, shows and even on military service, whole trains were especially composed to transport the Hunt from the kennels to the Meet, thereby avoiding long journeys by the Master, Whips, hunt followers and of course, the hounds.

Having been involved in equestrian matters for many years and after *Company's Servants* was published (Wild Swan), I thought a companion volume dealing with the other forgotten railway workers, those with four legs, a mane and a tail, would perhaps prove interesting to both the railway enthusiast and horse-lover alike.

To my knowledge, the subject has never been written about in depth before. Like the *Company's Servants*, surely the part played by the horse on the Great Western Railway in the past is not only of considerable importance, but very intriguing.

It was not until I carried out detailed research at Kew, and interviewed several former GWR employees, that I realised just how much these noble animals were essential to the smooth and successful operation of the Great Western Railway. Unfortunately there are pitifully few photographs of the working horses, but those that were still in a fit state to be reproduced have been included. I have found the exercise fascinating and I hope my readers will feel that it has been worthwhile, and that a small missing chapter of railway history has at last had some attention.

I would like to dedicate the work to all those uncomplaining quadrupeds, who for a bale of hay and a bucket of corn, helped the wheels of the railway to turn.

History

Crudely designed but sturdily built vehicles were used to transport coal and other minerals away from the mines. This Northern mine wagon of 1764 carried 53 cwt of coal and was pulled by a single horse down to the docks for shipment – *Fig. 1*. The weight and vehicle became standardised and were called the 'Newcastle Chaldron'.

Inside the mines Welsh cobs and New Forest ponies hauled small trains of mine tubs from the mine face to the shaft on narrow gauge wooden rails. Both breeds are renowned for their sturdiness and strength in relation to their size. The ponies were comfortably stabled underground and received excellent care. It is recorded that a miner could be fined for mistreating a pit pony. In 1881 the five horses at Cilely Colliery in Glamorgan were added to the register of Great Western owned horses. Recent press articles report that there are still some 60 ponies employed in Britain's mines. They enjoy two weeks' holiday on the surface when their eyes are protected by soft blinkers against the unaccustomed glare of the surface daylight.

The South Wales coal wagon of 1773 – *Fig. 2*, is of a

Fig. 1

Fig. 2

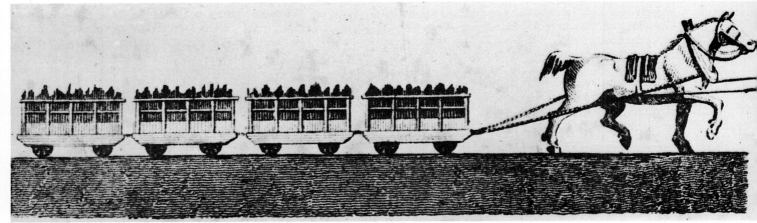

Fig. 3

very similar design to the upper photograph and held a comparable quantity of coal. One of George Stephenson's earliest memories was of keeping his four brothers and sisters out of the way of the horse-drawn wagons which ran on the wooden rails almost immediately in front of the cottage door. He recalled that coal was hauled from the local pits at Wylam by "enormous horses". Bearing in mind that he was only five years old at the time, they were probably well muscled horses of 15 to 16 hands high. (A hand is four inches.)

In order that the maximum load could be hauled by each horse, several wagons were fastened together to form a 'train', *Fig. 3*. It is mentioned in the archives that at the opening of the Croydon, Merstham & Godstone Railway in 1805, one horse pulled a load of 55 tons 6½ cwt in 16 wagons. A more common weight for a horse to pull on rails was 10 tons, an increase of 9 tons over the much less economic road wagon holding one ton.

When metal tracks were introduced on the early railways, each horse pulled a train of four trucks for an average of 174 miles each week. The railway was frequently on a falling gradient where the trucks could travel solely by gravity. In order for the horse to be conveyed to the bottom of the gradient, a small special vehicle was designed to enable the horse to ride down with the train, instead of being walked, and this was known as a Dandy Cart.

When a Dandy Cart was included in the train, the horse was detached at the top of the descent and installed in the Dandy. The whole train then ran downhill at considerable speed. In this way the weekly mileage of the horse was increased to 240 miles, an increase of some 40%. The horses quickly recognised the points where they mounted the Dandy. So much so, that when it was not included in the train they still ceased to pull and attempted to get into an ordinary coal wagon! The sequence is shown in *Fig. 4*.

One delightful story was related about a grey horse who sensed danger approaching in the form of a runaway train heading directly for his own Dandy Cart.

Fig. 4

Diagram shewing Method of Using

DANDY CART

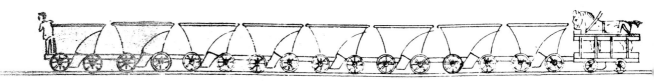

He immediately leapt out and saved his own skin. On another occasion he was unable to leap out so he transferred to the coal wagon in front and continued his journey in a somewhat precarious fashion on top of the coal like a statue!

Fig. 5. A more detailed diagram of the construction of a Dandy Cart. The harness worn by the rather idealised horse was extremely simple. Quarter straps supported a broad leather band passing round the quarters of the horse to which a single short chain and hook were attached for pulling the wagons uphill. The strain was transferred to the collar by means of two short lengths of chain. The tug chain from the hames to the saddle or back pad, and a short length of trace chain from the saddle ring buckled on to the broad leather band at the point where it was attached to the loin strap. No blinkers were worn and the driver perched on the frame of the leading coal wagon wielding a short whip with which to encourage the horse.

The vehicle illustrated in *Fig. 6* was designed to avoid the necessity of tipping the small mine tubs. They were placed sideways on a flat carriage and travelled direct to the port, returning empty or with mining supplies. These were often privately owned and ran on company railway lines for a small fee.

In 1821 George Stephenson and Mr Pease of the Liverpool & Manchester Railway debated the choice of building a railway or a tramway for the recently approved Stockton & Darlington Railway. Stephenson was requested to re-survey the proposed route prior to being responsible for its construction. Despite being firmly convinced that one locomotive was worth fifty horses and would 'entirely supersede all horse power on the railways' he did not boast of his own experiments and recommended the use of stationary engines to haul the goods wagons up the gradients when horses could not cope.

The building of a railway involved the transport of the workers to the site, the carriage of materials such as sleepers, ballast, tools and rails. Many horses were used for haulage in all weathers and camps were set up on the route of the proposed railway to house both men and horses. A blacksmith at each camp cared for the feet of the horses as well as making and repairing tools required for the construction gang.

Fig. 7 shows the excavation of a cutting to produce a more even gradient. A tremendous amount of manual labour was involved as the digging was done by 'navvies'. As the depth increased the spoil was removed in barrows. A series of sloping boards was arranged up the sides on

Fig. 5

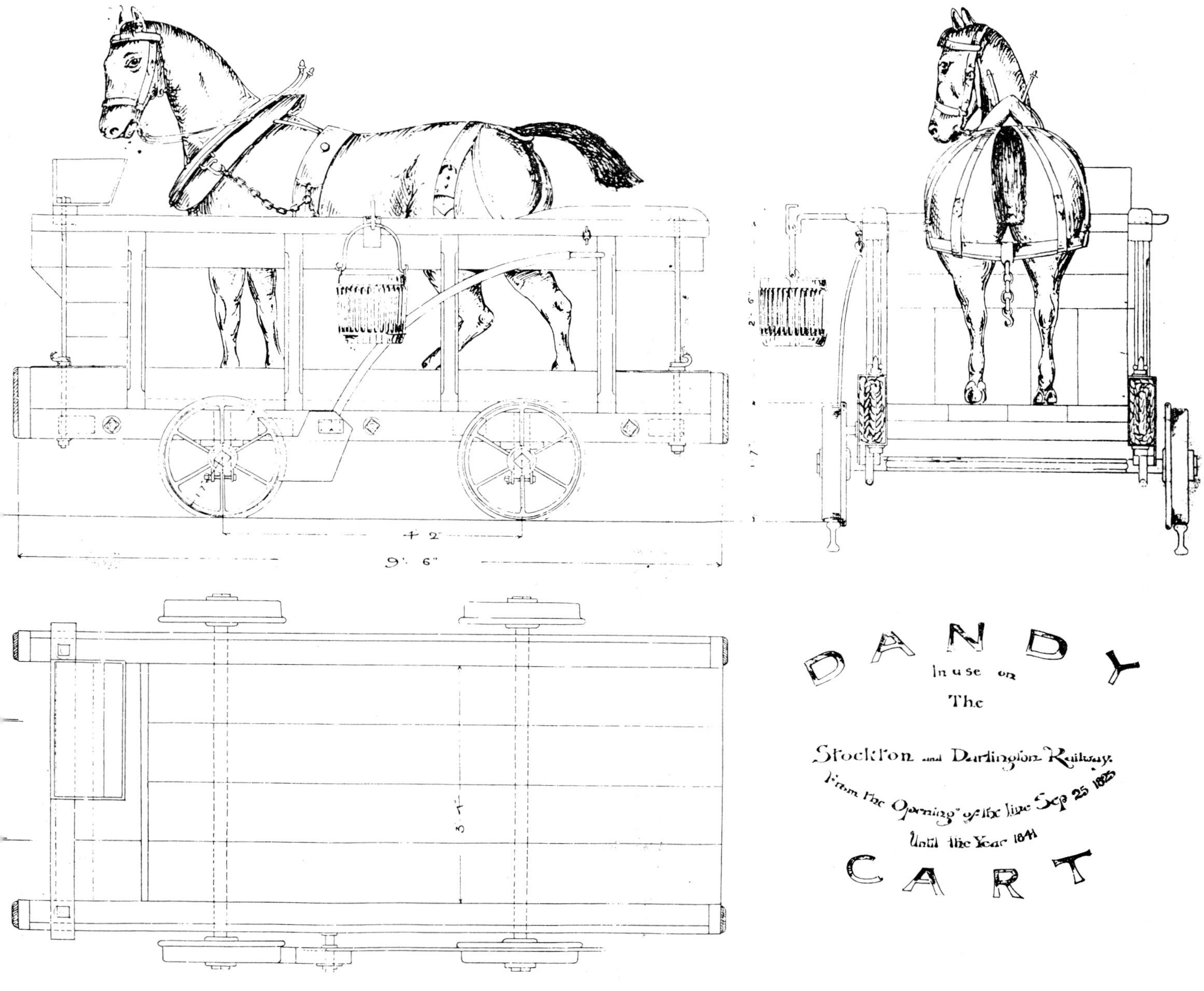

DANDY
In use on
The
Stockton and Darlington Railway.
From the Opening of the line Sep 25 1825
Until the Year 1841
CART

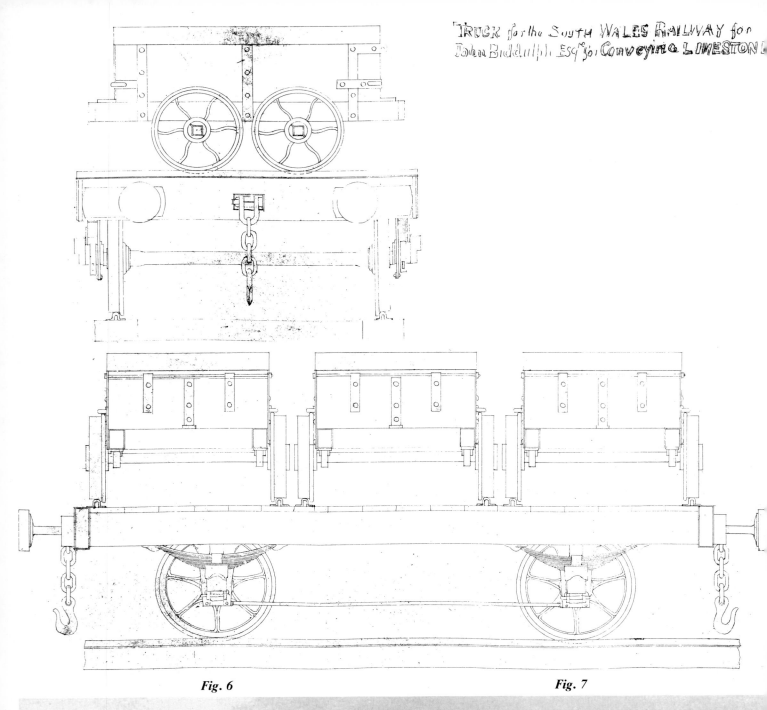

TRUCK for the South WALES RAILWAY for
John Biddulph Esq.^o, Conveying LIMESTONE

Fig. 6　　　　　　　　　　　　　　　　　　*Fig. 7*

which the full wheelbarrows were pushed. A horse walked along the top of the cutting, almost parallel to the course of the railway and hauled the barrow up by a long rope passing over a pulley wheel above the line of the boards. Each barrow was guided up the slippery slope by a man, but the slightest slip or untimely jerk by the horse or man would upset the precarious balance of the barrow and result in an accident. Later horse-powered gins enabled the rope to be wound round a large horizontal drum while the horse walked in a circular track or 'gin race'.

Fig. 8. Gradually the methods became slightly more sophisticated. In this photograph the horses are pulling tip carts full of spoil dug from a cutting which is needed here to create a level embankment on the Leatherhead branch of the Surbiton & Guildford Railway in 1884.

The very first steam locomotive to move upon rails was recorded on 11th February 1804, when Richard Trevithick drove his 'Tram Waggon' weighing 4½ tons on the plate rails of the Penydaren mine railway. Its speed over the nine miles averaged less than 5 mph and it was removed from the track after many of the plate rails had broken. The principal success of the early locomotive depended on their economy compared with horsepower. Careful calculations were made between the two methods of haulage which were shown to be on a par after one year. It was only after the introduction and fitting of the blast pipe in 1830, and which it was thought would terrify grazing horses and cattle, that the speed of the locomotive exceeded the walking pace of a horse. Constant reference was made to the amount that a locomotive could haul in comparison to the more generally accepted horses. This was the origin of the widely accepted term 'horsepower' which is used even today to denote the power potential of any machine used in transport.

The opening of the Stockton & Darlington Railway in 1825, *Fig. 9*, went some way towards tipping the balance of public opinion in favour of steam locomotion. To the delight of the crowd, George Stephenson's *Locomotion* pulled a long train of assorted passenger wagons, pre-ceded by the obligatory horse and rider bearing a red flag! It should be noted at this point that the first horse-drawn passenger train was on the Mumbles Railway, Swansea, in 1807.

Railways were much opposed during the required Parliamentary procedure, and this continued during construction. Not only were the turnpike keepers at cross-roads afraid of losing part of their income, but coach builders, saddle and harness makers thought they might be out of business if steam locomotion was encouraged.

The carriage makers were therefore greatly mollified when it was discovered that their skills could be put to use making vehicles for the railway companies. The coaches used for the railway passengers travelling the twelve miles of the Stockton & Darlington Railway on a regular basis conveyed fifteen people and proceeded at 10–14 miles per hour, pulled by horses, the engine loaned by Stephenson having been used solely for the inauguration of the service – *Fig. 10*.

The Liverpool & Manchester Railway was almost complete when a decision was taken by the Board of Directors in 1825 that horsepower was no longer a practical proposition for hauling the wagons. Whether to employ fixed or locomotive power was however, still undecided. It is worth noting at this juncture that in 1829 the Newcastle & Carlisle Railway Act was passed on the express condition that it be worked by *horses* only!

After further inspection of other railways, the Board of the Liverpool & Manchester Railway elected to use 21 stationary engines on the 19-mile stretch of railway. Stephenson was naturally disappointed in their decision, but continued to press for a fair trial. Indeed he was so persuasive that the Directors agreed to offer a prize of £500 for the best locomotive to be presented for a contest at the Liverpool end of the line on 1st October 1829. The *Rocket* designed and driven by Robert Stephenson won the race easily. Five enginees were presented on the day but *Cycloped*, weighing three tons, was eliminated when it was discovered to be powered by a horse working a treadmill within a frame. *Fig. 11*.

Fig. 8

Fig. 9

Fig. 10

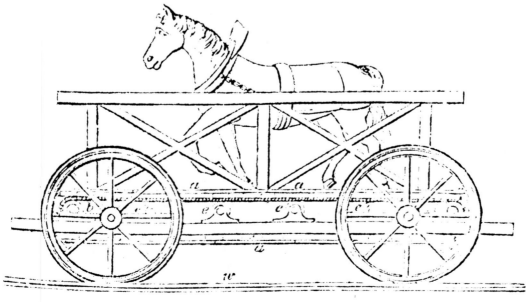

Fig. 11

BRANDRETH'S PATENT 'CYCLOPEDE'

The early railways drew support from passengers who wanted to experience a novel method of transport. One of the first vehicles designed expressly for the conveyance of railway passengers was called *Experiment*. It resembled a modern garden shed, with three windows on either side and a rear doorway without a door. The driver's seat was secured to the front of the vehicle which proved to be too heavy for one horse to pull until modified in subsequent models.

As can be seen from **Fig. 12**, the design of railway carriages at this time, 1834, was based largely on the well-known and tried 'Stage coach' which had operated on the roads for years past. A seat was provided at each end for a driver and guard.

Under the terms of the Railways Act, passengers could be conveyed along the track by anyone with a suitable vehicle on payment of a toll to the railway company. However, the companies quickly realised the potential income from operating such a service themselves and prevented other entrepreneurial carriers from using their track by pointing out that as there were few passing places, the Company's goods wagons required the line free of local passenger vehicles in order to prevent delays. In 1845 the Railway Clauses Act authorised the railway companies to act as carriers of goods, "providing reasonable facilities for receiving, forwarding and delivery of goods". This mandate was confirmed by the Rail & Canal Traffic Act of 1854 and the Great Western Railway successfully built up a reputation for courteous and efficient service all over their system.

The first proposal for a railway to be worked by locomotives between London and Bristol was made in 1824, nearly a year before the opening of the Stockton & Darlington Railway. John Loudun McAdam, a director of the newly formed 'London & Bristol Railroad Co.' was employed as engineer to survey and lay out the line. He recommended that a parallel turnpike road be constructed which would carry the passenger traffic directly into the towns as the railway was intended primarily for

goods traffic. Several similar schemes were suggested, but only two came into being – a horse tramway from Coalpit Heath rather grandly called the Bristol & Gloucester Railway, and the Avon & Gloucester Railway, again more of a horse-powered tramway than the name suggests.

With the general acceptance of the existing railways, interest was renewed in the idea of a railway from Bristol to London. Insufficient financial backing was available until 1833 when Isambard Kingdom Brunel was employed as engineer and a third survey was accepted at a meeting in August of the same year. The title 'Great Western Railway', was then adopted.

Among numerous sketches submitted to the Directors were these two drawings of the proposed terminus at Bristol Temple Meads, **Figs 13** and **14**, a station to be shared with the Midland Railway Company. In the upper sketch the Company titles can be clearly seen inscribed above the archways.

The lower illustration features a Great Western omnibus driving towards the archway above which are two coats of arms.

Fig. 15. Philip Shepherd RWS painted this impression of an omnibus leaving Bristol Temple Meads station, and is reproduced with the kind permission of the artist. It shows the Great Western side of the station as it was actually built and captures the atmosphere and activity of the 1870s.

Fig. 16. Brunel designed the modifications for a britzka coach in order that he could oversee the construction of the railway without relying on hired hacks or journeying on a public coach. Nicknamed the "Flying Hearse", this vehicle was to become a familiar sight to the contractors and construction gangs. There was room for his plans and engineering instruments as well as facilities for refreshment and a stock of his now famous cigars. The seating upholstery extended into the 'boot' under the driver's seat so that he could rest during the journey.

Fig. 17. *Galloper* was built between 1830 and 1840 for

Fig. 12

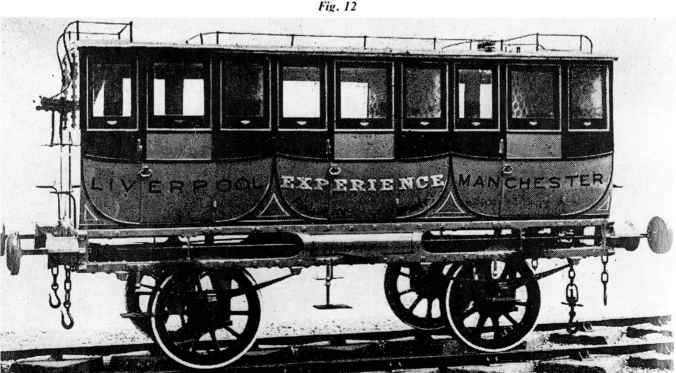

Fig. 13   *Fig. 14*

Fig. 15

Fig. 16

use by Brunel and the directors. It was pulled by two horses or four when greater speed was required. This photograph was taken in 1897. Ornamental wheel bosses added a further touch of individuality to the vehicle.

During the lengthy Parliamentary debate as to the necessity for a railway between London and Bristol, the landowners pointed out that there was already a canal connecting the two cities. Goods traffic took three days to travel 80 miles which could be shortened to three hours on a railway and despite the objections of the farmers and landowners whose property would be affected, the Great Western Railway received the Royal Assent on 1st August 1835.

Another early railway to be granted a licence to operate by Parliament was the Paisley & Renfrew Railway, opened in 1837 using a few steam-powered locomotives. However, in 1842 horse haulage was substituted and worked the line for the next 24 years when alterations to the line enabled locomotives to be re-instated. The length of the line involved was some 3½ miles from Paisley to Renfrew, later part of the Glasgow & South Western Railway.

Fig. 17

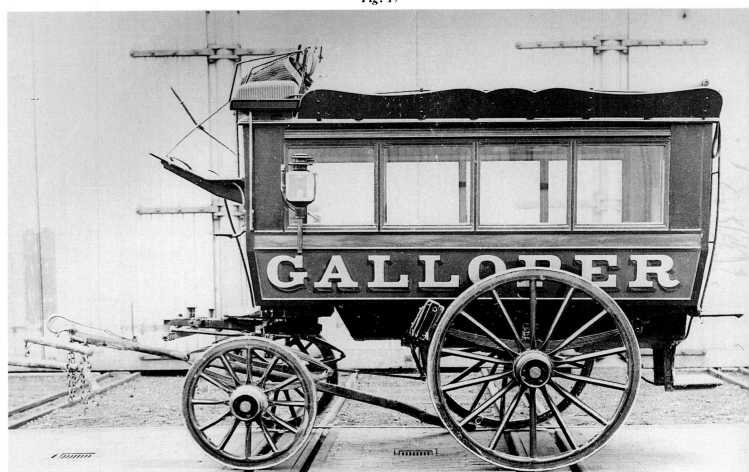

The route finally selected for the Great Western Railway was almost flat. The highest point of the whole line being only as high as the dome of St Paul's Cathedral. Brunel decided on 7 ft 0$\frac{1}{4}$ in as the gauge to be employed in order to keep the centre of gravity for wagons and locomotives as low as possible. There are many excellent books already published which set out the details of the extensive construction of the Great Western Railway. It only remains for me to point out that during this construction period, horses were employed in vast numbers to haul wagon loads of materials to the railhead and bring the waste or spoil away for redistribution where it was required.

Fig. 18 shows work in progress on the line at Fox's Wood near Bristol. Two horses are hauling a timber wagon towards the mouth of the tunnel and another cart is being unloaded alongside the tracks. Barges on the Kennet & Avon Canal may also have been used as a convenient method of bringing materials to the construction site. Between Bath and Bristol horse-drawn barges took a whole day which would be cut to a one hour journey on the railway. The Great Western Railway was the first railway upon which it was definitely stated right from its inception that locomotives would be the source of power to be employed to haul wagons on the tracks as soon as the line was complete.

Another tunnel constructed during the early days of the Great Western Railway was Boxhill, started in 1836 under William Glennie as Resident Engineer, formerly assistant to Brunel. Under his direction the contractor, Mr George Burge used 1,100 men and more than one hundred horses on his half of the tunnel. During the last six months of construction, 400 men and three hundred horses worked in the tunnel in order to meet the opening deadline. The excavated material was hoisted up the air shafts by wretched horses walking round and round turning gins or drums onto which the rope was wound. The tunnel was finally opened in June 1841.

As late as 1910 horses were still used to assist with transporting the materials for constructing permanent way. This photograph, *Fig. 19*, shows a horse hauling an empty wagon away from the newly excavated Shepherds Bush line.

When the first part of the Great Western Railway opened between London and Maidenhead on 4th June 1838, there were four classes of passenger fare – posting carriage, 1st class coach, 2nd class coach and 3rd class open carriage. The posting carriage was later adapted to a saloon carriage for the conveyance of family parties. Many passengers preferred to travel in their own horse-drawn road carriage secured on a carriage truck or wagon. *Fig. 20*. A note in the 1863 timetable set out the following scale of fees and conditions for such passengers who were averse to using upholstery that had been sat on by unknown persons:

"Passengers in Private Carriages (not being servants) are required to take first-class tickets, and such passengers may remove during the journey to the Company's First-class carriages if there be sufficient room in them.

Servants travelling on private carriages are required to take second-class tickets and they may remove to second-class carriages provided there be room. A groom travelling in a horse-box in charge of a horse is allowed to travel at third-class fare. Horses and carriages will be conveyed by the Parliamentary trains at a reduction of $\frac{1}{5}$th on the ordinary fare."

Fig. 18

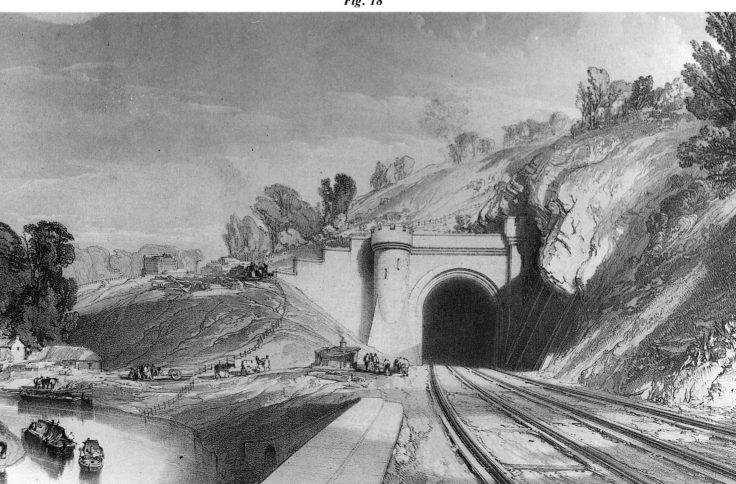

Fig. 19

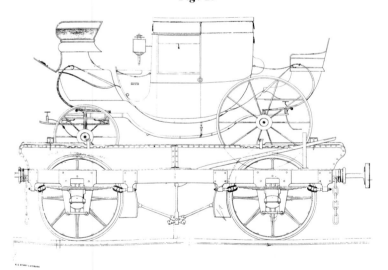

Fig. 20

Fig. 21

The practice continued until 1913. By 1845 the Great Western Railway Company owned 161 carriage trucks which cost £151 15s 3d each to build and 96 horseboxes which had been constructed at a cost of £198 17s 9d each.

Fig. 21. Privately owned coaches pulled by two or four well-matched quality horses were still very common despite the annual carriage tax of £4. Many factors were taken into consideration such as the size of the vehicle, the number of horses required to pull it, the number of passengers carried, the number of wheels, whether the vehicle was open or closed and the weight. A pair horse omnibus or coach costing between £320 and £650 to build, weighing between three and four cwt had been taxed since 1747 at two guineas. The increase in the tax in 1869 caused large numbers of bigger vehicles to be discarded in favour of the smaller types. In order to save tax, additional bodies were purchased for one wheelbase, but this attempt at tax evasion was stopped by levying an extra three guineas for each additional body.

The 1850s brought an increase in the toll payable to turnpike owners. Two pounds was now payable by the owner or driver of a horse-drawn coach which in some way compensated the landowners for the loss of business caused by the ever increasing numbers of private carriages that travelled in relative comfort by rail.

The Red Flag Act of 1865 reduced the speeds permissible of steam vehicles to 4 mph in rural areas and 2 mph in urban areas. It was also decreed that in addition to three persons being required to drive a locomotive, a man "shall precede such locomotive on foot by not less than 60 yards and shall carry a red flag constantly displayed, and shall warn drivers of horses and riders of the approach of such locomotive and shall signal the driver thereof when it is necessary to stop and shall assist the horses and carriages drawn by horses, passing the same".

This Act was slightly amended in 1878 with fewer words but still required a man to precede every mechanical road or rail vehicle. The red flag requirement was omitted from the text. In the painting of the opening of the Stockton & Darlington Railway (*Fig. 9*) a man can be seen preceding the locomotive. He has taken the liberty of riding a horse instead of walking in front as the law later decreed.

Fig. 22 shows the construction of an 1866 carriage truck or wagon which could be covered if necessary to protect the paintwork of the private coach if the occupants were travelling in a saloon or 1st class carriage.

New carriages were also conveyed from the coachbuilder's works to the buyer. If the works was situated close to the station it would probably have been driven there by an experienced and trusted employee and loaded at the station. Longer journeys to the station were overcome by loading the new carriage onto special low-loading carriage trolleys which could be covered to protect the gleaming paintwork of the new vehicle. The trolley was 14 ft 6 in long and 5 ft 6 in wide, with two ramps to raise the carriage and later, the motor car, onto the floor of the trolley which was 2 ft 8 in off the ground. The vehicle was then hauled by two steady horses.

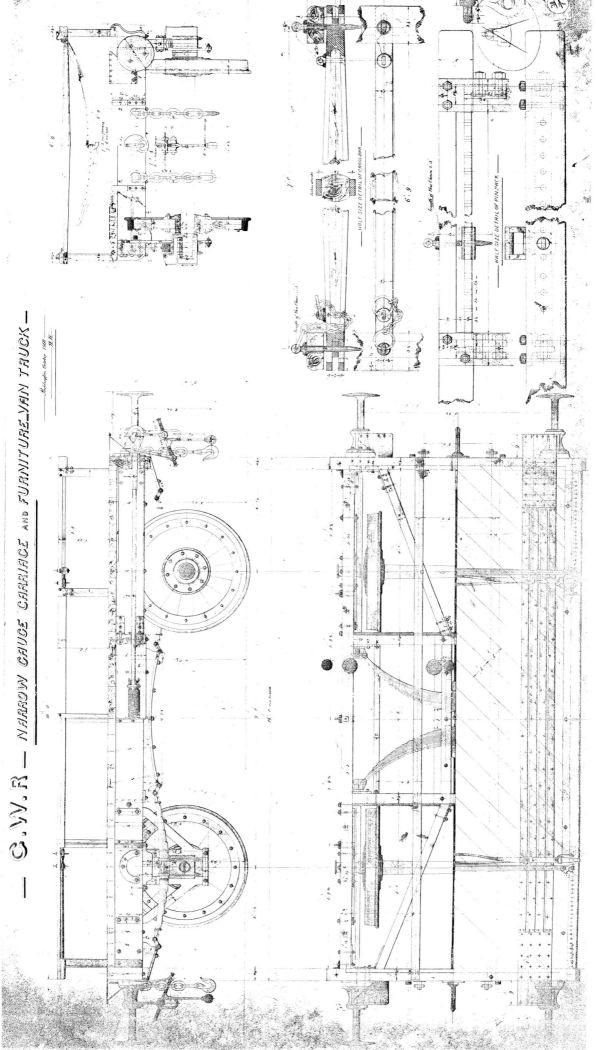

— G.W.R — NARROW GAUGE CARRIAGE AND FURNITURE VAN TRUCK —

HALF SIZE DETAIL OF CROSS BAR

HALF SIZE DETAIL OF PIN JACK

Fig. 22

Horseboxes and Carriage Wagons

The first GWR horseboxes of 1842 were strange looking vehicles, wider than they were long. Their dimensions were 9 ft 8 in long (12 ft 8 in over buffers) by 10 ft 8 in wide and 7 ft 6 in high. They ran on four 3 ft diameter wheels with a wheelbase of only 6 ft, and to the broad gauge of 7 ft $0\frac{1}{4}$ in between the rails. *Fig. 23* (opposite). As the vehicles weighed over 4 tons they rocked from side to side and must have been most uncomfortable for the occupants.

Later boxes were made narrower and three horses travelled side by side facing forwards, as opposed to the previous method of packing four horses in the box and travelling sideways. The horseboxes were painted brown to match the passenger vehicles with the letters G.W.R. picked out in a creamy-yellow. Those trains which included these horseboxes and carriage trucks were designated slow trains and departed from main stations and some London suburbs such as Marlow Road, Wooburn Green, Wycombe and Windsor.

Fig. 24. On the earliest standard gauge horseboxes of 1860, the horses travelled lengthways, the headcollars being attached to rings near the roof of the vehicle. There was no provision for a groom to travel with the horses and there is little in the way of comfort for the occupants. This photograph of the interior of an 1860 horsebox shows the rather primitive conditions in which the horse travelled. However, food and water could be given to the animals through the trapdoors over the mangers when the train was standing at a station.

Two diagrams of broad gauge horseboxes dated about 1848. In *Fig. 25* the horses travelled across the width of the vehicle. In *Fig. 26* (page 23), the three horses faced

Fig. 24

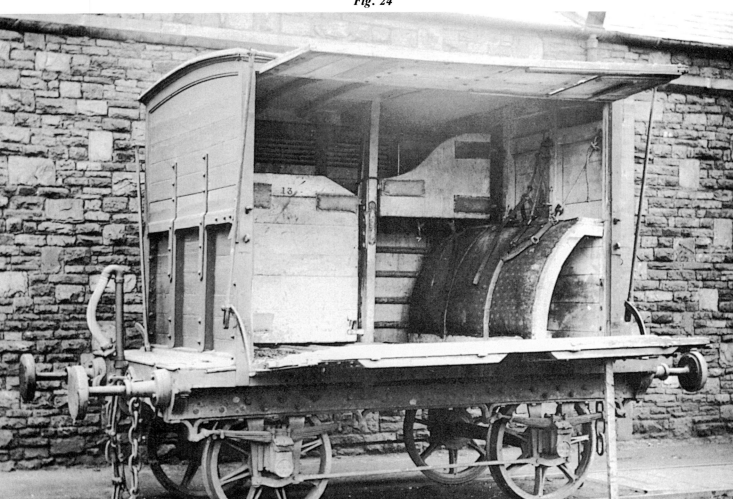

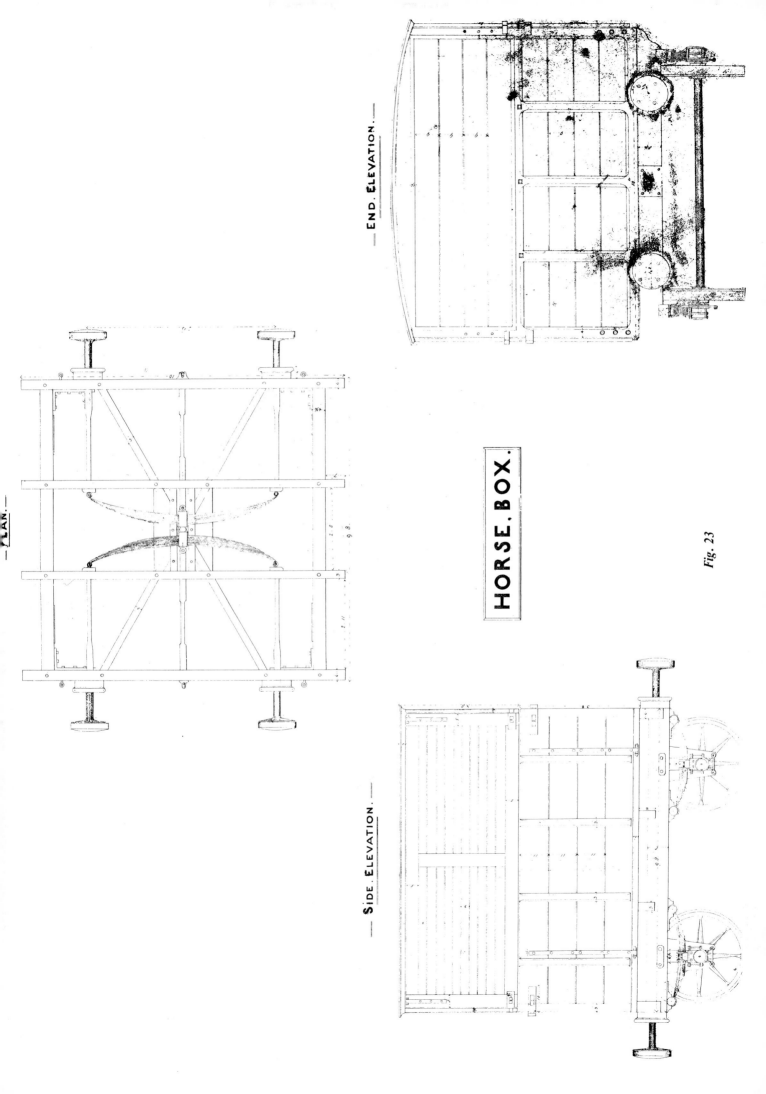

PLAN.

END. ELEVATION.

SIDE. ELEVATION.

HORSE. BOX.

Fig. 23

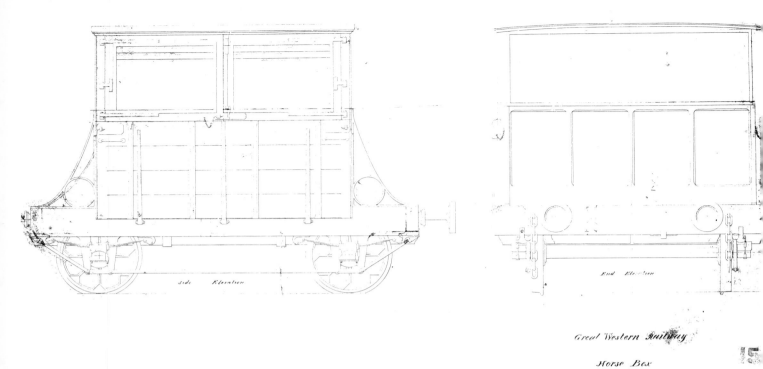

Great Western Railway

Horse Box

Fig. 25

the way they were travelling. By this date the GWR owned 385 passenger carriages and 170 horseboxes, carriage trucks and brake vans.

Fig. 27. This undated cartoon will give the reader some idea of the difficulty of loading high spirited carriage horses into railway horseboxes. Although the cap badges indicate that this is a Great Western operation, I have been unable to find a diagram which conforms to the artist's impression of the horsebox!

Fig. 28. The 'narrow gauge' (4 ft 8½ in) horsebox had three stalls inside for the horses, together with a grooms' compartment. Note the small hatch on the left hand side which was for the family pet dog or carriage dog. This modification was added to some horseboxes after 1861.

Fig. 29. Considered at the time to be the epitome of equine luxury, this 1888 broad gauge horsebox had leather padded stall dividers between the horses and an upholstered seat for their attendants.

Fig. 27

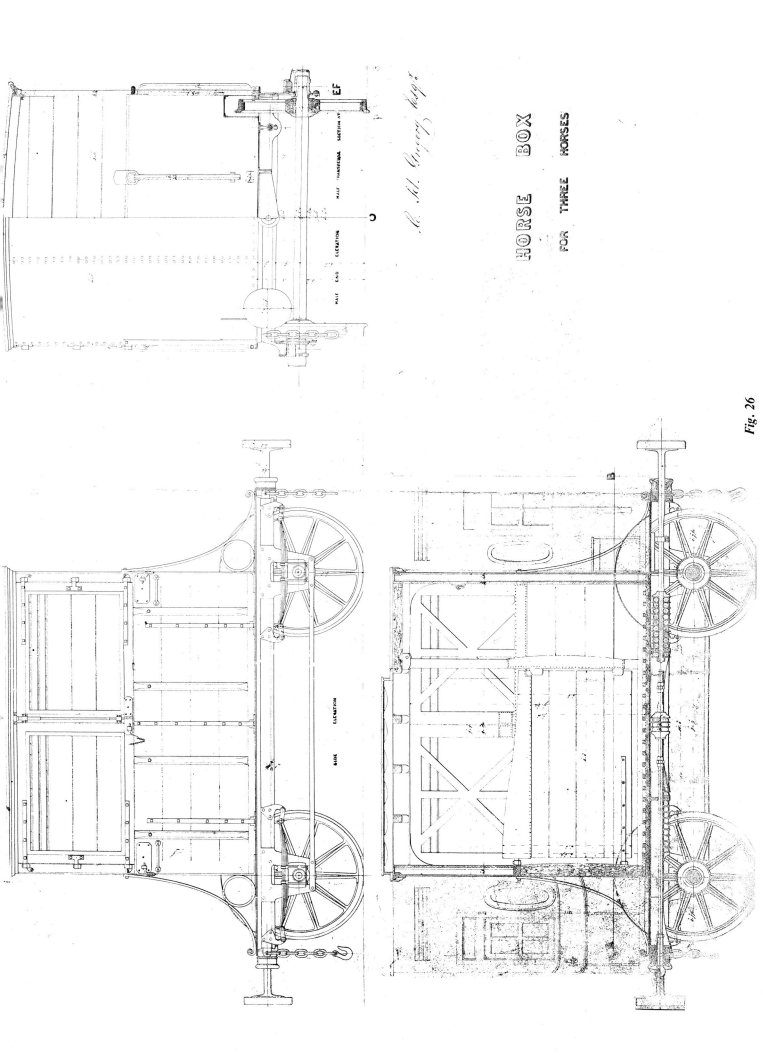

HORSE BOX

FOR THREE HORSES

HALF TRANSVERSE SECTION AT EF

HALF END ELEVATION

SIDE ELEVATION

Fig. 26

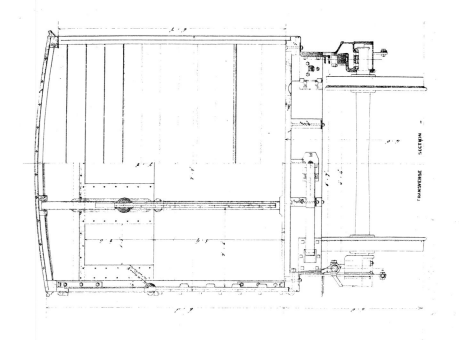

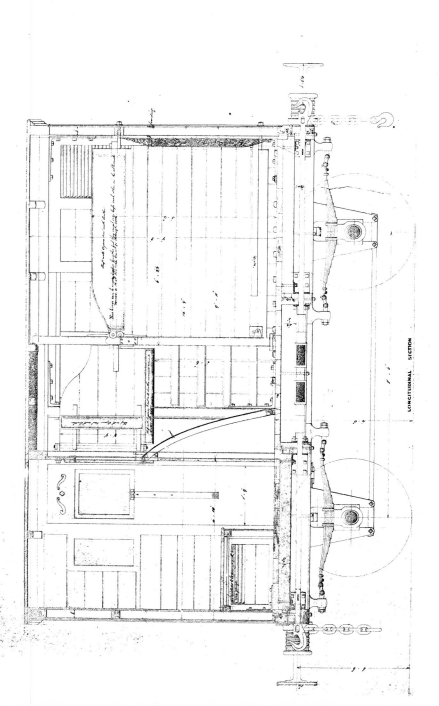

GREAT WESTERN RAILWAY

NARROW GAUGE ✳ HORSE BOX

Fig. 28

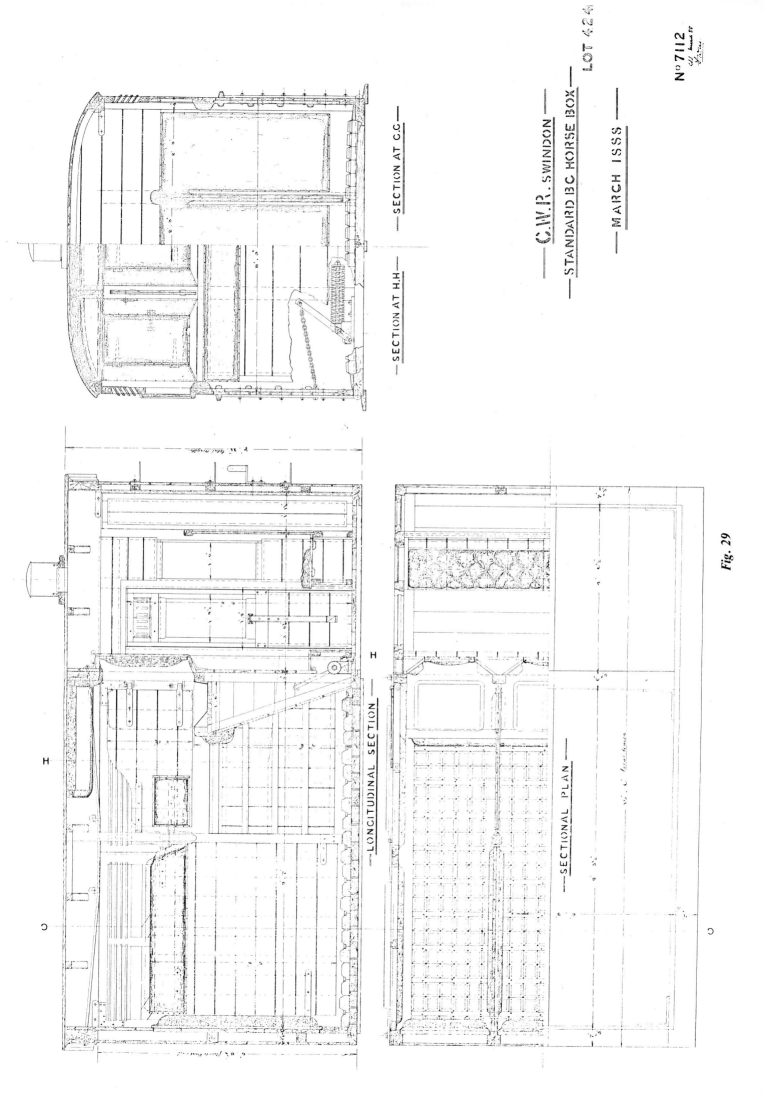

SECTION AT C.C

SECTION AT H.H

G.W.R. SWINDON

STANDARD 13C HORSE BOX

LOT 424

MARCH 1888

No 7112

LONGITUDINAL SECTION

SECTIONAL PLAN

Fig. 29

Fig. 30. Only minor modifications had been made one year later to the design of this horsebox. The additional locker, shown on the left of the vehicle, could be used to store the partitions should a mare and foal be travelling together. The diagram gives basic dimensions.

Fig. 31. This 1901 design added one foot to the length of the vehicle and a second handbrake. The grooms could attend their charges through the hatches during the journey. Also shown in the drawing is the facility for lighting oil lamps in the compartments at night. Many of these vehicles were used regularly until 1940 when they were dumped at Old Oak Common.

Carriage truck design also improved during the late 1880s. This 1909 version, ***Fig. 32*** was 21 ft in overall length with a Westinghouse brake and a 12 ft wheelbase, capable of transporting the standard four wheel carriage.

Fig. 33. In this photograph of a carriage truck, the fixing points for securing a load are shown clearly.

Fig. 34. Chains and bars or straps and bars were used for securing carriages and later the motor car on an open carriage truck.

Fig. 35. There was also a need for a much longer vehicle which could carry two vehicles at once, or even a tramcar. It was 45 ft long with ample fixing points for its load.

Fig. 36. Horseboxes also became longer. This 1907 version rebuilt in 1937, had an additional compartment for carrying fodder for the horses. It could also be used for carrying the harness and luggage if more space was needed. This was in addition to the 'slot' mentioned previously, which was used for storing the stall dividers.

Fig. 37. A scale drawing of the above vehicle. Note the increased height allowed for the horse's headroom.

Fig. 38. From the interior view of the same vehicle the reader will get an impression of the standard of comfort provided for the occupant. Leather padding on the stall dividers prevented bruising. The ramp would have rested on the platform or on the edge of a loading ramp to enable the horses to walk in more easily. Note the vehicle number stamped on the stall divider.

Fig. 30

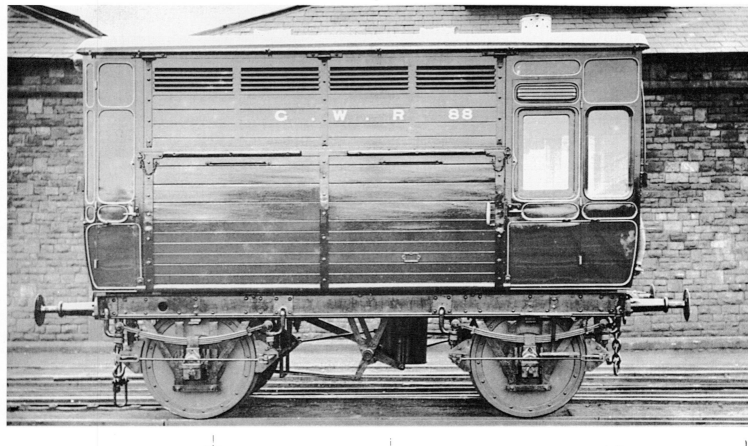

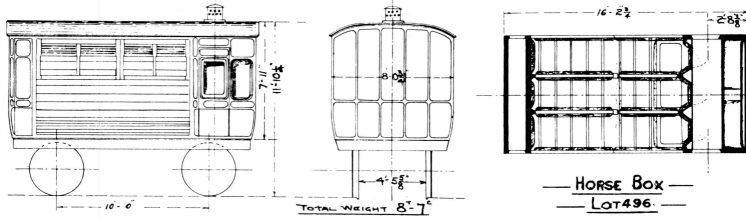

Total Weight 8ᵀ-7ᶜ

Horse Box
Lot 496

Fig. 31

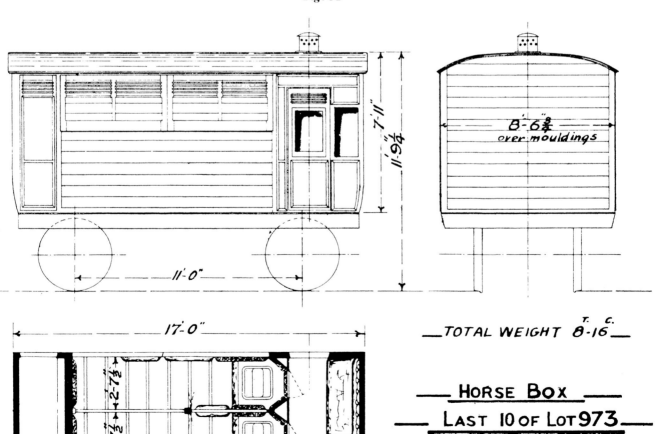

7'-11"

11'-9¼"

8'-6⅜" over mouldings

11'-0"

17'-0"

2'-7¾"

2'-7¾"

2'-7¾"

2'-8½"

__ TOTAL WEIGHT 8-16 __
T.   C.

__ HORSE BOX __

__ LAST 10 OF LOT 973 __

(Offical Drawing)

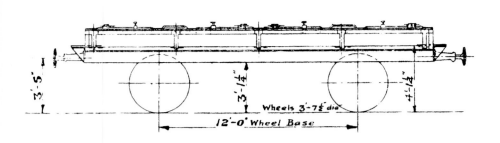
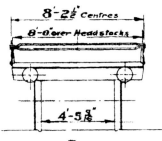

Total Weight 7ᵀ-7ᶜ

Load to carry 8 Tons.

CARRIAGE TRUCK

LOT 1158
1206   1217   12

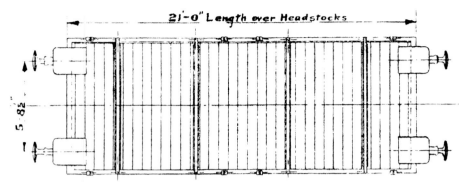

"SCORPION B" Vac & Westinghouse Brake   LOTS 1158, 1206, 1217, 1245

Fig. 32

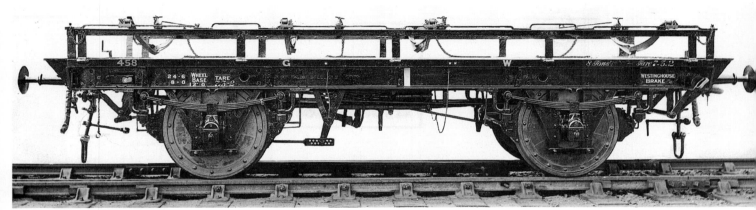

Fig. 33

Fig. 34

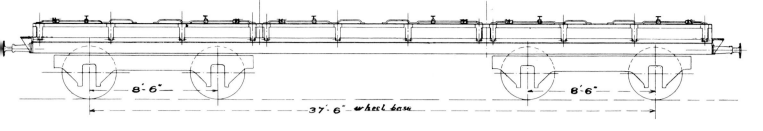

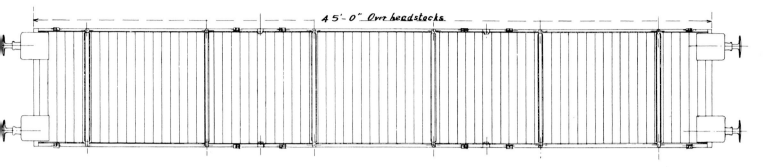

8'-6"   8'-6"

37'-6" wheel base

45'-0" Over headstocks

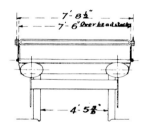

7'-8½"
7'-6" Over headstocks

4'-5⅝"

— CARRIAGE TRUCK —
— LOT 1025 —
— " 1104 —

DIA 119

(Official Drawing)

Fig. 35

Fig. 36

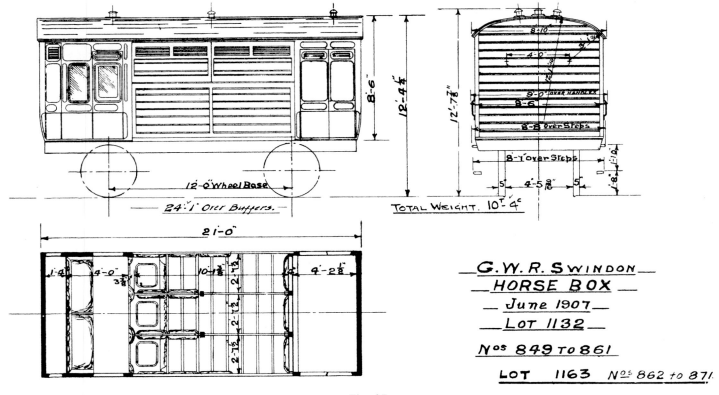

G.W.R. SWINDON
HORSE BOX
June 1907
LOT 1132
Nos 849 TO 861
LOT 1163 Nos 862 to 871.

12'-0" Wheel Base

24'-1" Over Buffers.

21'-0"

8'-6"

12'-4½"

12'-7⅝"

8'-10"

4'-0"

9'-0" OVER HANDLES

8'-6"

8'-8" OVER STEPS

8'-1" OVER STEPS

4'-5⅛"

TOTAL WEIGHT. 10ᵀ-4ᶜ

Fig. 37

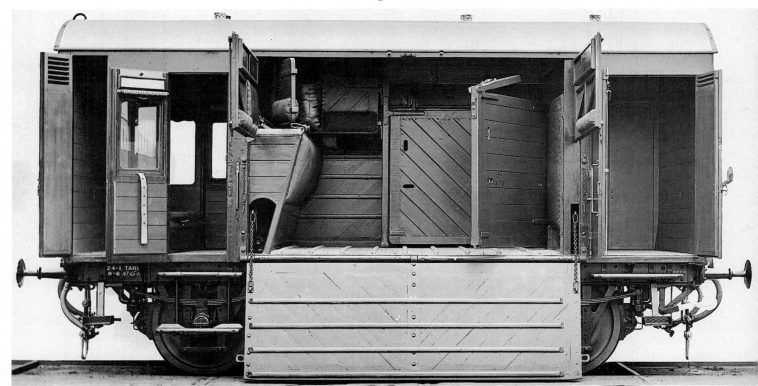

Fig. 38

Fig. 39. This is also a 1907 horsebox shown in the livery of 1920 but not nearly as modern in appearance as the previous vehicle. The letters are 24 in high whereas the roundel motif was used on most vehicles in the 1930s. Heating is available to both the grooms' compartment and the stalls via the steam heating pipe. Some of these vehicles were still in use in 1950 under British Railways ownership.

At the outbreak of the 1914–18 War, the Army were empowered to requisition hundreds of privately owned horses. The Government designated collecting places and horses selected by the Army were listed and then loaded onto every available horsebox. One such collection point was the 'Quay' at Kingsbridge, the horses being taken to South Hams depot for re-training and branding with their Army identification. They were transported in every available horsebox and also in modified open wagons when they were taken from the barracks to the docks.

Fig. 40. This 1889 covered carriage truck was only just over 8 ft in width. In the photograph, the end doors can be seen. These were used for loading the vehicle directly from the end of a siding or loading bay with ramps placed over the buffers. **Fig. 41** gives the dimensions.

Fig. 39

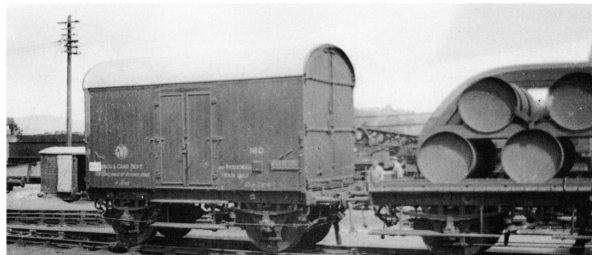

Fig. 40

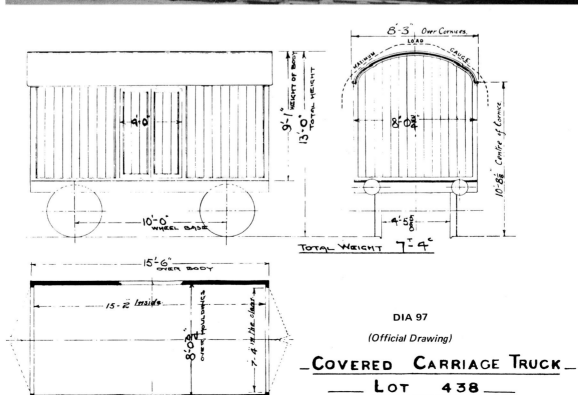

Fig. 41

DIA 97

(Official Drawing)

COVERED CARRIAGE TRUCK

LOT 438

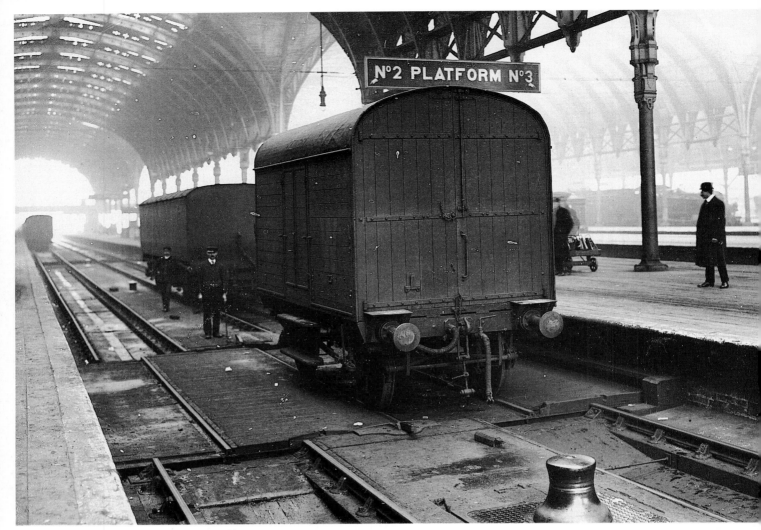

Fig. 42

Fig. 42. Photographed at Paddington station, this covered carriage truck was built to a design dated 1909 as shown in the diagram.

Fig. 43. Only one truck could be loaded at once from the end of the platform so the section of track was movable to allow the loaded vehicle to be pushed away from the ramp, crossed on to the other track and so allow another empty vehicle access to the loading ramp with minimum delay.

Built shortly after the First World War, these two horseboxes have obviously been used extensively. Internally the design had not altered significantly to the pre-war versions. **Fig. 44** of No. 398 shows the compartment end, and **Fig. 45** gives the fodder locker end of No. 420.

Fig. 43

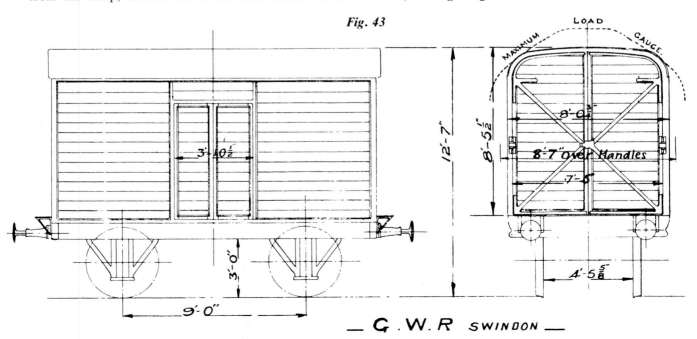

(Official Drawing)

G.W.R SWINDON

CARRIAGE TRUCK

LOT 4

Fig. 44

Fig. 45

Fig. 46. The photograph shows two medium to heavy-weight horses about to be loaded onto a horsebox at Aynho station. Although the picture was taken in 1932, the dimensions and fittings of the vehicle have changed little since the designs of 1907. The horse nearest to the camera is wearing a headcollar fitted with a bit, while the other horse appears to be wearing a full driving bridle. Extra neck ropes are lying on the ground for use when the horses have been installed in the horsebox. The vehicle number can be seen stamped on the stall divider – GW 330.

Fig. 47. This horsebox was photographed at Didcot in 1955 and shows the amount of space given to each horse in a comparatively modern vehicle. The basic fittings however, appear to remain unchanged. Only two horses travelled inside.

Fig. 46

Fig. 47

Fig. 48

Fig. 48. The horse travelled lengthways in this 1920 horsebox. While there is plenty of padding to protect the animal against bruising, there appears to be very little headroom despite the elliptical or arched roof, for such a large horse. Above the manger were half-doors which could be opened by the groom or attendant travelling with the horse in the adjoining compartment. Note the two headcollars, one leather and one a rope halter or headcollar, and the additional neck rope to restrain and secure the horse. The Rules of the Company stipulated that two halter ropes must be used. One tied to the ring on the corner of the manger and the other to the centre strut between the two half doors. Detailed instructions were also laid down as to the watering and exercising of animals travelling by rail.

Fig. 49. A horse's eye view of his travelling stall! Through the hatch he could see the grooms in their narrow compartment, but the padded dividers prevented him from either stealing his neighbour's feed, or nipping them. The two halter ropes and fixing points are again clearly visible. The photograph was taken inside vehicle No. 546, a more usual view of the interior being shown in **Fig. 50**, one of the modern horseboxes of British Rail made in 1954 and painted in British Rail maroon livery. This Western Region horsebox was built with the comfort of both horses and grooms in mind. The grooms' travelling conditions have been greatly improved by the addition of a toilet compartment. The headcollar can be seen hanging from the securing ring in the first stall. Many of the GWR rules for the treatment and care of the horses were still in force.

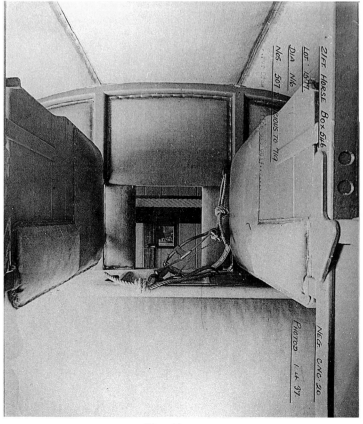

Fig. 49

Fig. 50

Fig. 51

The covered carriage truck found many uses on the railway. Very few of this length were built but they were constructed so soundly that circus elephants could be transported inside. After the end of horse and carriage traffic, motor vehicles were driven or pushed on board. The vehicle was 31 ft long, loaded like the smaller trucks, by opening the end doors. *Fig. 51.* The name of 'Python' was the code identification of these vehicles in the GWR telegraphic system.

Fig. 52. After many years of use, vehicle No. 523, built in 1905, was photographed at Paddington in 1947. The

GWR roundel has almost disappeared from the paintwork.

Figs 53 and *54.* Another version of the 'Python' carriage truck specially strengthened is shown in the photograph and the accompanying scale drawing is dated 1906.

Fig. 55. This 'Monster' (another code name) carriage truck, could carry several vehicles at once and these were also adapted to carry cars when carriages ceased to be carried in large numbers. HM Queen Victoria had a covered carriage truck specially built in 1895 for her four-

Fig. 52

Fig. 53

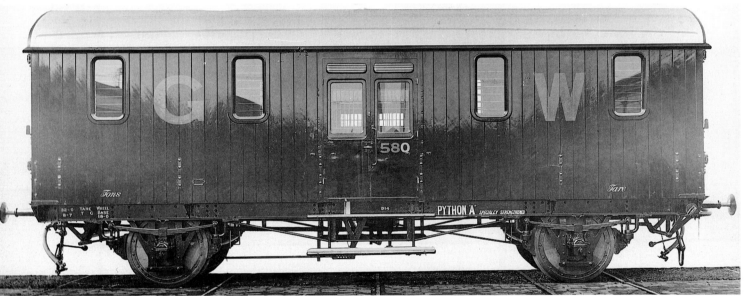

Fig. 54

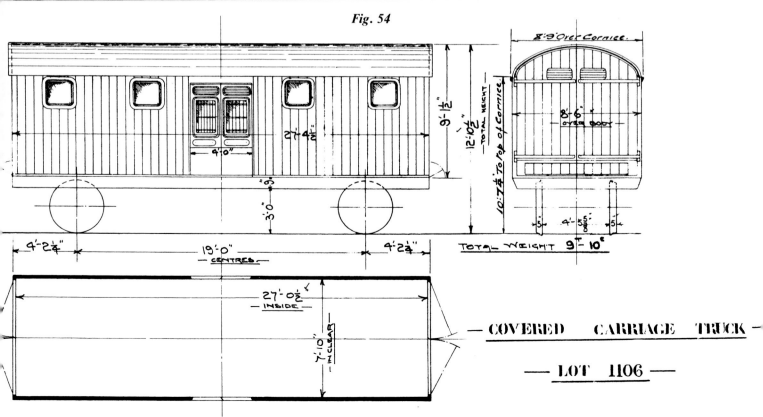

COVERED CARRIAGE TRUCK

LOT 1106

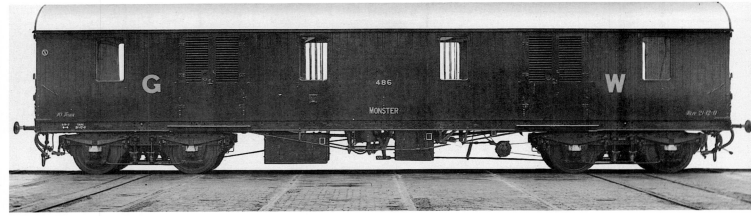

Fig. 55

Fig. 56

Fig. 57

wheel carriage which was taken with her in the same train. It was painted to match the Royal Train and had windows of similar shape and size. It weighed 12 tons, was 30 ft long, 9 ft 2 in high and just over 8 ft wide inside. It is very likely that some of the royal baggage would also have been packed inside.

Fig. 56. The interior view of the 'Monster' carriage truck shows the fixing bars for securing vehicles and the end doors through which loading took place.

Figs 57, 58 and *59.* Three views of the motorised horse boxes owned by British Railways Western Region in 1951. Horses could be loaded from the back and walked off through the side ramp towards the front of the vehicle. Alternatively, additional horses could be carried, travelling sideways in the front compartment, although this was not favoured by racehorse owners who liked their animals to face the way they were travelling at all times.

Racehorses were transported by rail from the station nearest the trainers' stables to the station nearest the racecourse. The racehorses from the Chilcombe stables under their foreman, Mr Hibberd, often loaded horse-boxes at the horse dock situated at the southern end of the main platform. The racehorse traffic on the Didcot, Newbury & Southampton Railway was so important that the GWR, who had running powers on this line,

often stopped their passenger trains to pick up entrants on race days.

Racehorses formed a high percentage of the trains passing through Compton, Hampstead Norris and Kings Worthy. Up to 28 boxes were recorded on days when racing was to take place at Newbury. Most of the horses were brought to the station by the stable lads from the local stables at Littleton and Burntwood. Where

Fig. 58

Fig. 59

there was no horse dock for loading, either the railway vehicle was drawn to the passenger platform and loaded there, or a gangway similar to this North Eastern Railway one (*Fig. 60*) was wheeled to the wagon to enable loading to take place from ground level.

Upton and Blewbury loaded horseboxes directly from the passenger platform. During 1909 it was recorded that 229 racehorses were loaded there and the following year a proper ramp was provided. Most of the horses came from the Chilton, East Hendred and Streatley stables.

Racehorses from the Lambourn district were loaded at Lambourn station. Many of the local trainers owned their own boxes, painted in their racing colours and

naturally demanded that their horses be suitably treated during loading, taking precedence over those using GWR horseboxes. The staff at this station earned a considerable sum in overtime payments, especially if a Race Special had to be provided for Sunday. All the boxes had to be cleaned and disinfected after each occupancy and the correct amount of oats put in each manger.

On arrival at Newbury station there was a resident farrier at the forge for emergency shoeing of any racehorse. As there were no Great Western horses at this station, this service was provided purely for the racehorse traffic.

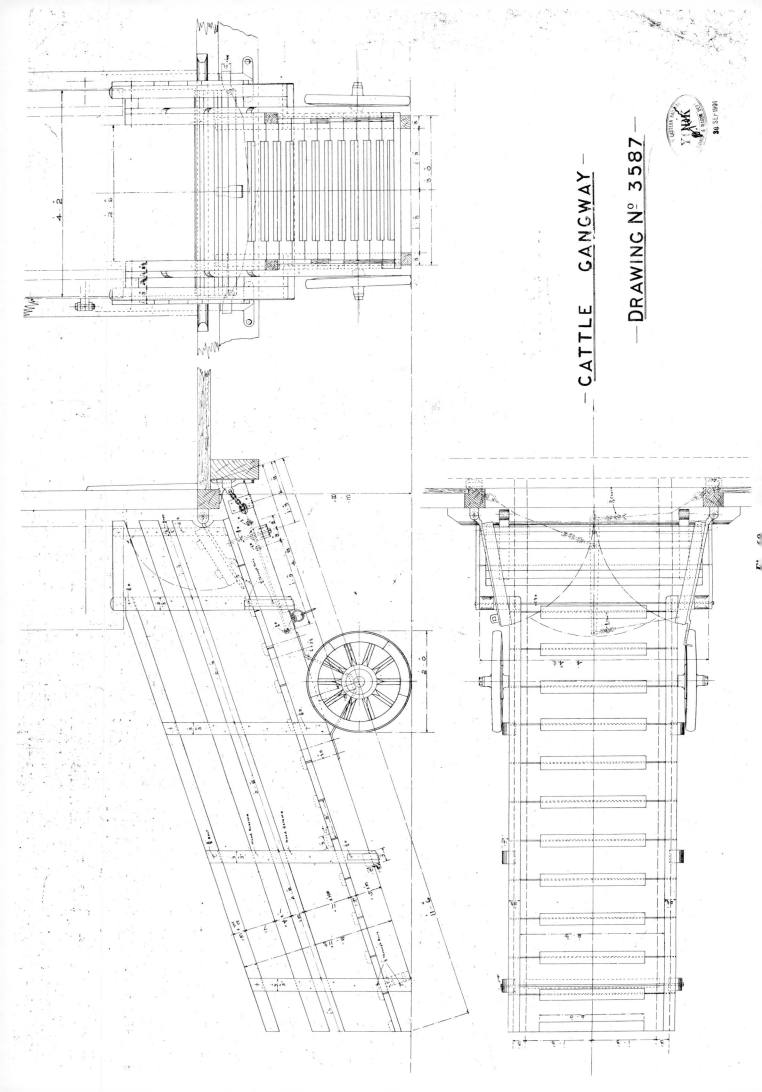

- CATTLE GANGWAY -

- DRAWING Nº 3587 -

Fig. 61

Fig. 61. Racehorses rugged up for their journey to the racecourse being loaded into horseboxes. The horse nearest the camera is wearing a tailored 'mask' designed to incorporate blinkers and ear protectors.

One hundred years ago, in the 1880s, special trains left Paddington (Platform 5) on Tuesday and Thursday during the hunting season to take members to meets at Slough, Taplow, Maidenhead and other Thames Valley stations. Other special trains were also arranged for meets at West Drayton or Uxbridge. The Huntsmen, hounds, horses and hunt servants could board the train at a station near their kennels and travel to a meet in a similar manner, the hounds travelling in a closed wagon, probably accompanied by the whipper-in. Ordinary members of the travelling public were excluded from hunt specials. At the end of the day the procedure was reversed, no doubt causing a great deal of work for the station staff who had to clean the vehicles out.

Tramcars

Many of the early GWR stations were constructed some distance from the actual town. Local carters quickly grasped the opportunity to increase their trade by ferrying passengers and goods from the town to the station and vice versa. Some towns built tramways to perform this service. One such town was Wantage. The first scheme to link Wantage with the main railway system was the Wantage & Great Western Railway Co, incorporated in July 1866 to construct a branch railway from the station to the town. Ten years later the scheme was still only on paper. A tramway was therefore constructed by local interests without GWR involvement and completed in 1875. It took some fifteen minutes for the tram journey of 2½ miles from the town centre to Wantage Road station and was worked by horses initially.

In 1879 the railway was approached with a view to operating the entire tramway but the proposal was turned down, partly because the railway company had no wish to involve themselves in passenger tramways and partly for economic reasons.

The cost of a horse-drawn tram was approximately £180 for an open top vehicle and £167 10s for a single decker. Both vehicles were hauled by one horse which would have cost about £20.

The Great Western Railway Company Board then permitted the tramway rails to be connected to the railway line and appointed the Tramway Company their agents for receiving and delivery of goods. Six horses worked the line, four on a passenger service, and two for goods. Stabling at an adjacent public house cost 4s (20p) per week!

An extract from a GWR rule book of the period points out "that in the event of a horse being frightened when near any steam engine of the Company on the tramways, the driver of such steam engine shall immediately bring such an engine to a stand".

Fig. 62. The photograph shows a tramcar belonging to the Port Carlisle Railway which was very similar to those used on the Wantage Tramway, for which no photographs suitable for reproduction could be found. The tramcar would not normally be quite so crowded, but the opportunity to be recorded for posterity by a photograph was not a chance to be missed!

Fig. 62

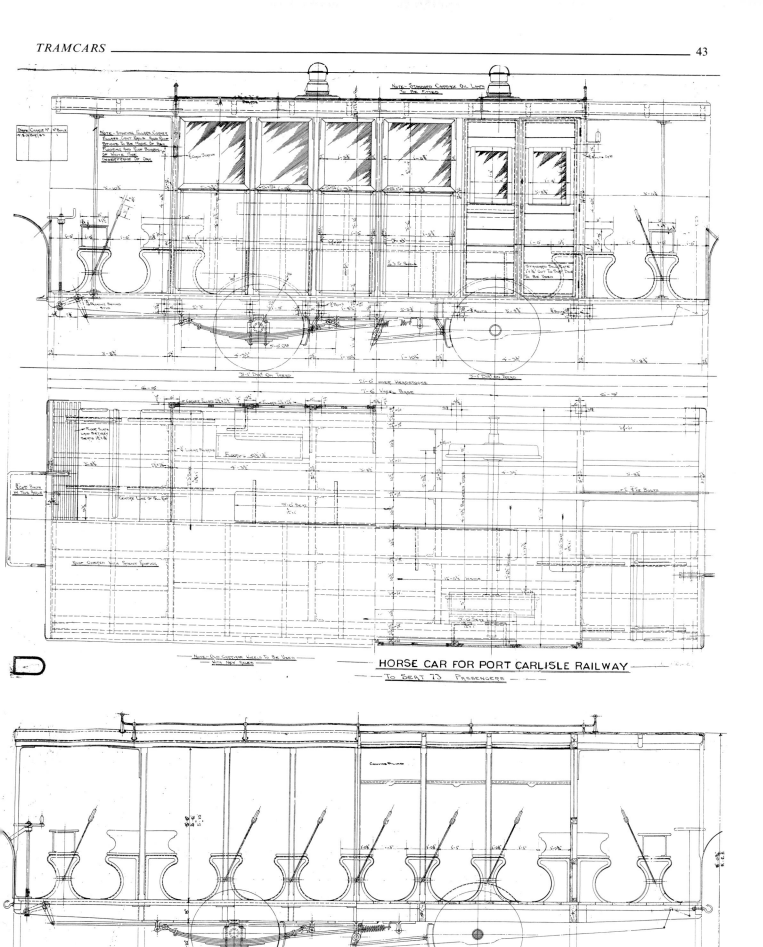

HORSE CAR FOR PORT CARLISLE RAILWAY

To Seat 73 Passengers

Fig. 63

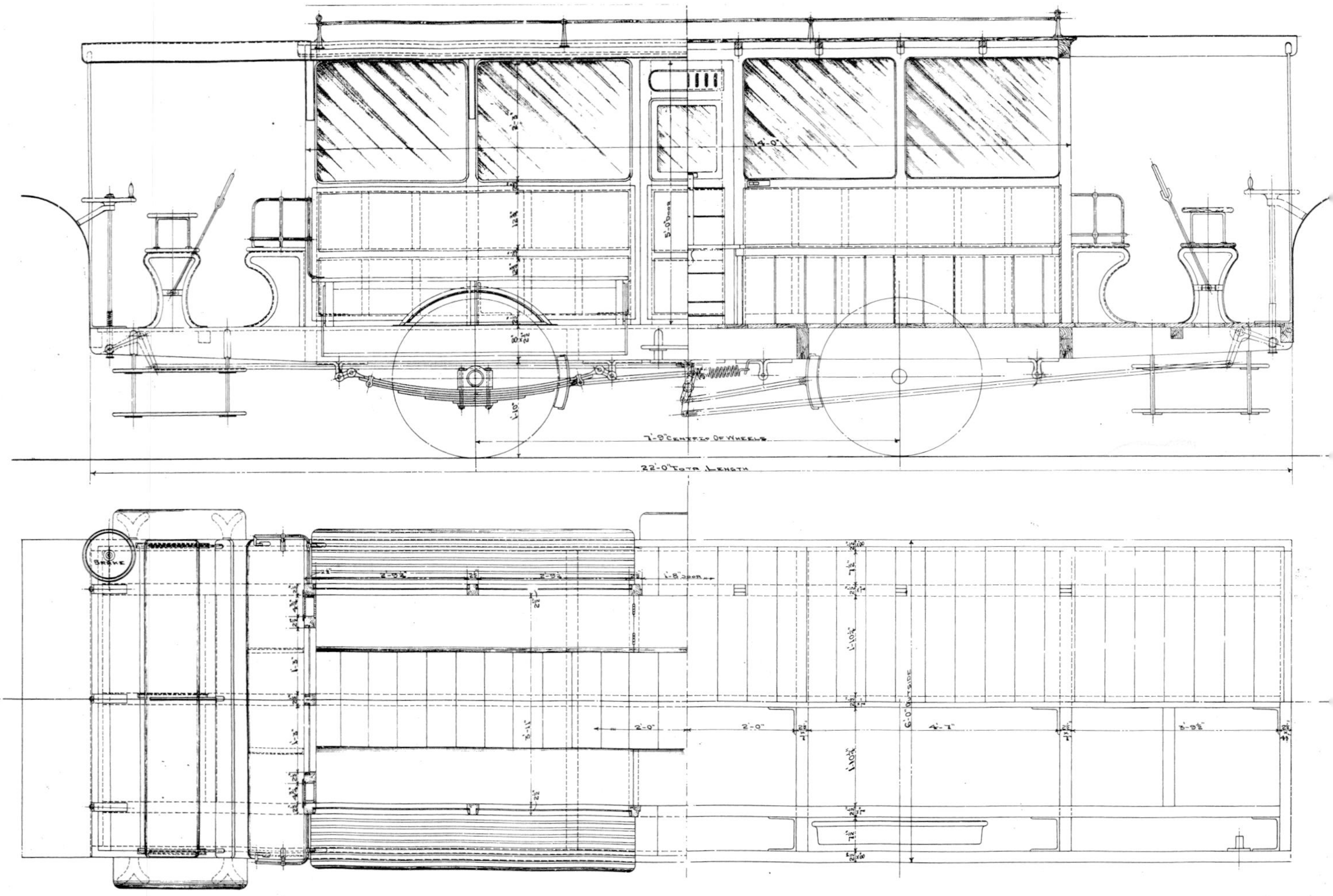

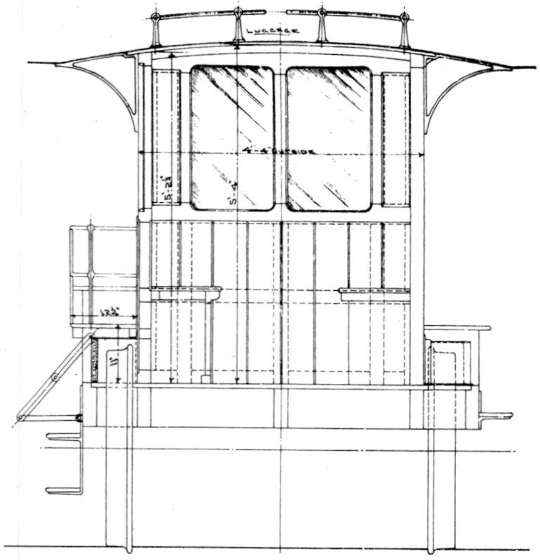

TO SEAT 4 PASSENGERS.

Fig. 64

Fig. 63 shows the construction of the tramcar. Of interest to the cost conscious reader is the note under the scale drawing of the subframe and floor – "old carriage wheels to be used with new axles".

Fig. 64 is a diagram of a proposed horse car for the Port Carlisle Railway. Whether it was ever constructed is not recorded. Bear in mind that it was intended that one horse would be pulling the vehicle!

The horse car could be pulled by one or two horses and by the 1890s, 249 horses were employed by the Wantage Tramway to haul their stock of 58 trams. A screw type brake operated by the driver assisted the horses on downhill gradients.

Vehicles of this type were used on the multitude of tramways connecting stations to villages, or as in the case of the Swansea & Mumbles Railway, from the station to the pier. Horses pulled the tramcars on this particular line right up to mid-Victorian days, and at Wantage Road, even after the tramway had steam engines to pull the trams, many horses were still used by the GWR to pull slip coaches into the station until 1920.

Fig. 65 shows a double decker tramcar pulled by one horse, possibly of Clydesdale extraction. The effort required to initiate the forward motion of such a weight often produced poor knees and their working life was shorter than horses working in more hectic situations, but with smaller vehicles or lighter loads.

Fig. 66. The lower photograph is of the Pwllheli to Llanbedrog tramway which took passengers from the GWR terminus at Pwllheli along the coast to the nearby seaside resort. The line opened in 1895 with six horses and closed in 1928 when the 3 ft 6 in gauge lines were taken up.

In addition to the closely associated tramways of Wantage and The Mumbles, several small railway branch lines were horse-operated, either during ownership by the GWR or at times when the Company had running powers over the line while in the ownership of a smaller company.

1841 – Weston Junction to Weston-super-Mare, a distance of 1¼ miles. Three four-wheeled carriages were pulled by three horses in tandem and ridden by boys. The practice was discontinued in 1851 two years after the Bristol and Exeter line had been taken over by the Great Western Railway.

1853 – Laira Junction to Sutton Harbour, 1⅔ miles was worked by the GWR although owned by the South Devon Railway. In 1856 the line was closed for a year but continued being worked by horses until locomotives were introduced in April 1869.

1873 – Buckfastleigh–Totnes railway used only horses on this short stretch until some locomotives were added to the strength late in 1874. The company was part of the South Devon Railway which was taken over by the GWR in 1875, although they had had running powers

over the line for almost 30 years.

A special vehicle was manufactured at Swindon for the conveyance of trams on the road, pulled by two horses. Its design is similar to that of the timber wagons made in the same works. Diagram (*Fig. 67*) page 46, shows the loadbearing section and construction details while *Fig. 68* is a photograph of the vehicle taken in 1906.

Many stations relied on a tramway or private road carriage operator to transport passengers to and from the station. It was not long before the Company realised the potential of this service and set up their own omnibus and passenger coach service from many of their larger stations.

Fig. 65

Fig. 66

Fig. 68

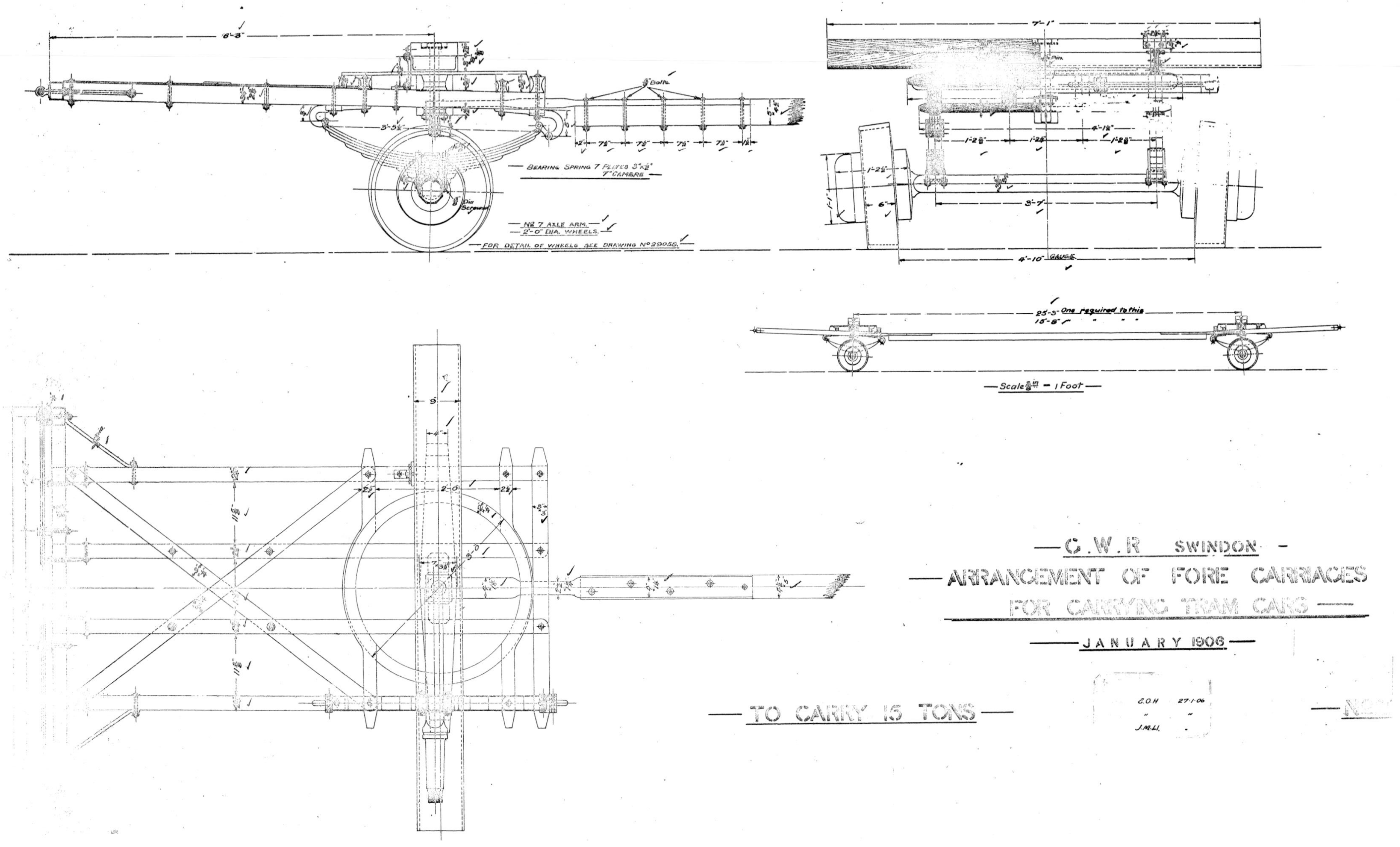
C.W.R SWINDON
ARRANGEMENT OF FORE CARRIAGES
FOR CARRYING TRAM CARS
JANUARY 1906
TO CARRY 15 TONS
BEARING SPRING 7 PLATES 3" x ½"
7" CAMBRE
Nº 7 AXLE ARM.
2'-0" DIA. WHEELS.
FOR DETAIL OF WHEELS SEE DRAWING Nº 29055.
Scale ⅜ in - 1 Foot
25'-5" One required to this
15'-8"
4'-10" GAUGE
6'-8"
7'-1"
3'-7"
C.O.H 27.1.06
J.M.Ll.

Fig. 67

Omnibuses

By 1889 the vehicles displayed an element of style, rather than purely utilitarian lines. The steps to the upper deck were not popular with the ladies as their ankles were revealed to the male eye as they mounted the stairs. In deference to their sensibilities, the Company fixed boards on the outside of the stairs which were then used for advertising and nicknamed 'Modesty Boards'.

Fig. 69. This 1908 photograph of Paddington station shows a variety of vehicles used for the conveyance of train passengers. Notice the destination board, bottom left. The majority of vehicles in the picture are one-horse omnibuses, smaller than many of the Great Western vehicles which required two horses.

Fig. 70 is of an 1889 omnibus requiring four horses and taking as many as 20 passengers and their luggage.

Fig. 71. An omnibus or cab photographed in 1895 belonged to the GWR. It was built about 20 years before being photographed as it still has 'C' springs beneath the body of the vehicle. This type of spring was superseded by semi-elliptical springs before the 1880s. It is quite likely that when the vehicle was full, an extra horse would have been required to assist on steep hills. A number of these horses were stationed at the bottom of such hills and were harnessed in front of the shaft horse. At the top of the hill, the chain horse would be released and return to his post at the bottom of the hill to await the next coach or wagon requiring extra horsepower.

Fig. 72. This is a 'cab' built by the Gloucester Railway Carriage & Wagon Company, who made vehicles for both railway companies and private individuals. The vehicle can be drawn by one or two horses. Note the lining out on the shafts and pole propped against the wall in the background. With the exception of the side windows, this vehicle is fairly similar in construction to

Fig. 69

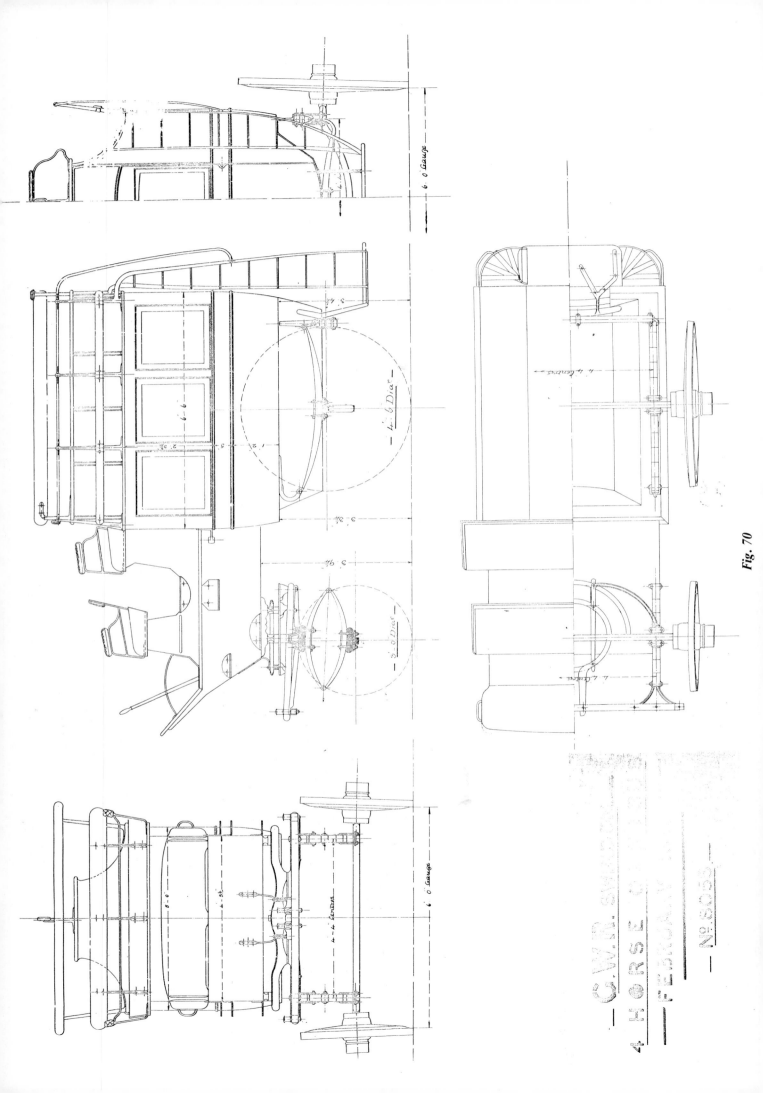

Fig. 70

G.W.R. SWINDON.

4 HORSE OMNIBUS

No. 8095

Fig. 71

Fig. 72

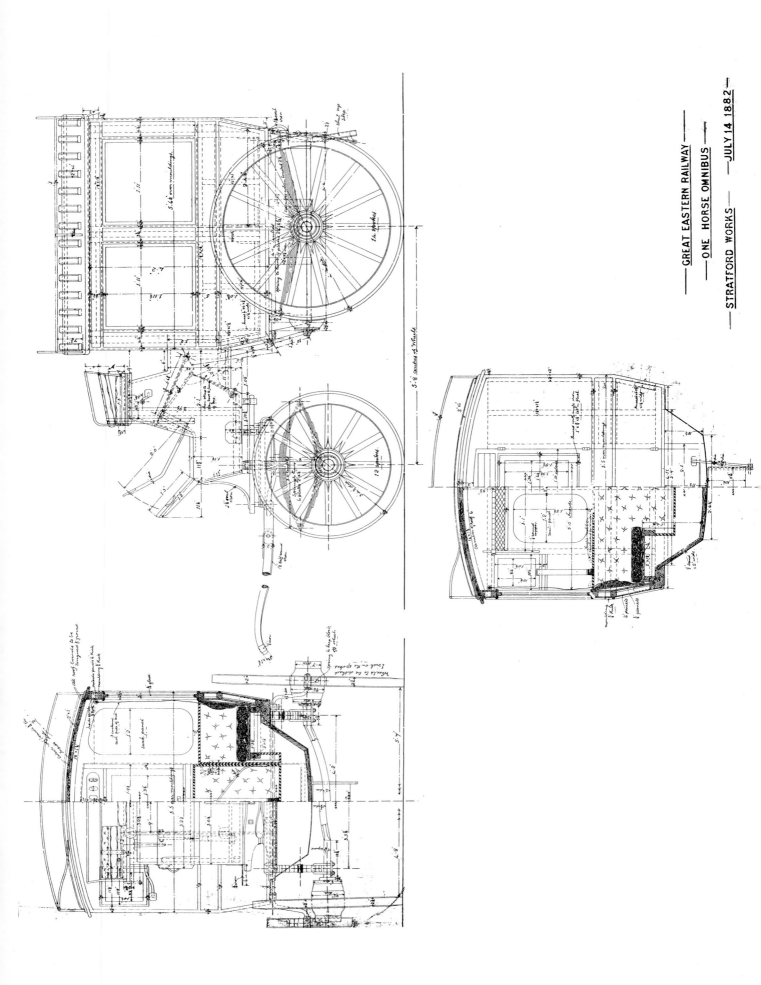

GREAT EASTERN RAILWAY

ONE HORSE OMNIBUS

STRATFORD WORKS — JULY 14 1882

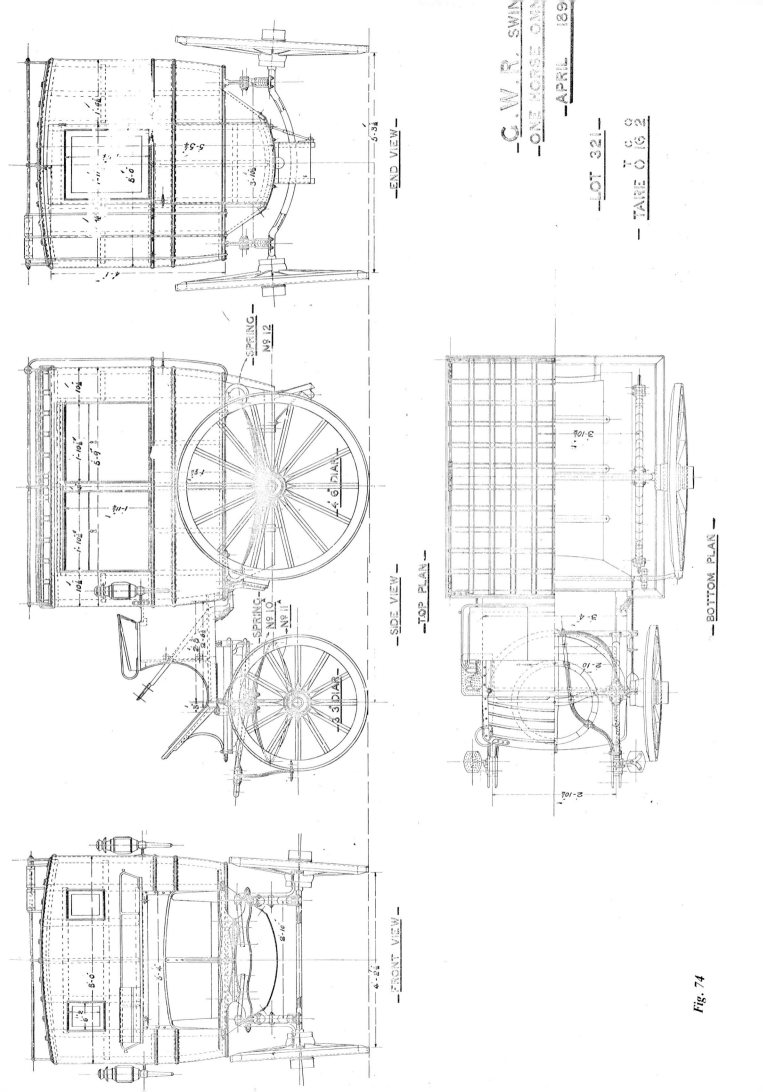

Fig. 74

Fig. 75

the drawing prepared by the Great Eastern Railway in 1882, *Fig. 73.*

Fig. 74. In 1894 the Great Western also adopted the two side window design shown in the previous drawing. The vehicle would have been manufactured at Swindon at the Carriage & Wagon Works which was opened in 1869. Passengers sat three or four to each side. The vehicle was mounted on semi-elliptical springs and had the added refinement of a handbrake. Single shafts for one horse were fitted.

Fig. 75. The two horse omnibus made at Swindon, was a standard vehicle and manufactured in considerable numbers. Only the final paint, lettering and interior furnishing distinguished them from private omnibuses. Twelve to fourteen passengers were seated inside, parcels were carried on the railed area on top. Because of the weight of the vehicle, horses were used in rotation with four other pairs, with an eleventh horse being kept as a reserve. Four days working and one rest day eked out a working life with the GWR of approximately four to five years for a London based horse. Harness was much simpler than that used for a normal draught horse and no breeching strap was required as the vehicle was fitted with a brake. Two horses were paired together for their working life. The majority of the London omnibus horses were mares while geldings were used for goods

traffic. In addition to Company horses and vehicles, the numbers were augmented by those owned by private contractors.

The London terminus of Paddington licensed a number of privately owned 'cabs' or omnibuses to serve the travelling public. In 1851 the number of private vehicles was increased from 80 to 100, ten of the additional vehicles to be supplied by new proprietors who had previously applied for the privilege pass, and the other ten by existing contractors having the best appointed vehicles.

The omnibus in *Fig. 76* is typical of the four to six-seater reserved almost exclusively for passengers staying at a Company-owned hotel. Many private hotels also had their own turnouts and stabling facilities for their own horses and those of its visitors. Some small hotels reserved a gig or barouche for this service. Hub brakes, applied by using the foot brake, can be seen on the inside of both rear wheels. Of interest to the driving fraternity is the conversion apparatus. The pole and movable splinter bar were for use with a two horse team when required. The square fitting for the pole can be seen between the forewheels of the omnibus and a roller bolt for the outside trace, which is visible on the end of the bar resting on the ground.

Fig. 76

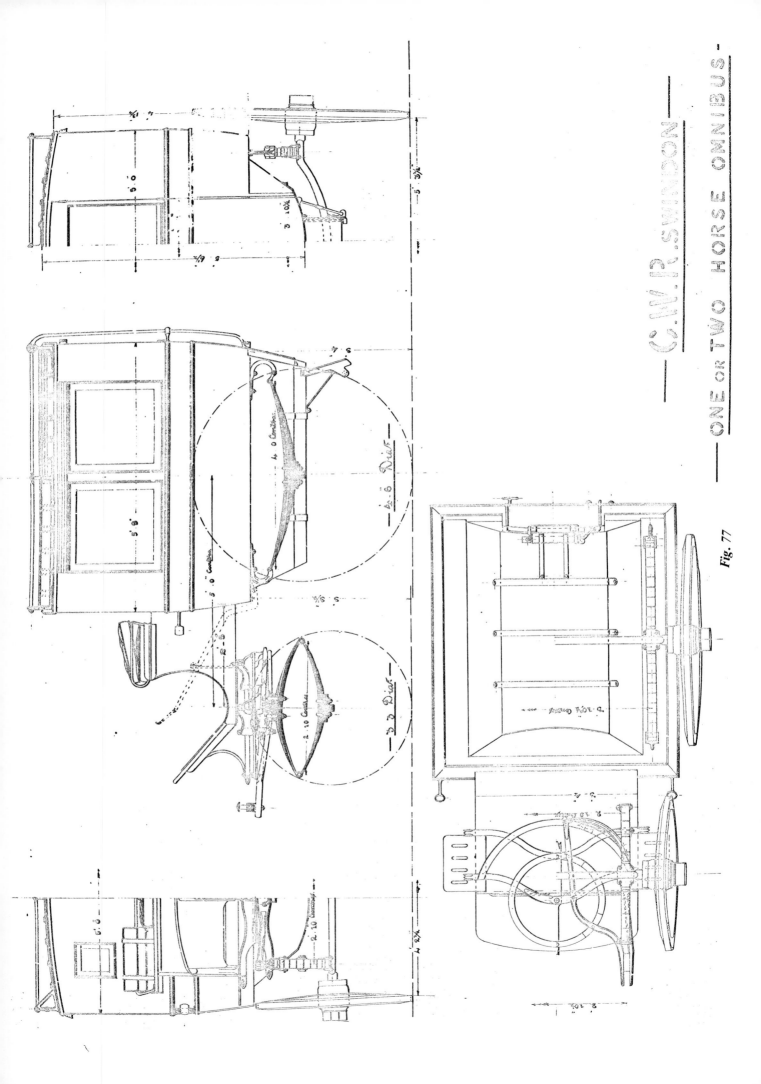

G.W.R. SWINDON.

ONE OR TWO HORSE OMNIBUS.

Fig. 77

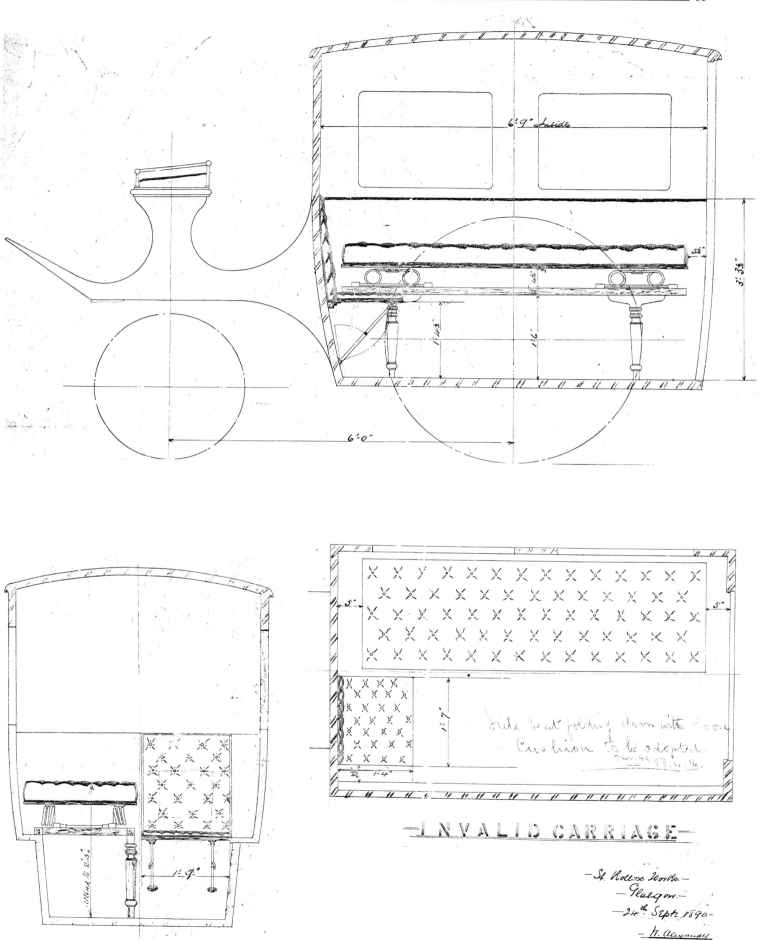

Fig. 78

Fig. 77. The scale drawing of the Great Western one or two horse omnibus is included to demonstrate the similarity between vehicles designed and manufactured for rival railway companies, in this instance, the London & North Western Railway.

Since the mid 1800s, further developments to pander to the comforts of the rich travelling public had been introduced. Distances covered could now involve night journeys. The mail was carried on a regular basis by the railways, both on trains and road coaches. A special carriage was designed to convey twelve passengers with the mail bags locked in a boot beneath the guard's feet. The Great Western sleeping car was a natural extension of this design. The boot was retained to accommodate the legs of the sleeping passengers. Only one example of the sleeping carriage is known to be preserved. It was built for Queen Adelaide in 1842 and was almost 22 ft long. The records of its method of movement are somewhat sketchy but there is little doubt that two or three horses were used to shunt the ornate vehicle into its position in the train which was then hauled by the locomotives of the day.

Passengers who were too infirm or sick to travel to the railway stations by normal omnibus were carried in invalid carriages. The diagram, ***Fig. 78***, shows an 1890 vehicle built for the Caledonian Railway but of a fairly standard design throughout most railway companies. A bed for the sick person, together with an upholstered seat for an attendant are shown clearly. Note the rollers for ease of transferring the patient from the road carriage into the railway carriage compartment. The body of the vehicle was considerably lower than the standard omnibus resulting in a smoother ride for the occupant.

The Ilfracombe and Barnstaple service was provided to cater for the holiday makers visiting the two resorts. This chart of 1888 (***Fig. 79***) shows four types of 'breaks' or omnibuses intended for the regular trips between the two towns, a regular service having been in use for many years under private ownership. It can be seen that at this time, 1888, there were nine vehicles allocated for this service, Nos 1–9.

The stables at Barnstaple had good accommodation for 34 horses, a harness room and a large store capable of holding a week's supply of provender and straw for the horses. Ilfracombe on the other hand, had rather poor stables for its ten horses. Feeding of the horses was a matter of considerable importance if they were to carry out the work expected of them. The rations given to the horses at both Ilfracombe and Barnstaple were different to that given to the horses used at other stations, and were made up of:

> 13 lb hay
> 16 lb oats
> 1 lb bran
> 2 lb beans
> ─────
> 32 lb of food per day

While most other stations were supplied with prepared provender from Handsworth and later Didcot, these two stations used locally purchased feedstuffs after 1879. Then, the proportions mentioned above were changed to allow the substitution of 4 lb maize for some of the oats and the doubling of the bran and bean content, again at the expense of the quantity of oats which had become very expensive.

Being primarily a summer service the numbers of staff and horses varied according to the season. Only one

driver was retained at Ilfracombe in the winter while three were employed in the summer months. Both stations were under the superintendent at Hockley and it is likely that the additional horses and manpower were drafted from there if possible.

Records for 1877 give the number of staff employed at Ilfracombe as:

Winter	Summer
1 coach driver	3 coach drivers
1 guard	3 guards
1 stable foreman	2 stable foremen
2 stablemen	7 stablemen

A list of the wages appears in the Minutes of the Horse Committee for November 1881 showing the winter wages for the Ilfracombe and Barnstaple service.

1 driver at 27s 6d (£1.37½) per week.
1 driver at 25s (£1.25) per week.
1 driver at 20s (£1.00) per week.
1 driver for *Galloper* omnibus at 25s (£1.25) per week.
1 conductor 10s (50p) per week (increased in 1882 to 12s (60p) per week).
1 shunter at 20s (£1.00) per week.
1 guard at 22s 6d (£1.12½) per week.
1 stable foreman at 25s (£1.25) per week.
3 stablemen at 20s (£1.00) each per week.

The minutes do not say whether these staff were based at Barnstaple or Ilfracombe, but as the *Galloper* was based at the former and shunting was also carried out there, it seems reasonable to assume that this was the list of winter staff at that station. In the summer there were 46 horses operating the service and a corresponding increase in staff would have been required.

Records do not show whether the *Galloper* was in fact the same coach used by Brunel but as it was photographed in 1897, see ***Fig. 17***, it is possible that it was the same vehicle put to good use after Brunel's death in 1859.

One coach went each way every day in winter, increasing to two each way during the month of May. From 1st June to September three trips were scheduled each way, but if traffic was heavy, the resting horses would be harnessed to the spare omnibus and an extra journey made. Horses that were unsuitable to be returned to the stud at Hockley at the end of the season were sold off at public auction.

Two additional horses were required for shunting purposes at Barnstaple later in the mid 1880s to replace those that had been hired, and these were stabled in the stalls allocated to coach horses which had been disposed of. New stables were built at Ilfracombe to accommodate 16 horses, together with a carriage shed to shelter the omnibuses and breaks. The building of such a complex cost approximately £200! The old stables were leased out at £35 per annum.

At the same time the Barnstaple provender store was proving insufficient, so an additional shed was erected to house and protect the straw from weathering and the yard was paved.

Having got its own shunting horses, the Barnstaple stable then required three additional coach horses to assist the loaded vehicles up the hills. These were kept at the Half-way Inn and either replaced exhausted horses or were harnessed in front of the team at the bottom of the hill and removed at the top.

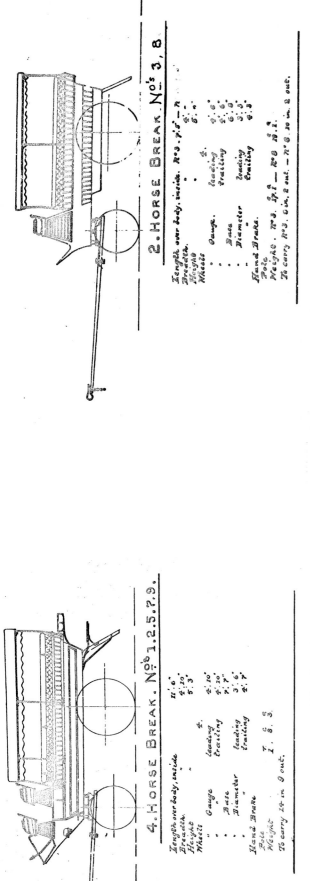

2. HORSE BREAK. Nºˢ 3, 8.

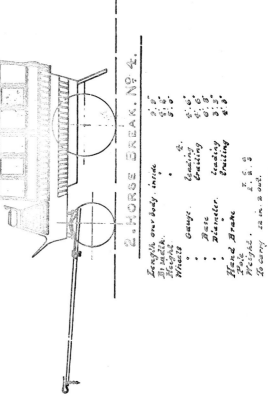

2. HORSE BREAK. Nº 4.

G.W.R. SWINDON
ILFRACOMBE & BARNSTAPLE
ROAD VEHICLES
JANUARY — 1888

4. HORSE BREAK. Nºˢ 1. 2. 5. 7. 9.

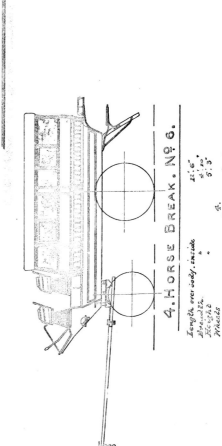

4. HORSE BREAK. Nº 6.

Fig. 79

Fig. 80

Fig. 81

Fig. 82

Fig. 84

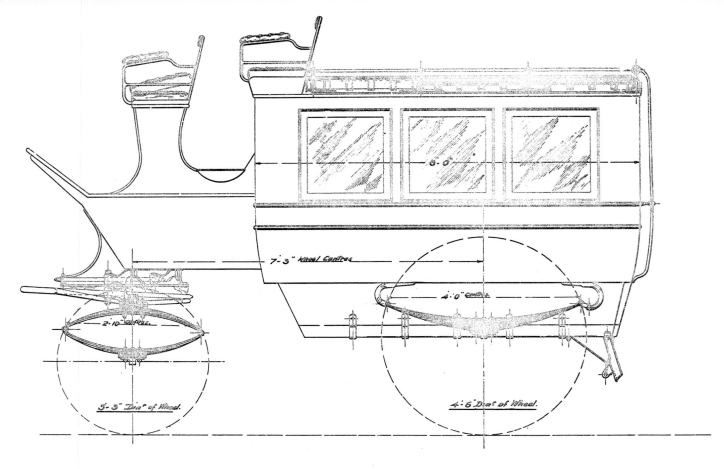

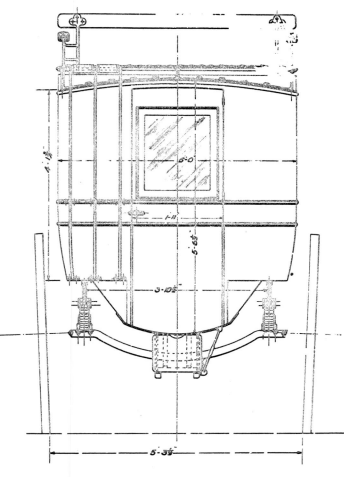

G. W. R. SWINDON

PROPOSED TWO HORSE OMNIBUS

Fig. 83

In June 1887 a short loop line permitted railway passengers to reach Ilfracombe by rail instead of being obliged to wait for the next coach, but the service was continued as a tourist attraction for another ten years. It is rather doubtful if the breaks shown on the diagram (*Fig. 79*) actually saw much service on this route.

Many years later breaks were still being used to take would-be passengers from Burnham Beeches to Slough station. This old photograph (*Fig. 80*) shows twelve passengers in a vehicle owned by Mr R. R. Hughes outside a tearoom. Similarly passengers were transported from St. Ives station to the nearby hotel which was owned by the Great Western Railway Company.

Fig. 81. This photograph, taken in 1925, shows a large Great Western omnibus just prior to scrapping. The design is reminiscent of much earlier vehicles, circa 1890 and may have been manufactured about that date as the standard of workmanship was such that vehicles were built to last many years of hard service. Note the braking system operated by the driver's left hand which applied an oak pad to the iron rim of the rear wheel.

Fig. 82. As in the previous photograph this vehicle had come to the end of its working life in 1925. The brake is hand-operated by the driver's right hand which would have enabled him to retain a correct grip on the reins in his left hand. The roller bolts for securing the traces are on the underside of the splinter bar which is a rather unusual arrangement. Modern driving vehicles have trace attachments on the upper surface.

Fig. 83. The accompanying diagram shows a proposed two horse omnibus drawn in 1903. If the design was approved, it appears to be the same vehicle as that in the photograph, giving the vehicle a working life of approximately 27 years.

Fig. 84 (page 59). The last omnibus photograph shows a two horse vehicle, again about to be scrapped. The driver sat in solitary state on the roof and operated a right hand brake acting on the iron rim of the rear wheel. A bracket for a lamp is shown beneath the driver's seat.

Springs

Springmakers were skilled craftsmen employed in all coach and carriage makers' workshops. It was their task to cut the wrought iron strips and bend them to form the springs as shown in the diagrams (*Figs 85* and *86*). By making standard items in the railway workshops, the springs could be made on a continuous basis and vehicles supplied with the requisite set or a replacement from stock, instead of being delayed while waiting for a spring to be made individually.

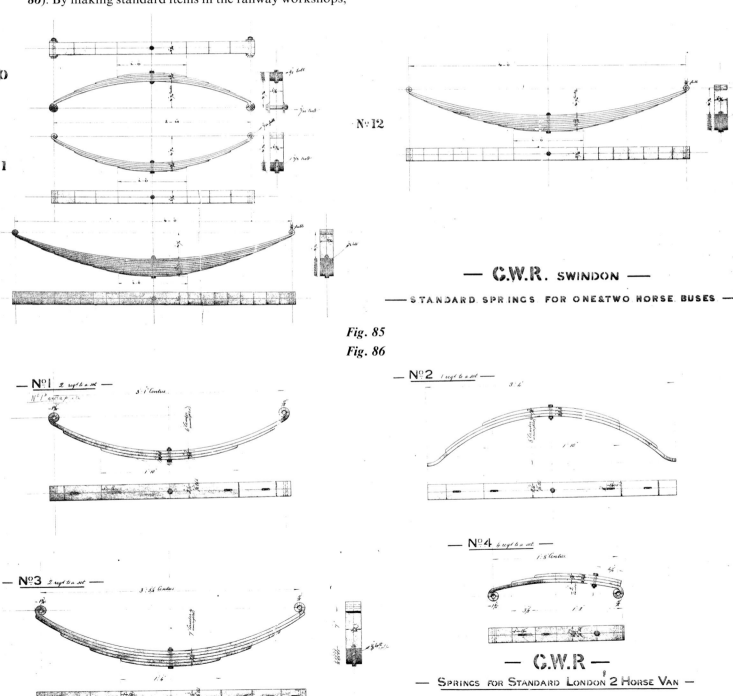

Fig. 85

Fig. 86

Fire Pumps

Railway companies were safety conscious. Usually grey horses were used to pull this 1895 fire pump to the scene of an accident or fire. (*Fig. 87*). The smaller hand version contained fire extinguishers and hose. This photograph was of the Swindon Works fire station, while *Fig. 88* shows the pump ready for action.

Fig. 89. The North Eastern Railway design of their 1895 fire pump tender was similar to those used on most railway companies property. It could be pulled by one or two horses, again often greys, while the firemen clung precariously to the handrail while standing on the 10 in wide step on either side of the hose pipe chest in the centre of the vehicle.

Fig. 87

Fig. 88

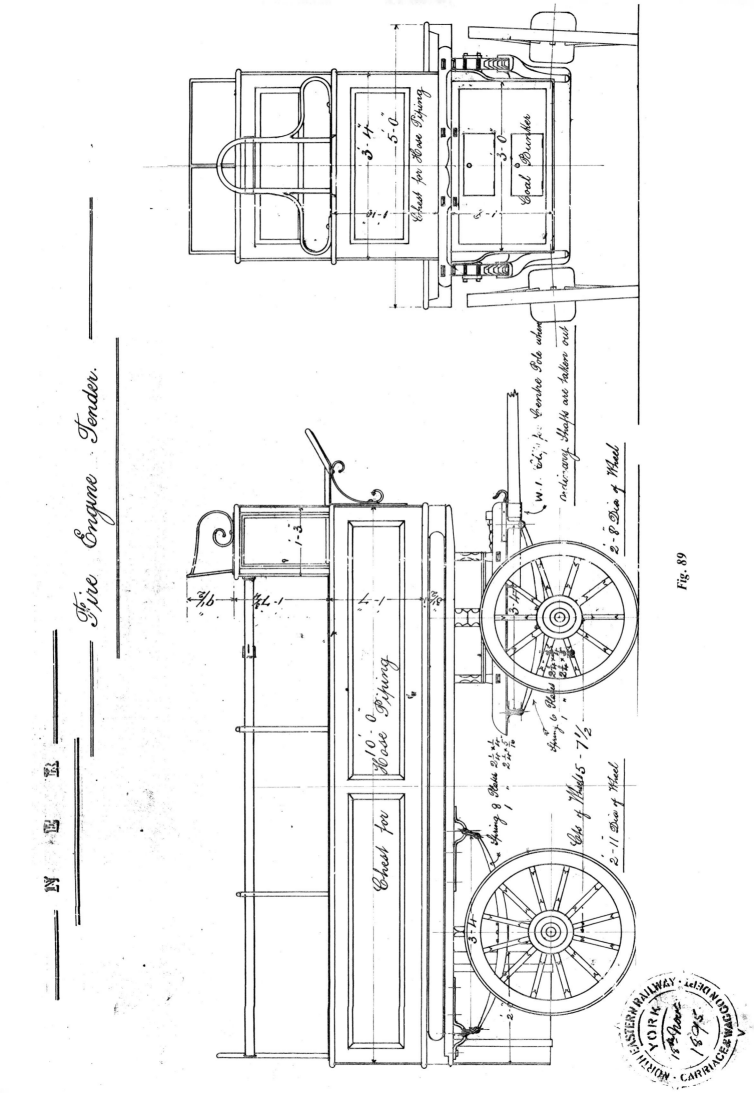

N E R

Fire Engine Tender.

Chest for Hose Piping

3'-4"
5'-0"

Coal Bunker
3'-0"

W.I. Eye for Centre Pole when
ordinary shafts are taken out

2'-8" Dia of Wheel

1'-3"

Chest for   10'-0" Hose Piping

1'-7½"
1'-1"

3'-4"

Spring 6 Plates 3½ × 5
3½ × 3

Spring 8 Plates 2½ × ⅞
2½ × ⁵⁄₁₆

Spring 1"

Dia of Wheels 5 - 7½

2'-11" Dia of Wheel

Fig. 89

Wheels

Wheels were made to standard designs by each of the railway companies. This chart belonging to the North Eastern Railway Co. and dated 1906, shows 15 patterns which covered most types of vehicles used for goods and parcel traffic. *Fig. 90* (page 65).

Wheels are made in such a way that the spokes slope outwards from the central hub to the felloe or rim. They are 'dished' in this way to prevent strain on the axle which is shaped so that the spokes below the hub remain vertical, while those above the hub slope outwards. The spokes are set in a staggered row round the hub, 'dodging' an imaginary line. The spokes radiate outwards from the hub and are driven into the fellow or wooden part of the wheel inside the iron tyre or hoop. Spokes were made of oak while the felloe was made of ash, steamed to the required curve. For many years the tyres were heated in a forge and applied to the felloe while still hot. The wheel was then plunged into water which cooled the tyre and effectively shrank it on to the wheel. Hydraulic tyre setters were introduced in 1895.

A hub cap was added to some wheels, which was frequently ornamental or embossed with company initials. This screwed into the thread of the axle box which stored lubricating oil, and prevented mud and dirt from entering.

From 1915, most Great Western wheels were made with twelve spokes, the 'Artillery' pattern, taken from the Army which had come to the conclusion that even if two or three spokes had been shot away or damaged, the wheel still had sufficient strength to turn satisfactorily. Three hundred wheels a week were made by the Great Western workshops, and even more were produced in wartime.

Fig. 91. This elegant parcel cart with its curved canopy and large wheels was probably used almost exclusively within the urban areas served by the London & North Western Railway. The shaped shafts and 'pigtails' for the traces, would have enhanced the appearance of the whole turnout.

Fig. 91

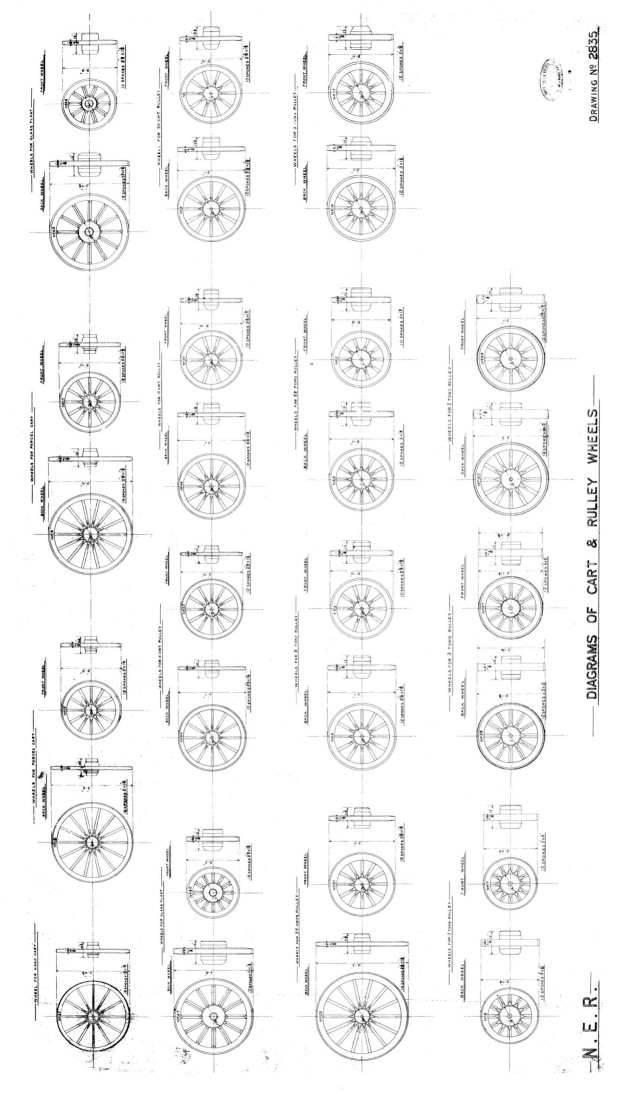

N. E. R. —— DIAGRAMS OF CART & RULLEY WHEELS ——

Fig. 90

Road Cartage Vehicles

In 1907 records show that over 3,500 horses were employed by the Great Western Railway for cartage, as well as the conveyance of passengers within urban areas by horse-drawn vehicles. The types of vehicles were as varied as the loads they carried.

Fig. 92 (opposite). A plate glass trolley, drawn by two horses, was a substantially constructed vehicle. The design had not altered significantly since the first proto-types were constructed in the early 1880s. The drawing shows an unusually small front wheel and a skid chain hanging to the side of the rear wheel. This chain was locked round the wheel to prevent it turning on steep hills when the skid shoe was used. It could also be used when the vehicle was stationary.

Fig. 93 shows a photograph of the vehicle in 1934. It is fitted with single shafts which could be removed for conversion for a two horse team.

Earlier models (*Fig. 94*) frequently had a splinter bar attached to an extended, reinforced bar protruding three to four feet from the front of the vehicle, with *DANGER* printed clearly on each side. The traces were attached to roller bolts on the splinter bar which would have required longer reins than usual to compensate for the extra distance from the horses's heads to the driver's hands.

Fig. 95. GWR vehicle No. 1270 has a similar base to the preceding glass floats, but is a horse box. Railway horses belonging to the Great Western Railway had a better health record than most of the other haulage and railway companies, but when a horse needed transport-ing to the company-owned horse hospital, the animal would be loaded at the stable and taken there as swiftly as two horses could pull it. It would also have been used for transporting a horse to or from a location not served by the railway if for some reason it could not be used in harness.

The illustration of a cattle float, (*Fig. 96*), is also mounted on a similar base to that of the glass floats. There is a small box attached to the nearside of the vehicle where details of the beasts loaded on the vehicle could be carried. The presence of the chain and winch suggests that the vehicle could also have been used for reluctant animals or even those who had pre-empted the knackers task and died naturally.

Fig. 93

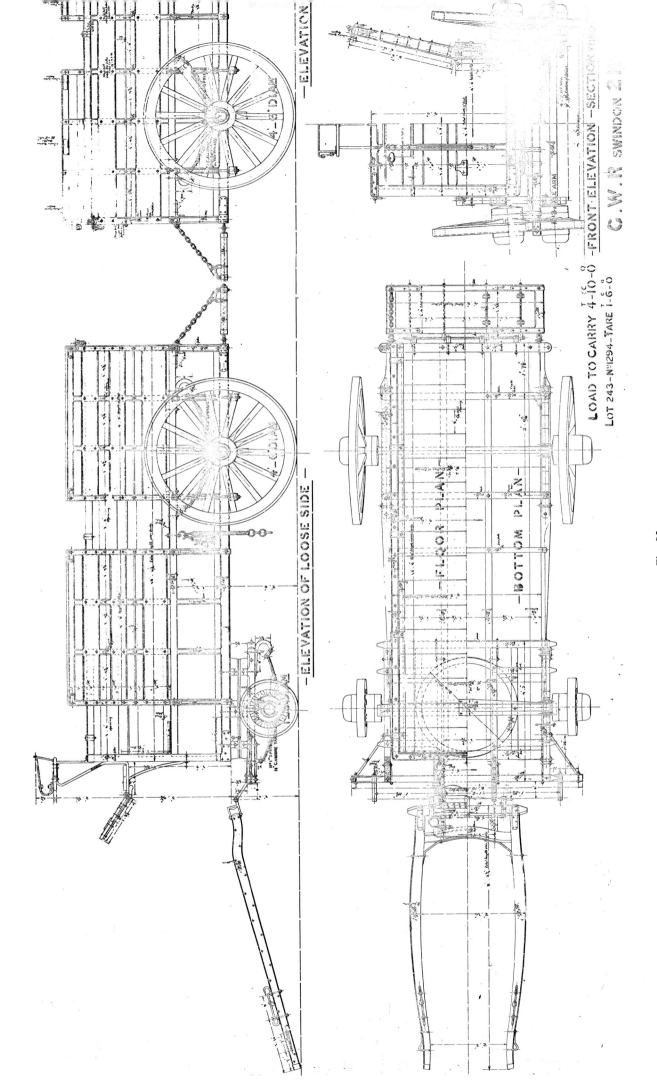

— ELEVATION —

— ELEVATION OF LOOSE SIDE —

— FLOOR PLAN —

— BOTTOM PLAN —

— FRONT ELEVATION — SECTION

G.W.R SWINDON

LOAD TO CARRY 4-10-0
LOT 243 — N° 1294 — TARE 1-6-0

Fig. 92

Fig. 94

Fig. 95

Note the presence of a skid hanging alongside the rear wheel. This metal shoe was carried on most vehicles not fitted with brakes to prevent the rear wheels from rolling. Correctly fitted this shoe produced enough friction to slow the descent of heavy loads downhill, and so assisted the horses to walk slowly and safely. The chain immediately in front of the rear wheel was passed between the wheel spokes to further prevent the rear wheels turning.

Sparks used to fly when this skid was being dragged along the road.

A team of eight horses was borrowed from the Paddington stud to pull this splendid coach to the trade exhibition in 1895 after it had travelled from the station at Gloucester. It is pictured here (*Fig. 97*) in front of Marble Arch with four drivers, one walking beside each pair of horses. The interior (*Fig. 98*) was a credit to the

Fig. 96

Fig. 97

Fig. 98

skill of the coach builders and trimmers, known nowadays as upholsterers, of the Gloucester Railway Carriage & Wagon Co. Ltd, for whom the vehicle was an advertising enterprise. As can be seen, the carriage body was supported on two special road bogies for the journey through the streets.

Fig. 99. This diagram is of an elegant mail phaeton built by the GWR in 1888, it was a fast, light vehicle. It was probably only used for urgent letters and did not remain in service for any great length of time, being superseded by the more practical and robust vehicles of the 1900s. The mail horse did not commence duties in London until he was five or six years old. He worked a seven day week and was likely to be called to collect foreign mail from the station at unexpected times. Despite irregular rest periods, the horses lasted for about six years. This was mainly due to the attention lavished on them at the stables and also at the station.

Fig. 99

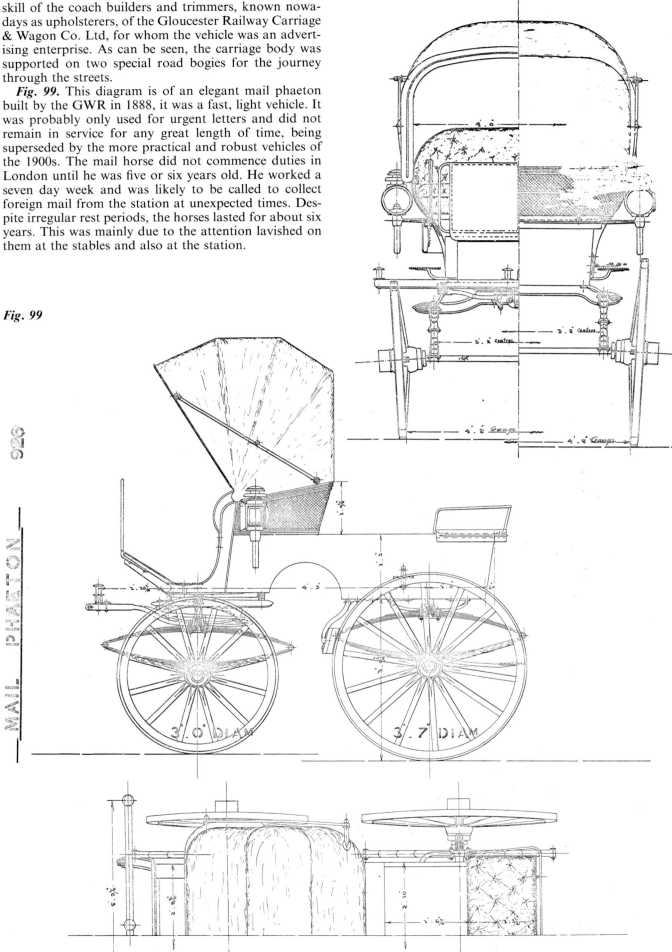

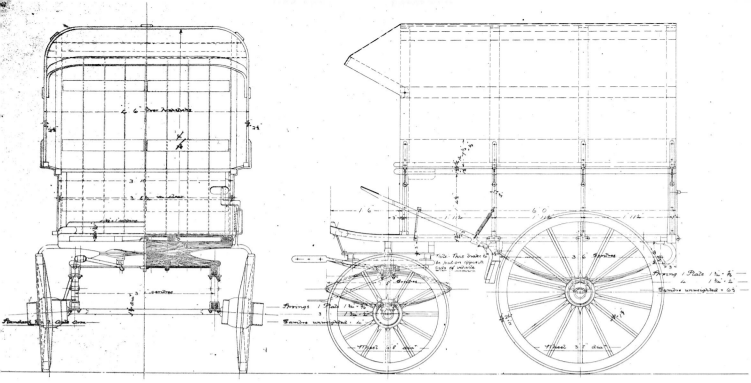

Fig. 100

The diagram (*Fig. 100*) and photograph (*Fig. 101*) depict a pony parcel van built between 1899 and 1901, for the Henley-on-Thames area. The driver was afforded some shelter by the small hood and the tarpaulin could be fastened down at the rear to protect the contents from rain. A right hand brake acting on the rim of the rear wheel is shown in the photograph. The drawing outlines a foot pedal-operated brake. Similar vehicles were sent to Bath, Newton Abbot and Exeter.

There were approximately 300,000 horses working in and around London at this time, their tasks covering coal haulage, fire fighting, funerals, cabs, omnibuses, goods traffic and a multitude of parcel carts. Private carters owned almost two thirds of these.

Fig. 101

Fig. 102

The photograph and diagram, *Fig. 102*, are of a light parcel cart intended for use in Manchester, Frome, Bath and Yeovil. It was built in the early 1900s and the body was of more rigid construction than the previous ex-ample, having an arched wood roof projecting forward to protect the driver. The cost of building such a vehicle was in the region of £60.

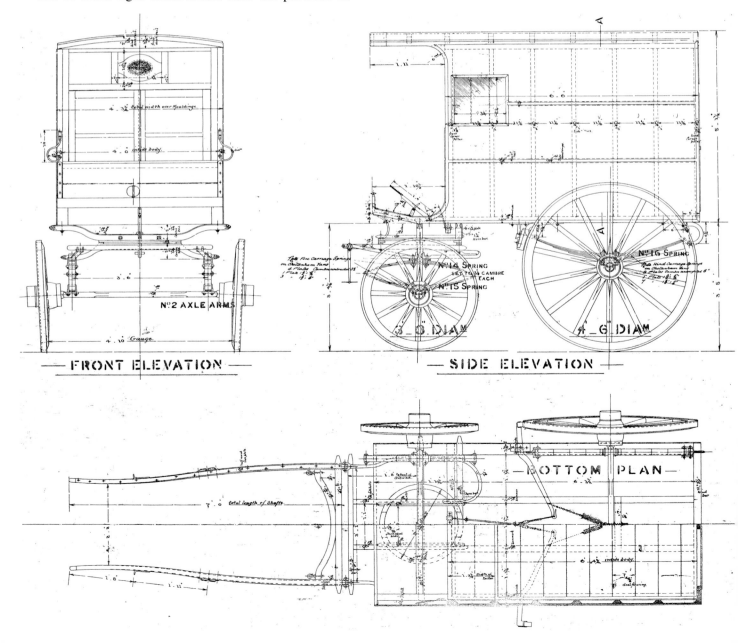

— FRONT ELEVATION —

— SIDE ELEVATION —

— BOTTOM PLAN —

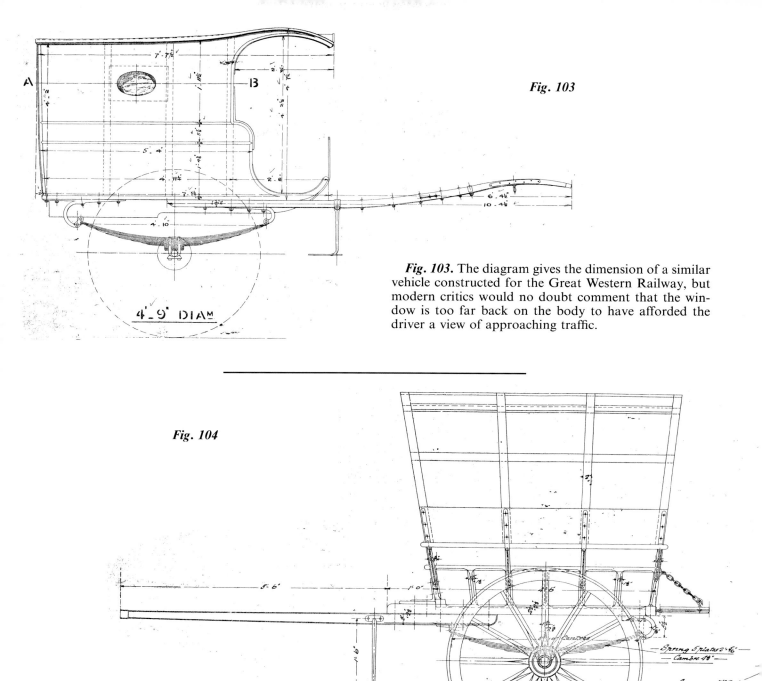

Fig. 103

Fig. 103. The diagram gives the dimension of a similar vehicle constructed for the Great Western Railway, but modern critics would no doubt comment that the window is too far back on the body to have afforded the driver a view of approaching traffic.

Fig. 104

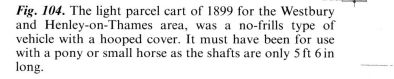

Fig. 104. The light parcel cart of 1899 for the Westbury and Henley-on-Thames area, was a no-frills type of vehicle with a hooped cover. It must have been for use with a pony or small horse as the shafts are only 5 ft 6 in long.

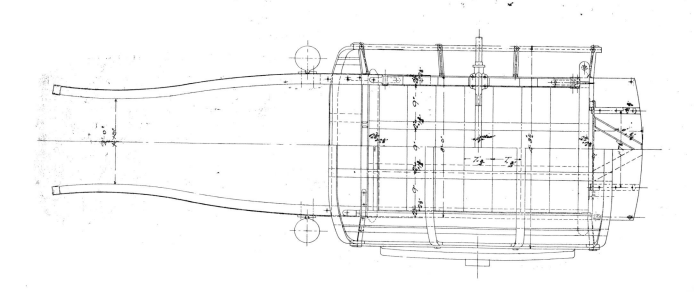

Fig. 105

Fig. 105. A list of possible destinations for goods and parcels is painted on the rear doors of this four-wheeled parcel cart, belonging to the Great Central Railway, built in the early 1900s. The wheels and shafts have been lined out by the manufacturers, the Gloucester Carriage & Wagon Co.

Fig. 106. The 1889 diagram of a Great Western town parcel cart shows a single door in the rear of the two wheel model, and steps set in the coachwork for the driver or his boy to reach to goods carried on the railed area on top of the vehicle. The driver's seat appears to be a rather basic box seat set into the body of the cart.

Fig. 107. Photographed in the summer of 1909, this parcels van has no less than ten different types of lettering on the sides of the vehicle. The overall message will leave the reader in no doubt as to the type of service the driver was empowered to offer to the public! After an initial delivery of parcels the van would spend the rest of the day collecting loads and returning to the Strand prior to returning to Paddington at the end of the day. The driver's seat is obviously nothing more than a hard plank of wood level with the splinterboard or front of the vehicle.

Fig. 108. This express parcels delivery van photographed in 1933 shows the numerous improvements which had been introduced to add to the comfort of the driver and his horse. One piece traces pass directly from the collar to the vehicle instead of being attached to the shafts, thereby lightening the harness. Note that the

driver appears to be sitting on a padded seat! The uniformed staff have obviously posed for this picture, hence the mare's oiled hooves and ultra clean, overall appearance. Apart from the lack of blinkers, the harness will be recognisable by modern horse-driving enthusiasts.

Fig. 109. Photographed when brand new in 1937, this vehicle was thought to be the epitome of luxury for both horse and driver. Pneumatic tyres, padded driving seat, electric lights and modern braking all combined to ease the work of the horse on the streets of London. The vehicle was based at Paddington.

Fig. 110. This photograph is of the same van seen early in 1938 when an advertising poster had been added to the side panel. The horse appears to be one of the poorer animals in the stable having bad knees and a generally sloppy appearance.

Fig. 111. A van built at the same time as the previous example and consecutively numbered. Driven by Mr T. Hoare, the horse won a prize at the London Van Horse Parade in 1938. The medals awarded by the RSPCA are hanging from the shafts, and were for the best horse with undocked tail. A very different condition of horse to that of the previous photograph.

Fig. 112. Another entrant for a competition using a parcels van. This time for the Windsor Horse Show in 1947. Still in GWR livery, this turnout was entered in the Heavy Trade class but records do not show whether the turnout was awarded a prize. The vehicle is very similar

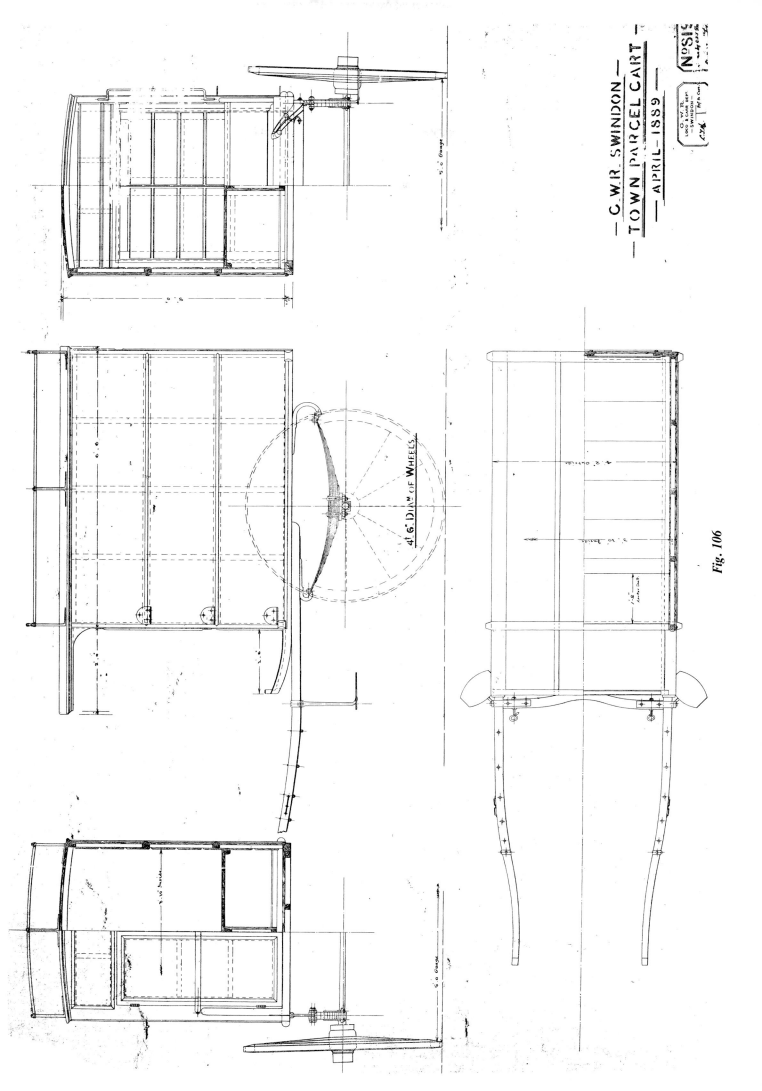

— G.WR. SWINDON —
— TOWN PARCEL CART —
— APRIL 1889 —

4ft 6in DIAM OF WHEELS

Fig. 106

Fig. 107

Fig. 108

Fig. 109

Fig. 110

Fig. 111

Fig. 112

Fig. 113

Fig. 114

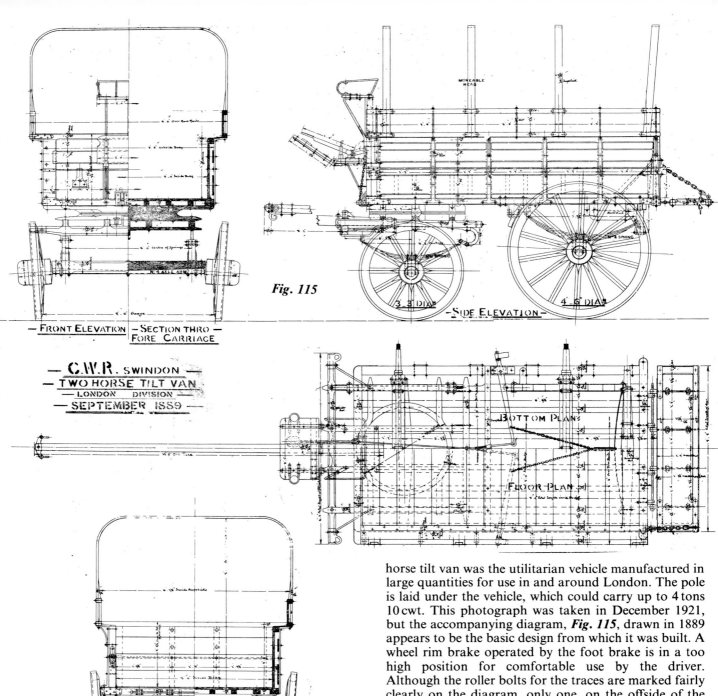

Fig. 115

— FRONT ELEVATION — —SECTION THRO —
FORE CARRIAGE

—C.W.R. SWINDON —
—TWO HORSE TILT VAN—
—LONDON DIVISION—
—SEPTEMBER 1889—

—SIDE ELEVATION—

BOTTOM PLAN

FLOOR PLAN

—HIND ELEVATION— —SECTION THRO—
HIND CARRIAGE

to that shown in *Fig. 108*, except that the lettering and number denote a much earlier version. Note the ornate bosses on the bridle and the wide setting of the blinkers. The driver was able to pull the collapsible canopy forward during wet weather.

Fig. 113. Although this vehicle was built just before the turn of the century, a considerable number were still in use in the 1940s, drawn by two horses. Although some were relegated to heavy duties in the goods department, the remainder continued to carry parcel traffic alongside their more modern vehicles. No protection was provided for the driver.

Fig. 114. Moving on now to heavier vehicles, this two

horse tilt van was the utilitarian vehicle manufactured in large quantities for use in and around London. The pole is laid under the vehicle, which could carry up to 4 tons 10 cwt. This photograph was taken in December 1921, but the accompanying diagram, *Fig. 115*, drawn in 1889 appears to be the basic design from which it was built. A wheel rim brake operated by the foot brake is in a too high position for comfortable use by the driver. Although the roller bolts for the traces are marked fairly clearly on the diagram, only one, on the offside of the splinter bar, can be seen in the photograph.

Fig. 116. A lighter, one horse tilt van was also very common round the London area from the early 1890s onwards. Again the oak block acting on the iron rimmed rear wheels is operated by the driver using a foot brake. The beautifully groomed gelding is unusual in that his tail is not docked, but looped into a braided knot. Well oiled hooves make it very difficult to distinguish a number branded into one hoof which was the practice at the time in the Great Western stables. There was no seat for the carter's lad who is perched on the tail gate of the vehicle, photographed in 1921. The chain over the back pad was connected to the 'D' ring on the shafts. A short chain from the collar transferred the pull or tractive effort to the shafts and the breeching gear prevents the cart from pushing the horse unevenly. There are no traces in evidence, the use of the various short lengths of chain making their use unnecessary. Modern drivers may be divided as to the efficiency of this type of harness as opposed to using tugs and traces to carry the shaft weight and transfer the forward movement respectively. A diagram of a similar vehicle is shown which demonstrates why GWR vehicles lasted many years in service. *Fig. 117.*

Fig. 116

Fig. 117

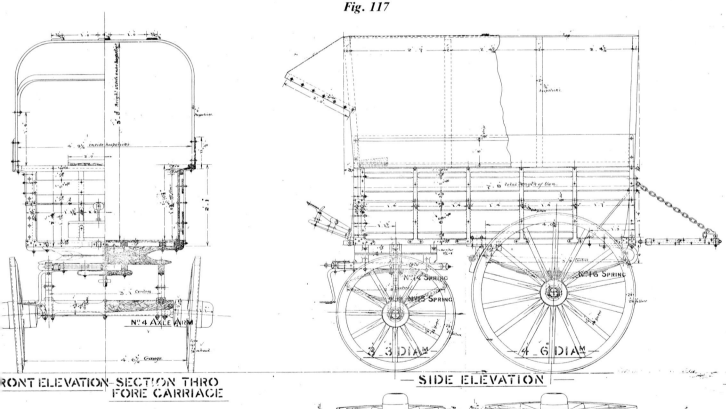

GREAT WESTERN RAILWAY

2490. PADDINGTON STATION 2490

No 4 AXLE ARM

4. 6½ Gauge

FRONT ELEVATION-SECTION THRO
FORE CARRIAGE

SIDE ELEVATION

No 4 SPRING

No 16 SPRING

No 15 SPRING

3. 3 DIAM

4. 6 DIAM

FRAME PLAN

FLOOR PLAN

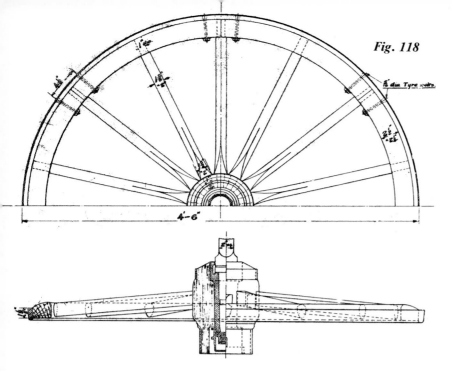

Fig. 118

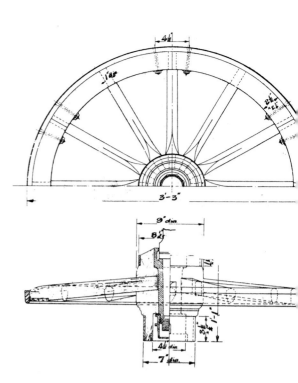

Fig. 118. This scale drawing of the wheels for the one horse tilt van shows the detail of their construction. All parts were manufactured from the raw materials received at the works.

Fig. 119. Vehicles were altered to serve a different purpose when the need arose. The necessary horses were purchased from any available source or in case of war service, commandeered. This train of horse-drawn ambulances based on the two horse tilt van design were made by the Gloucester Railway Carriage & Wagon Company in 1900 for the Boer War casualties. Both the horses and wagons were taken down to the docks in Great Western wagons on special trains, and shipped to South Africa for the duration of the War.

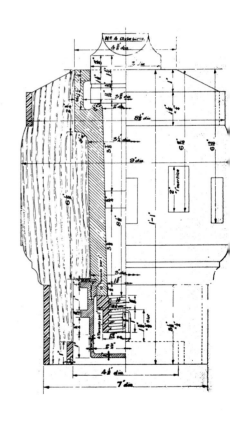

_ G.W.R _
_ STANDARD WHEELS _
_FOR ONE HORSE TILT VAN
_ SWINDON _ MAY 1909

_ N.º 39320 _

Fig. 119

Fig. 120. Lord Roberts, Commander-in-Chief of the armed forces engaged in the Boer War had one of the ambulances converted for his own use as a command vehicle. Similar to the britzka used by Brunel, it had sleeping and refreshment accommodation built in, together with the all-important table and convertible seating. Pulled by two horses, the overall appearance of these wagons is that of a sturdy and practical vehicle. Two swingletrees are suspended from hooks on the leading edge of the vehicle with four roller bolts on the upper surface of the splinter bar as an alternative method of attaching the traces.

Fig. 121. This photograph, taken in 1923 is of a van for carrying empties. These vans were designed before 1900 and from the number, 140, this would have been constructed within the first two or three years of the production at Swindon. The slightly ornate hames were no longer standard issue at this time and had perhaps been transferred to this collar for the occasion! The chain for securing the wheel is still in place, although a wheel rim brake is shown on the rear wheels. One point of particular interest is the lack of traces or long leather straps from the collar to the cart. In modern driving harness these are usually the only method of transferring the pull from the collar to the turnout. The broad saddle has a chain passing across the groove from the large 'D' shaped ring on the shaft. From the leading edge of the ring, another short chain is connected to the hame ring on each side of the collar. In order to reverse, or hold the vehicle back when going down a hill, another short piece of chain is connected to the quarterstrap buckle on the breeching gear and secured to the rear end of the 'D' ring. The horse's effort was therefore transmitted to the vehicle along the shafts, the weight of the shafts being carried by the saddle which appears to have been re-stuffed recently.

Fig. 122. A photograph taken at the Royal Windsor Horse Show in May 1949, shows the same type of vehicle repainted and entered in the Trade Single Heavy Turnout class in British Railways livery. The harness is a fine example of the care which was lavished on the leather-work, and the gelding's coat and condition are a credit to the stables. Although docking of working horses' tails was by now frowned upon, it was still fairly common practice.

Fig. 123. The diagram shows the main dimensions of the vehicle including details of the required springs for each wheel. The handbrake is shown somewhat fore-shortened which may explain why the photograph of vehicle No. 140 has a foot brake and the show vehicle, No. 197 has a handbrake clearly shown by the driver's left-hand side.

Fig. 124. This view of Paddington Goods Yard was photographed on 14th September 1906 when the new offices were under construction. Even the removal of the outer wall was not allowed to prevent work proceeding normally. Most of the vehicles nearest to the camera appear to be empty, while those in the distance are loaded with a variety of crates, barrels and bundles.

Fig. 120

Fig. 121

Fig. 122

Fig. 123

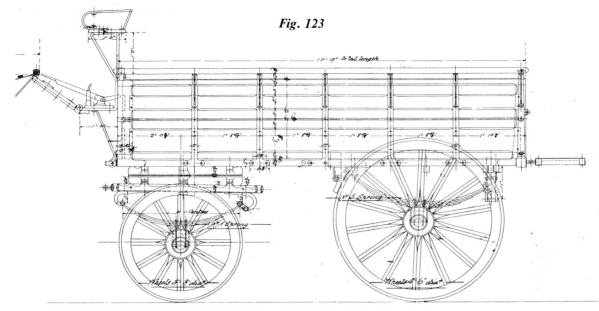

Fig. 124

Fig. 125. Two more detailed drawings of use in the wheelwrights' department. A 4 ft diameter wheel, specifically for use in rural areas, and details of the cast iron centre for a road wagon wheel drawn in 1910.

Fig. 126. This standard two-horse van for the London area of the GWR was drawn in 1912 and built at Swindon in large numbers. The hoops could either support a canvas cover or act as the framework for a more solidly constructed wooden top for the vehicle. Many of these vehicles lasted for 30 years in service and were capable of carrying 4 tons 10 cwt of goods from the station loading bay to a wide range of destinations. The carter would supervise the procedure, checking the items to be carried against his list, but it was not general practice for him to assist physically. The boy in the photograph, *Fig. 127*, looks as though he would be in his mid-teens. It was unusual for the cover of a vehicle to display a different number to that of the cart. Most likely it had been used to replace the original on a temporary basis, perhaps while a repair was made. All detachable parts of a cart were numbered with the vehicle number, and were not supposed to be interchangeable. Chain traces were easier to adjust to the correct length than the more modern leather pattern. The chain is passed round the drawbar and fastened back onto itself with a hook.

Of particular interest is the fact that these mares are being driven without blinkers. It was the horsemaster's decision whether this was advisable or not, even though he may never have driven this particular team. The horsemaster, in control of the stable, was often a man with a considerable knowledge of horses, including the treatment of simple ailments, but he was seldom recruited from the ranks of the carters or stablemen from that particular stable.

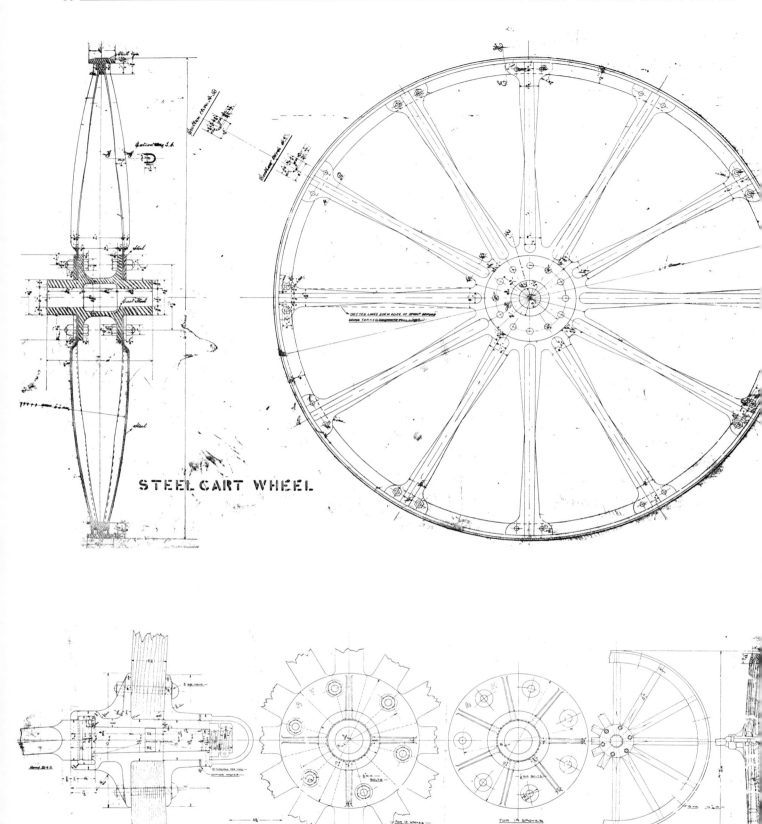

STEEL CART WHEEL

C. W. R SWINDON
CAST IRON CENTRE FOR ROAD WAGON WHEEL
Nº 4 AXLE ARM
FEBRUARY 1910
Nº 41203

Fig. 125

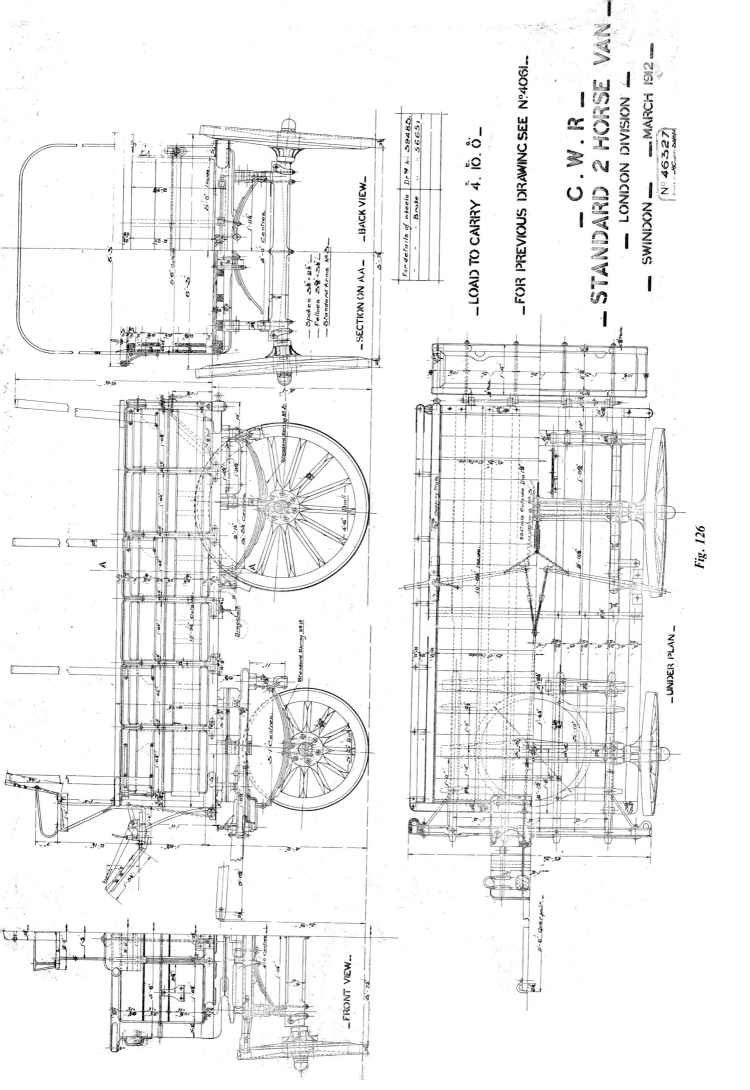

— BACK VIEW —

— SECTION ON AA —

Spokes 2⅝" × 2⅝'
Felloes 2⅝" × 2⅝'
Standard Arms Nº 3.

| For details of wheels | Dr.ᵂ Nº 39485. |
| Brake | „ 56651 |

— LOAD TO CARRY 4. 10. 0 —

— FOR PREVIOUS DRAWING SEE Nº4061 —

— C. W. R —

— STANDARD 2 HORSE VAN —

— LONDON DIVISION —

— SWINDON — MARCH 1912 —

Nº 46327

— FRONT VIEW —

— UNDER PLAN —

Fig. 126

Fig. 127

Fig. 128 shows two grey mares who have been teamed up to pull this slightly shorter van with a lightweight permanent top of wood, which has been used to advertise its use at Paddington station. The harness is considerably simpler than modern driving harness, there being no breeching gear. Leather traces with chain ends are shackled onto themselves after passing round the draw-bar of the vehicle. The 'lad' standing on the tailgate is not wearing the usual overall, and was probably of the age when they were allowed to take the reins when permitted to do so by the carter, who remained responsible for the horses, cart and load.

Fig. 128

Fig. 129

Fig. 130

Fig. 129. Unloading the flat trolley of potatoes required little skill but plenty of muscle. The use of the ubiquitous sack trucks by the porters speeded up a tedious operation. Note the skid shoe under the rear wheel furthest from the camera, although the drag chain has been left hanging.

The driver in the photograph, **Fig. 130**, stands by the horse's head. The horse bears a strong resemblance to a shire horse and is probably 16 hands high. It was quite rare for a horse of a particular breed to be purchased by the Company who preferred a 'common' horse with little feathering about the legs. Diagrams of three vehicles designed before 1900 which continued in use for several decades are shown on this page.

Fig. 131 is a light pair horse van, designed in 1885, and could be used with a hooped cover or as an open vehicle. The load carried by this vehicle would have been up to 1 ton 10 cwt, a comparatively light load for a two-horse team.

Fig. 132 is of a two-horse pole van. Note the ample provision for stopping the vehicle. In addition to the normal drag shoe and wheel chain, there are wheel rollers which acted on the rear wheel to prevent it running back on a hill. The roller, made of ash, and bound by two metal bands, hung on a chain behind the wheel, turning as the wheel revolved. Should the wheel slip back when going up a steep hill, the roller jammed beneath the rim.

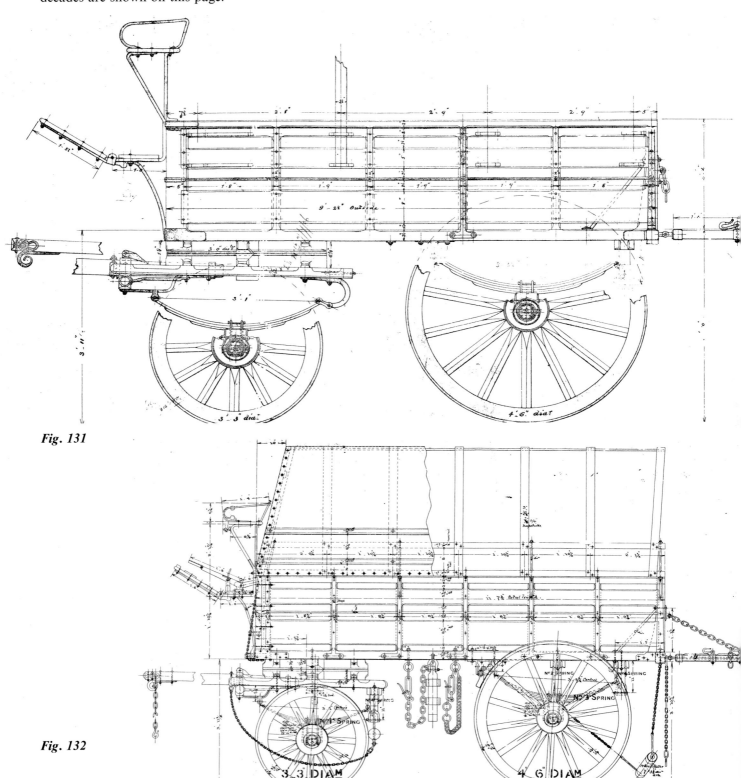

Fig. 131

Fig. 132

Fig. 133. This diagram is of a light trolley designed for carrying 1 ton 10 cwt of fruit or vegetables within the London area. Drawn in 1890, the pattern changed little during successive versions produced during the next 30 years or so. Constructed economically, the wheels were standard two-horse omnibus size, the forecarriage was taken from a one-horse tilt van, and the dickey seat from a one-horse van. The horses were expected to travel at 6 mph, and cover 20 miles in their day's work.

Fig. 134 is a photograph of a fruit and vegetable trolley of 1896. No brake is provided and the single horse could therefore have worn harness which included breeching gear to enable him to slow the descent of the vehicle when travelling downhill.

Fig. 135. This busy scene at Paddington goods loading bay in 1921, shows several one-horse trolleys being loaded with an assortment of boxes, crates, baskets and barrels. The drivers, or carmen, stand by the horse's head until the loading was complete, when he checked the list to ensure that goods were in the correct position to be unloaded in rotation according to the route to be taken. Two of the horses are eating from nosebags secured over their bridles, most of which have no blinkers attached. One side of the bit was usually unfastened to enable the horses to eat more naturally.

Above these loading bays was a second floor where a similar scene could be found. Goods stacked on the upper floor can be seen in the background of this picture, just left of centre.

Fig. 136. This scale drawing of a one-horse trolley dated 1904, shows an alternative splinterbar to take two pairs of shafts when required. Although brakes had been introduced on parcel vans by this date, there is no provision for a mechanical brake on this vehicle.

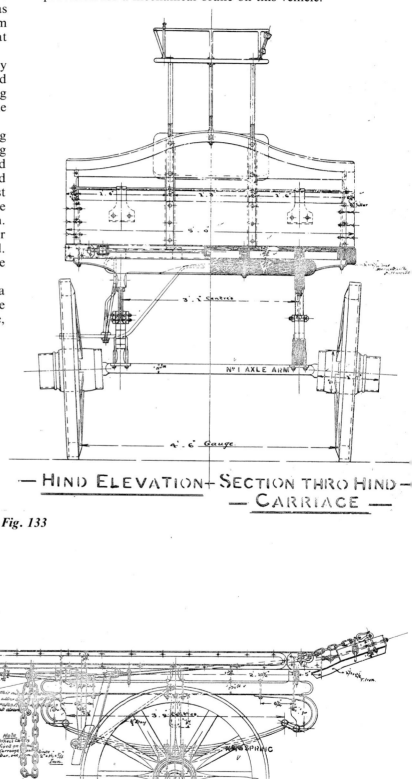

— HIND ELEVATION — SECTION THRO HIND —
— CARRIAGE —

Fig. 133

— SIDE ELEVATION —

Fig. 134
Fig. 135

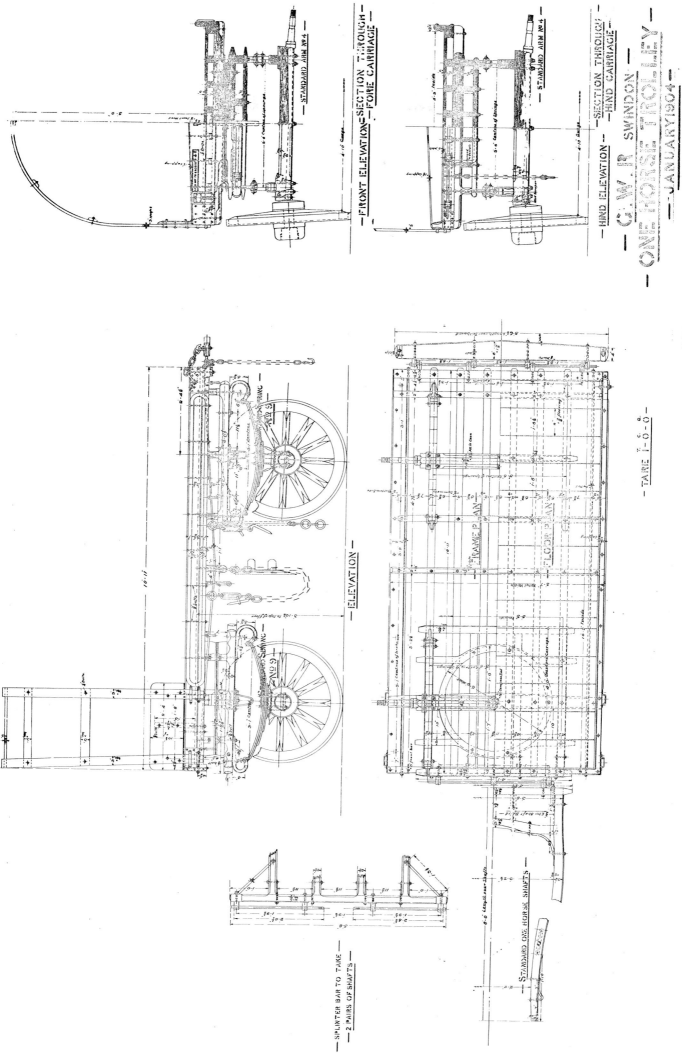

FRONT ELEVATION—SECTION THROUGH
FORE CARRIAGE

HIND ELEVATION—SECTION THROUGH
HIND CARRIAGE

G.W.R SWINDON

ONE HORSE TROLLEY

—JANUARY 1904—

STANDARD ARM Nº 4

ELEVATION

FRAME PLAN

FLOOR PLAN

—TARE 1-0-0—

—SPLINTER BAR TO TAKE—
—2 PAIRS OF SHAFTS—

STANDARD ONE HORSE SHAFTS

Fig. 136

Fig. 137

Fig. 137 is of a light one-horse trolley photographed in 1894 and was probably used for perishable goods. A canvas hood could be secured to the arched framework which would also have afforded a small degree of shelter to the driver. A modified version of this vehicle was used at Ilfracombe, it being 5 in narrower.

Fig. 138 (page 95). This 1920 drawing of a one-horse lorry for production at Swindon Works shows variations of design intended for different areas on the GWR system. The one intended for use at Paddington has a driving seat above the front board supported by a bracket, while the Birmingham pattern has a box seat raised some 10 in above the floor of the vehicle. The Liverpool version, built to carry 4 tons, had no seat at all. The South Wales version was 3 in wider and carried 2 tons 10 cwt. The vehicle made for the Manchester area was somewhat lighter with a longitudinal support for a canvas cover. Although the drawing is dated 1920, the drag shoe is still in use. A single horse was expected to pull upward of 36 cwt on this vehicle.

Fig. 139 is a drawing of a two-horse trolley for bagged or baled goods such as coal, cotton, cocoa or building materials and was designed in 1894 to carry a 7-ton load.

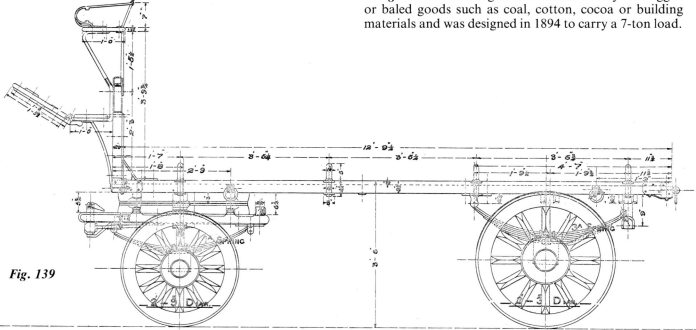

Fig. 139

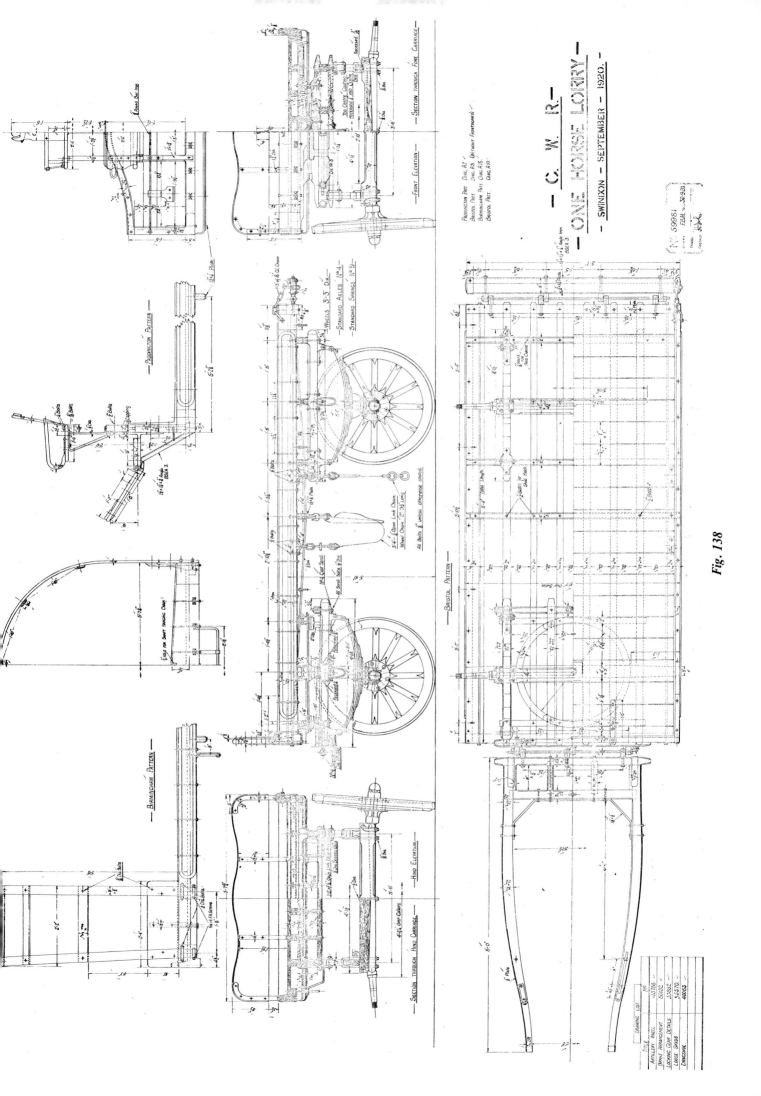

Fig. 138

Fig. 140 shows the design pictorially with No. 1082. Although an earlier vehicle than the 'lorry' of 1920, a handbrake is now provided. Note the ample securing points on the floor of the vehicle.

Fig. 141 depicts an 1894 trolley designed to be hauled by three horses. Two in the pair shafts, called the wheelers, while the third was in front attached by chain traces to the brackets on the shafts. The drag shoe and wheel roller can be clearly seen to the left and right of the rear wheel respectively. A wheel-operated brake is also shown and this would have been turned by the van lad while the driver held the team steady. Judging from the obvious strength of the vehicle, the maximum load for this trolley would probably have been in the region of 7 tons. The version built for Newton Abbot carried 8 tons 12 cwt.

Fig. 142 Off loading light, one-horse trolleys at Paddington in the early 1900s. Checkers are busy ticking all the items off, as they are loaded on to railway vehicles for

forwarding. Cranes are being used in addition to manpower in order to meet the hectic schedule, and little time has been lost while the photograph was taken.

Fig. 143. This photograph, taken in the yard at Paddington, shows a convoy of two-horse vans carrying a special consignment of blankets for the Maple's store in the centre of London. In order to protect the bales from the sides of the carts, straw has been used as padding. The carmen, or drivers, are wearing their uniform caps which were first issued on an annual basis to both carmen and van guards in March 1889. Driving aprons were issued once every two years to the carmen but whips were still supplied by the individual and appear to reflect their own financial status. The driver of the pair on the left holds a whip that is obviously home-made.

Nosebags hanging under the tailgate indicate that the horses will be away from the stables for a considerable length of time. Most of the horses' tails are left in their natural state and they are being driven without blinkers.

Fig. 140

Fig. 141

Fig. 142

Fig. 143

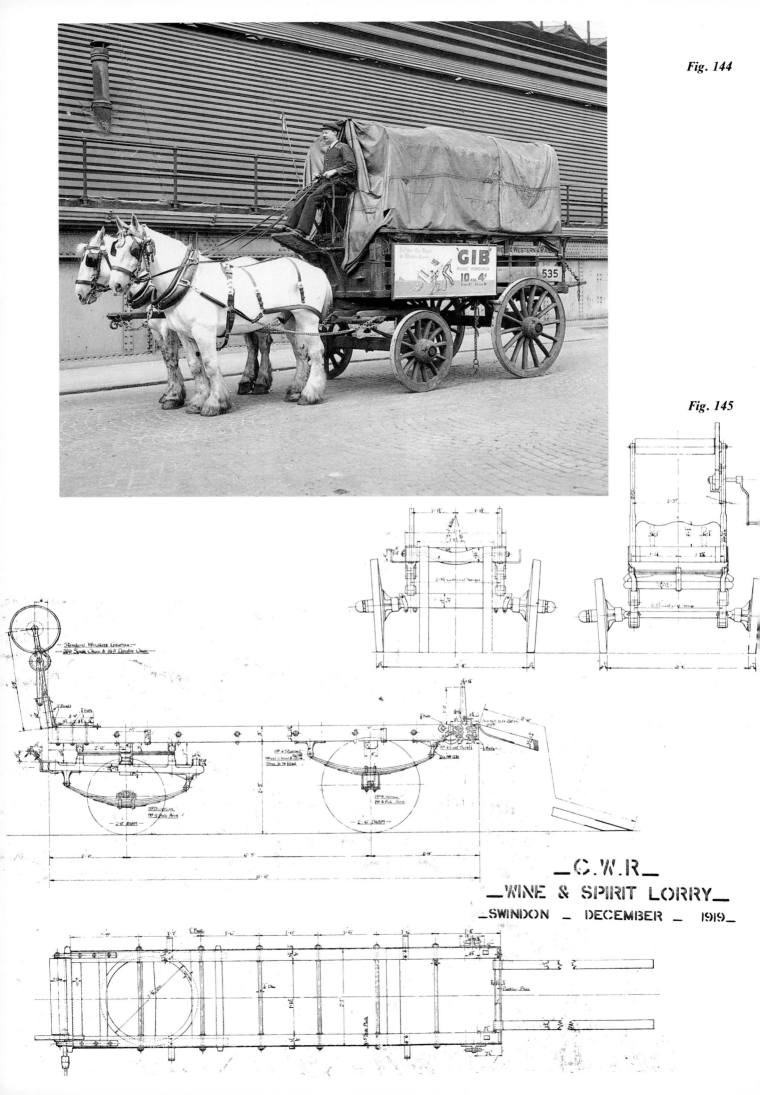

Fig. 144

Fig. 145

_C.W.R_
WINE & SPIRIT LORRY
_SWINDON _ DECEMBER _ 1919_

Fig. 144. By 1930 the Company had started to earn revenue from advertisements attached to the sides of their own vehicles. The photograph of a two-horse pole van shows two grey geldings wearing decorated harness. Most working harness was unadorned and severely practical, but for the purpose of this posed photograph, even the trace chains appear to be brand new. Under a magnifying glass the number of the nearside horse can be seen on the off-side fore hoof. The number was cut into the hoof as soon as the horse was allocated to a station or stable and records kept in the cartage manager's office as to the date of purchase, cost, efficiency and time off sick. When the particular animal was cast and disposed of at auction, the number was re-allocated to a new horse purchased to replace the one whose services had been dispensed with.

Fig. 145 is a diagram of a 1919 wine and spirit lorry manufactured at Swindon which had a manual winch fitted at the front with two lengths of chain to assist with loading. Skids 9 ft 6 in length were carried to act as a ramp for the barrels. These were tucked in brackets on the side of the vehicle which was 11 ft long. The fifth wheel for improved turning is clearly shown in the floor plan.

Fig. 146. In this 1920 photograph of a wine and spirit lorry the skid can be seen almost obliterating the 'GWR' painted on the nearside of the vehicle.

Fig. 147. Details of two sizes of skids are shown. They were manufactured from ash wood at the Slough Road Transport Depot and were supplied for use with the wine and spirit lorries (*Figs 145* and *146*), and for any other carts that loaded goods in barrels.

Fig. 148. This proposed two-horse van for carrying electric cables used a standard heavy pair horse van body with additional reinforcing above the front wheel, together with an additional lateral spring. Although the drawing is designated 'Proposed' which means that it was not necessarily built, the accompanying photograph proves that such a vehicle was actually produced and photographed the following year, 1906, *Fig. 149*.

Fig. 150. The ornate coal trolley was built in 1897 by the Gloucester Railway Carriage & Wagon Co. for a Mr E. Draisney who had rented a coal depot at Acton from the GWR. Single shafts are leaning up against the wall in the background.

Fig. 151. Another vehicle built in 1897 by the same company, was for a Tewkesbury flour milling company. Note the brake which was applied by turning the wheel by the driver's seat. Again it was intended that this vehicle was to be pulled by a single horse.

Fig. 152 is of a covered van of the late 1890s. The brake shoe and chain for holding the wheel when going down hills is shown clearly on the nearside. There does not appear to be any provision for the driver to sit in or on the vehicle, even in bad weather when the tarpauling cover would be closed. The practice of walking beside the horses was extremely unpopular but under the watchful eye of inspectors, the rules were rarely disobeyed. The lettering on the front sheets is unusual.

Fig. 153. This photograph, taken in 1921 shows a more modern two-horse covered van with a driver's seat. The pole is lying on the ground beneath the vehicle, and the wheels, although still metal rimmed, are of different sizes, the rear wheels having 14 spokes.

Fig. 146

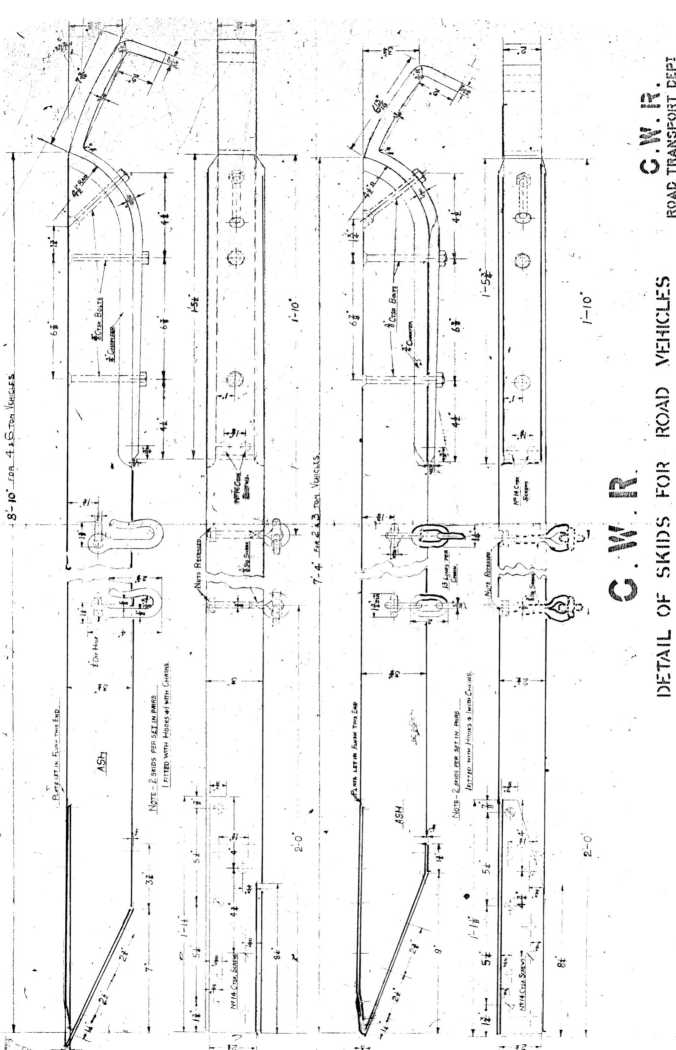

C. W. R.

DETAIL OF SKIDS FOR ROAD VEHICLES

G. W. R.
ROAD TRANSPORT DEPT.
DRAWN BY J.A.J. SLOUGH.
CHECKED BY
DATE 26-11-35.

Fig. 148

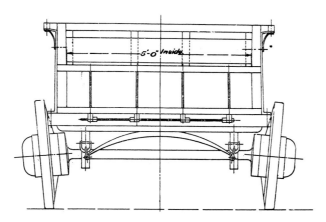

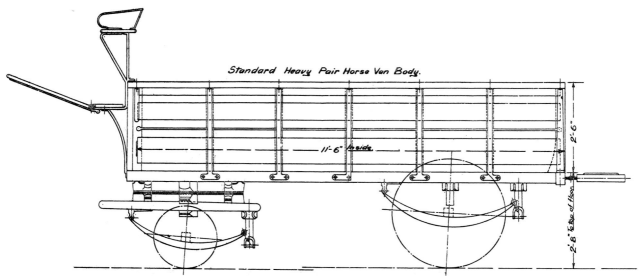

Standard Heavy Pair Horse Van Body.

5'-0" Inside.

11'-6" Inside.

2'-6"

2'-8" to top of floor.

Fig. 149

GREAT WESTERN RAILWAY
509 · PADDINGTON STATION 509

Fig. 150

Fig. 151

Fig. 152

Fig. 153

First World War

Fig. 154

Fig. 155

During the First World War, many of the railway company wagon works were turned over to the manufacture of vehicles for the armed services. *Fig. 154* shows the LNWR works at Wolverton is typical of the extent to which the change of purpose was accomplished. Approximately 50 two-horse supply wagons for army use are seen in a more or less finished state, and unfinished undercarriages are in the foreground, together with the body parts on the ground behind them on the right.

Fig. 155. In addition to supply wagons, the parcel cart diagrams shown earlier were altered to create a horse-drawn ambulance for battlefield casualties. Similar to the invalid coach provided by the Great Western Railway, rollers were used to facilitate the removal and insertion of stretcher cases inside the van whose doors opened the full width of the rear end of the cart. Fixed wood steps made lifting the stretchers in and out easier.

Fig. 156. Another horse-drawn ambulance manufactured by the Gloucester Railway Carriage & Wagon Co. for the War Department, gives details of the number it can accommodate on the side panel, i.e. four lying or twelve sitting.

Horses for the war were requisitioned from many sources including the Great Western Railway. Twenty-two heavy horses and 52 lighter animals were required for the First World War and they were sent to army camps by train in specially adapted open wagons.

The horses were branded with a new number and fitted with army harness which incorporated many quick release fastenings. All harness was the same size so that if one horse in a team was killed, another could immediately replace it without having to alter the length of the traces or rein. Whether this resulted in sore shoulders and other ailments does not seem to be recorded.

One fact that is documented is that millions of troops embarked through Avonmouth Docks, together with 350,000 horses and mules.

Fig. 157. Originally built in 1905 with seven-plank 4 ft 3 in sides, these open wagons were rebuilt in 1914 with an additional top rail to transport horses and mules required for army service during the First World War. Note the rings for tying up the animals which were carried across the width of the vehicle, their headcollars attached by two halter ropes to adjacent rings. They were loaded by cranes using slings.

Fig. 158. Another wagon which started life in 1912 as an open wagon had two extra rails added to carry military pack-horses and mules. There do not appear to be any rings on the outside for attaching halter ropes but the extra height afforded by the second rail may well have made them unnecessary. During the Second World War horses were again used to pull baggage trains and guns. During the first 18 months of the war 8,924 special trains were run and among the equipment transported by the Great Western Railway on these trains were 14,555 horses and mules, probably in vehicles similar to those adapted for use in the First World War.

Horse-drawn ambulance, 1915

Fig. 156

Fig. 157

Fig. 158

Fig. 159

Fig. 160

Fig. 159. Transport for the officers was provided by the railway workshops in the style of this rather elegant trap. Unusually, there are 16 spokes in the large wheels and the moulded shafts are carried right through the body of the vehicle. This particular vehicle was built just before the full austerity of the war effort became apparent, and is reflected in its appearance and furnishings.

Fig. 160. This photograph of a later version of a trap for wartime use clearly indicates that less expensive materials had been used to construct this more mundane vehicle.

Those horses which remained in Britain were also brought into service to replace petrol powered vehicles wherever possible. These two photographs show Great Western Railway trolleys being used to deliver Anderson shelters to householders in bombing areas, namely Cardiff in **Fig. 161** and London in **Fig. 162**. Some of the carts

look as though they have seen better days but every vehicle was pressed into service regardless of ownership or condition.

In addition to commandeering horses and property for the war effort, many Great Western employees were called up for periods of military service. Many GWR staff were awarded medals for gallantry. Among the long list are a few awarded to staff of the Horse Goods Department.

G. W. Cooper, Horse Foreman at Poplar station was awarded the B.E.M. before the end of the war.

F. E. Scanlon, Chief Horse Foreman at Birmingham was awarded the B.E.M.

W. Sparks, Horse Inspector at Plymouth was Commended.

J. G. Thomas, stableman at Plymouth was awarded the B.E.M.

Fig. 161

Fig. 162

Refuse Carts

Refuse was a big problem on and near railway property. *Fig. 163.* This 'slop' cart of 1920 could hold over 200 gallons of liquid and was emptied by using the chain passing round the centre drum when the handle by the nearside shaft was turned. The wheels of the cogs could be prevented from reversing by the small lever lying on the smaller of the two toothed wheels.

Stands are hinged to the shafts so that the vehicle could be used even if the horse was not in the shafts taking some of the weight on the chain which passed over the groove in the backpad, attached at each end to the bracket on the shafts.

Fig. 164 (page 109). The diagram of the LNER tumbler or 'slop' cart demonstrates the sturdy construction of this small but essential appliance.

Manure from the stables was sold to farm contractors for 1d per horse per week. They were responsible for collecting the by-product, and carting it away from the stable premises. At the Smithfield establishment, competition for the manure raised the price in the late 19th century to 2d per horse per week, but this was considered an exception to the normal price paid elsewhere.

Fig. 165 (page 110) is a diagram of a stronger vehicle designed in 1891. It was capable of carrying 300 gallons of liquid, but was still only destined to be drawn by one horse! Two hoses at the rear delivered the water to where it was required and was controlled by the upper foot pedal beneath the driver's seat. A foot brake was provided to restrict the speed of the vehicle when going downhill.

Fig. 166. This single horse tip cart photographed in 1897 had a sloping floor to the vehicle to enable the contents to be pulled out more easily. Shaft supports kept the vehicle steady even if the horse had been taken away for other work. This cart was commonly seen at many smaller stations where it had a multitude of uses.

Fig. 163

Fig. 166

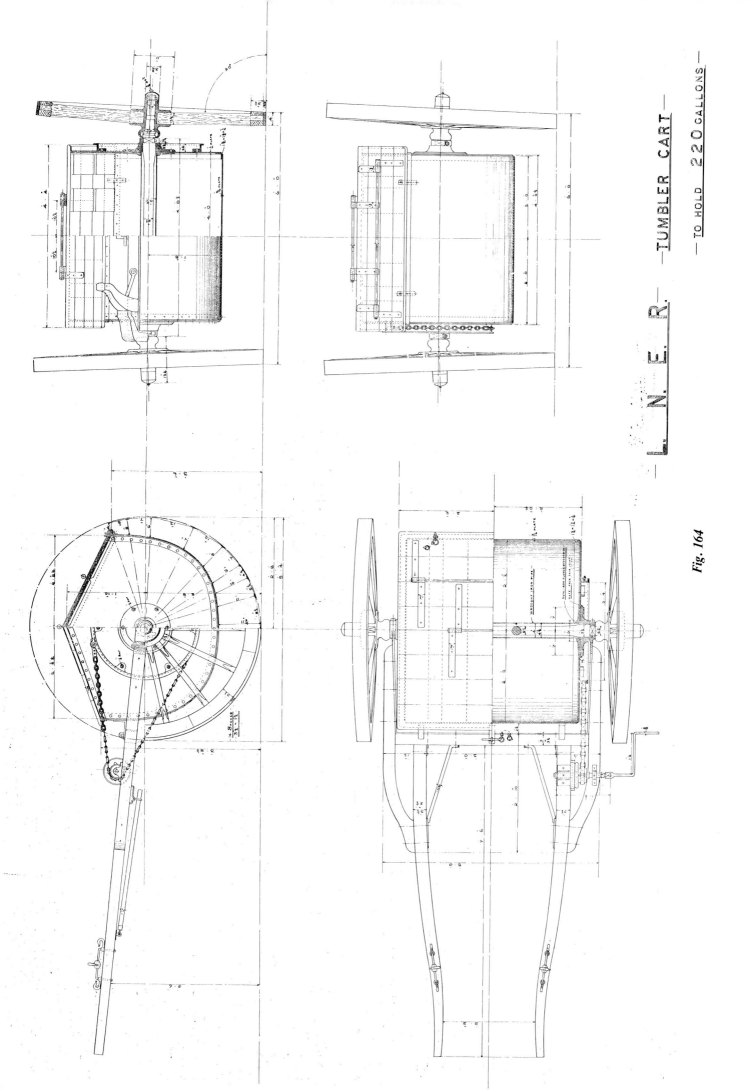

L. N. E. R. — TUMBLER CART —

— TO HOLD 220 GALLONS —

Fig. 164

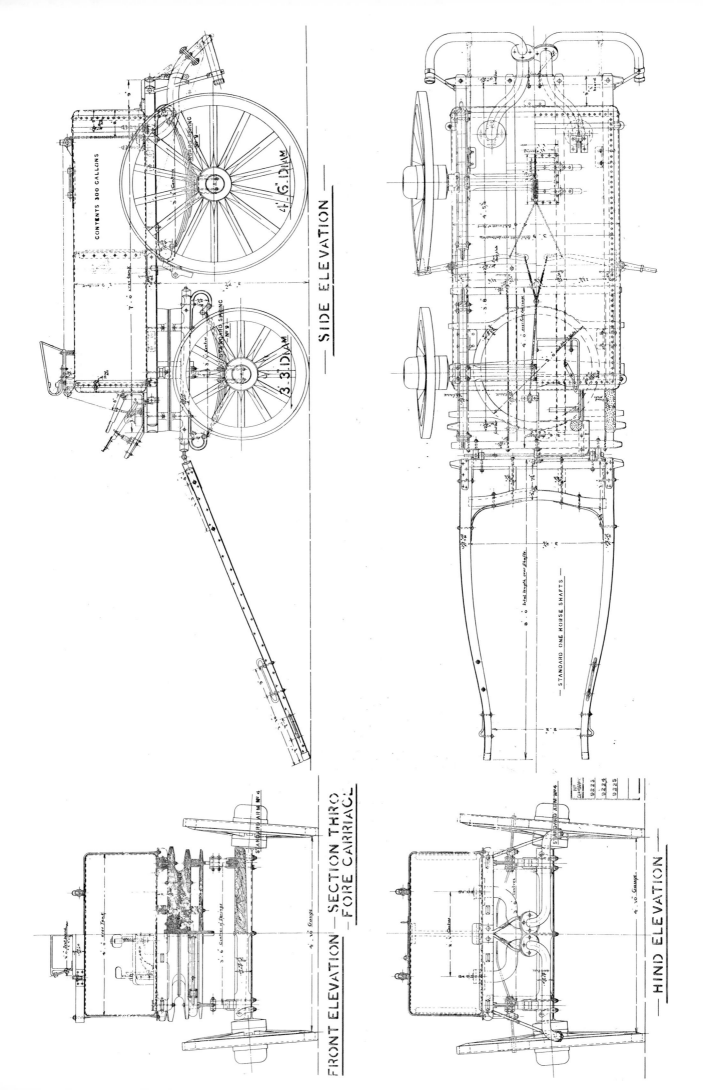

CONTENTS 300 GALLONS

4'·6" DIAM

3'·3" DIAM

— SIDE ELEVATION —

— STANDARD ONE HORSE SHAFTS —

Fig. 165

— FRONT ELEVATION — SECTION THRO FORE CARRIAGE —

STANDARD ARM Nº 4

— HIND ELEVATION —

STANDARD ARM Nº 4

Shafts

Fig. 167

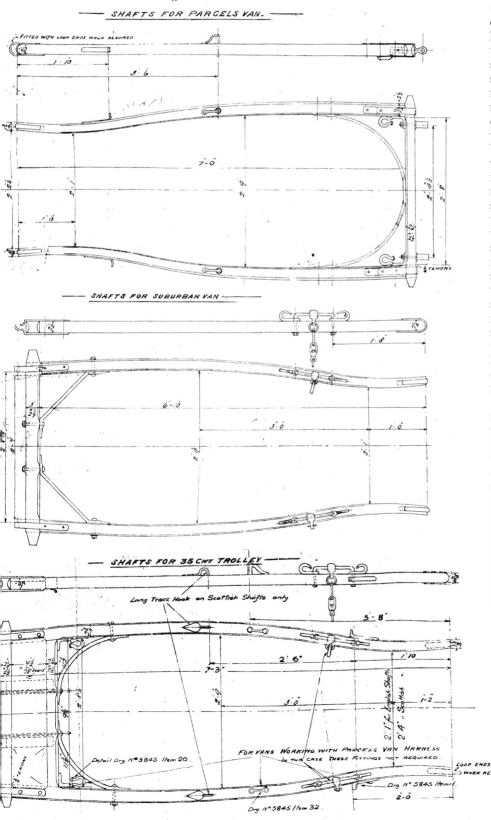

SHAFTS FOR PARCELS VAN.

SHAFTS FOR SUBURBAN VAN

SHAFTS FOR 35 CWT TROLLEY

Shafts for Great Western Railway vehicles were made at the Swindon Road Vehicle Shop. This Midland Railway chart, *Fig. 167*, shows the main variations required for seven different types of vehicles. By standardising the design, replacement shafts could be fitted in minutes instead of a vehicle being out of commission while an individual pair was made. The Great Western had a very similar chart which is unfortunately not available for reproduction. Shafts are usually made from ash wood which can be steamed to the required shape. When used with a two-wheeled vehicle, they afford balance and a measure of steering, being fastened to the harness by chain hooks or leather straps. Shafts on four wheel vehicles were attached to the harness in a similar fashion, but were not required for balance, only as a measure for steering and when attached to breeching harness, prevented the horse from being pushed by the body of the cart or wagon when proceeding downhill.

The back chains, trace hooks and shaft lengths vary according to the weight of the vehicle and therefore the size of horse that would draw the vehicle. The Great Western 'D' ring on the shafts was less ornate, being made without the hooks on either side, but the same rule applied with regard to the back chain not being required when a horse was using light or parcel van harness. Note that Scottish horses appear to need a wider gap between the shafts than English horses (2 ft 5 in as opposed to 2 ft 2 in).

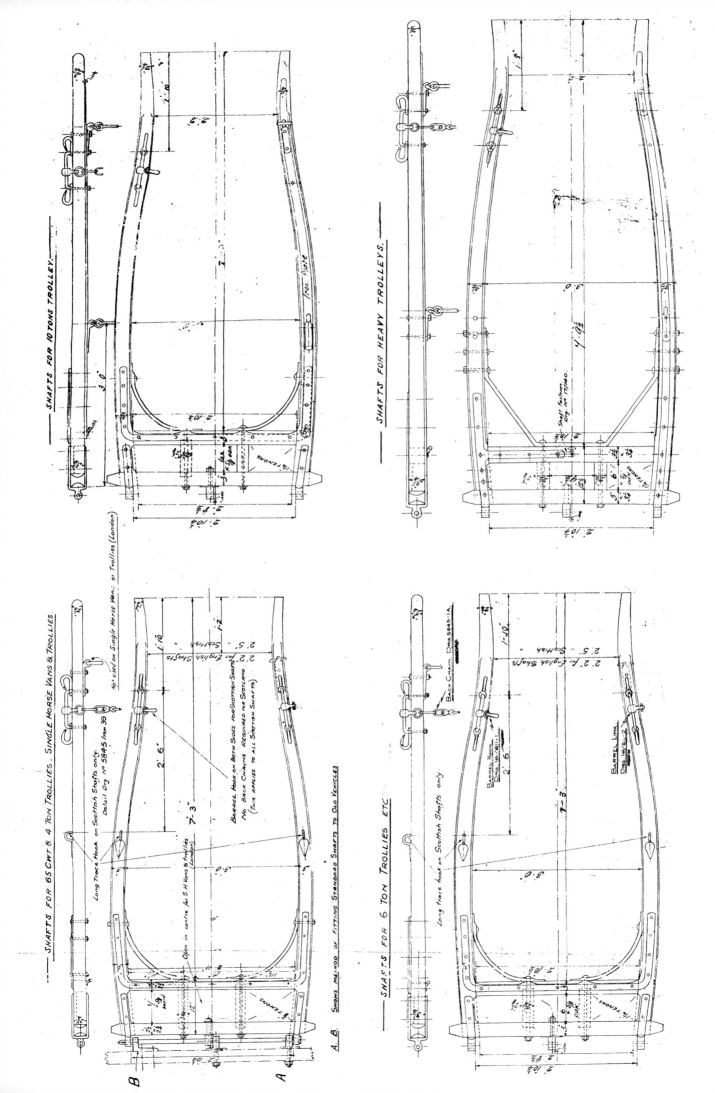

— SHAFTS FOR 10 TONS TROLLEY. —

— SHAFTS FOR HEAVY TROLLEYS. —

— SHAFTS FOR 65 CWT & 4 TON TROLLIES. SINGLE HORSE VANS & TROLLIES. —

— SHAFTS FOR 6 TON TROLLIES ETC —

A . B .   SHOWS METHOD OF FITTING STANDARD SHAFTS TO OLD VEHICLES

Fig. 167 (cont)

Special Vehicles

This simplified diagram of a mobile crane, *Fig. 168,* was hauled around the goods and marshalling yards by two strong horses with a third chain horse when required. It was made by Messrs Booth & Bros near Leeds, and regularly used for unloading railway wagons on the site of new building works.

Fig. 169. The photograph is of a 15-ton lorry base used for a crane. The double shafts are lying on the floor of the vehicle which has a wheel brake acting on the rear wheel and several securing points for the crane machinery when it was in position. Note the all-steel wheels and smooth flat tyres.

Fig. 170 shows a similar road vehicle in the lower right hand corner of the photograph. One horse is pulling a somewhat lighter crane base with the jib removed. Work was in progress at Worcester in 1925. Rather unusually, the horse appears to be unattended.

Fig. 171. A team of six horses was required to haul this unwieldy load of engineering machinery from Shepherds Bush yard. Three drivers were required to supervise the team, one driver walking at the head of each pair. Each pair was harnessed together but the reins are not coupled together for driving from the vehicle as in modern driving practice. The horses are equipped with heavy van horse harness which weighs about 40 lbs. Spreader bars used between the first two pairs of horses keep the trace chains at a uniform height and width before being attached to the tug ring of the next pair. The traces of the middle or swing pair are fastened to the 'D' shaped bracket on the shafts with sliding rings. Note the use of double shafts for this vehicle.

Fig. 172. Special trolleys or lorries were made to carry considerable loads such as the engineering machinery in the previous picture.

Fig. 173. The diagram on this page shows a vehicle capable of carrying ten tons, pulled by two horses in double shafts, or a pair of horses harnessed either side of a pole. The upright stanchions of the stone lorry were used to guide containers of brick or stones onto the floor of the vehicle.

Fig. 168

Fig. 169

Fig. 170

Fig. 171

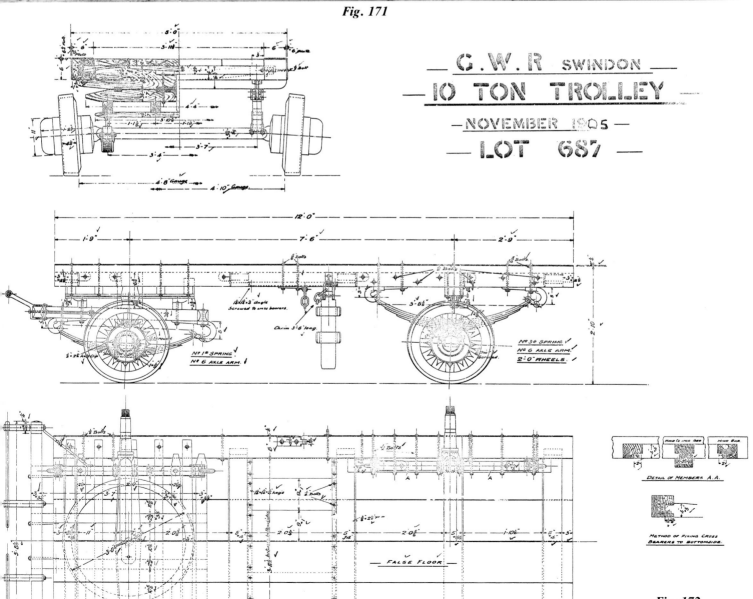

G.W.R SWINDON
10 TON TROLLEY
NOVEMBER 1905
LOT 687

Fig. 172

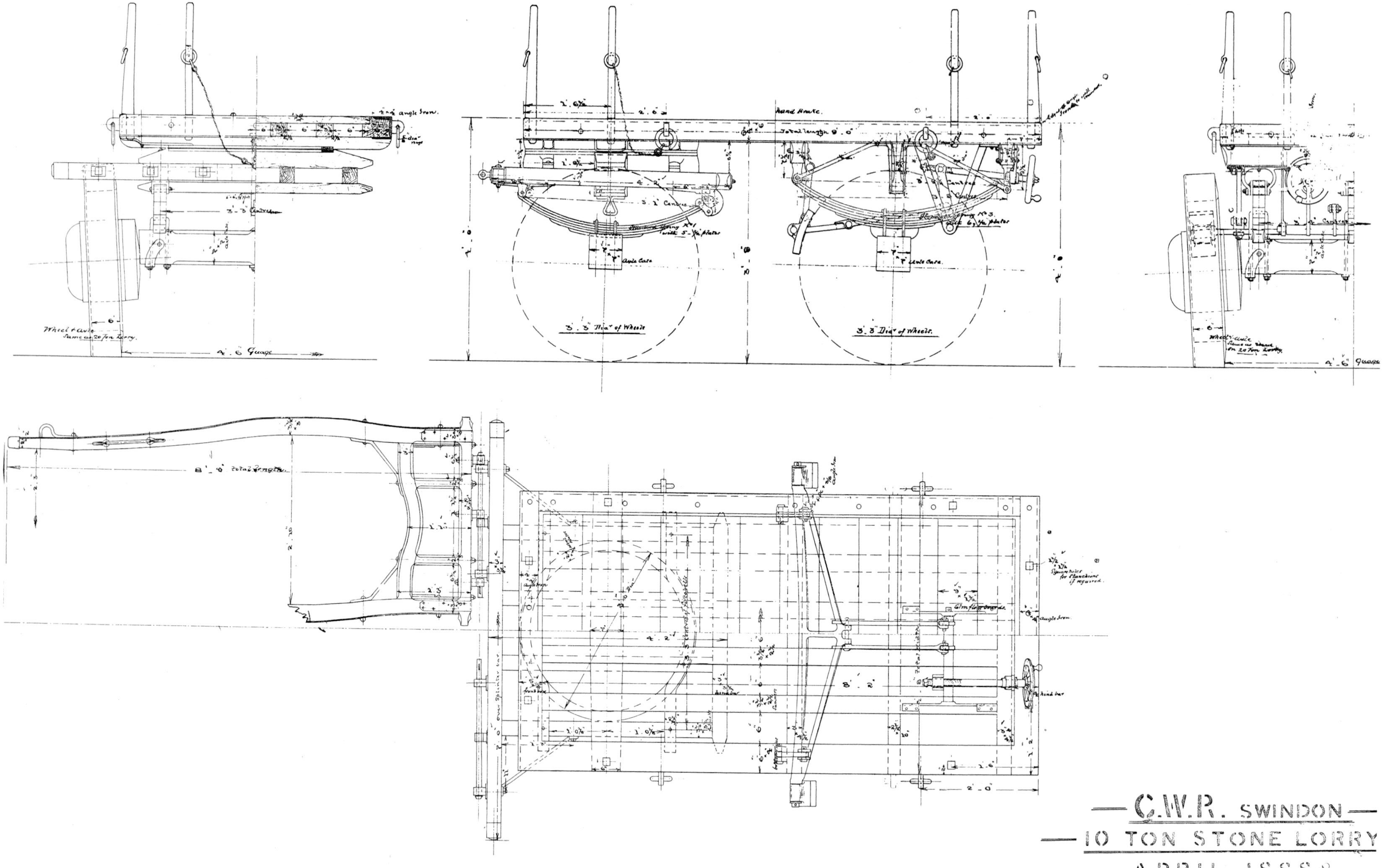
G.W.R. SWINDON
10 TON STONE LORRY
APRIL 1888
3'. 8" Dia^r of Wheels
Axle Case
Hand Brake
Total length 9'. 0"
4'. 6" Guage
Wheel & Axle Same as 20 Ton Lorry
8'. 0" total length
angle Iron
Elm floor boards

Fig. 173

Fig. 174

Fig. 174. The 1896 photograph of a stone lorry clearly shows the reinforced construction of the vehicle and the springs. Note that the shafts are attached beneath the floor of the vehicle. The driver would undoubtedly have walked beside his team when the maximum load was being pulled. Yeovil, Bath and Frome each had a stone lorry.

Fig. 175 (page 118). A proposed lift van for frozen meat traffic from Liverpool to London. It would have been the forerunner of the refrigerated container and was transferable to a train by using a crane. The vehicle was pulled by two horses. The drawing is dated 1910.

Fig. 176. In this picture a team of four horses under the charge of a driver or carman and a van guard are about to set out with a wagon laden with whisky. Two of the horses are in double shafts with heavy harness and back chains to support the shafts while the front two are chain horses with lighter harness. There does not appear to be a spreader bar behind the leading horses which keeps the chain traces at the correct distance apart, but the chains are supported by additional quarterstraps attached to the strap running along the centre of the horse's back. The chain on the far side of the team seems to be in a very slack position, but this would no doubt be corrected as soon as the team moved off. The local constabulary would be informed about the movement and intended route of such a vehicle and also the railway company's own police force. Wagons in the background belonging to a cartage contractor are loaded in a rather more precarious fashion than the GWR vehicles.

Fig. 176

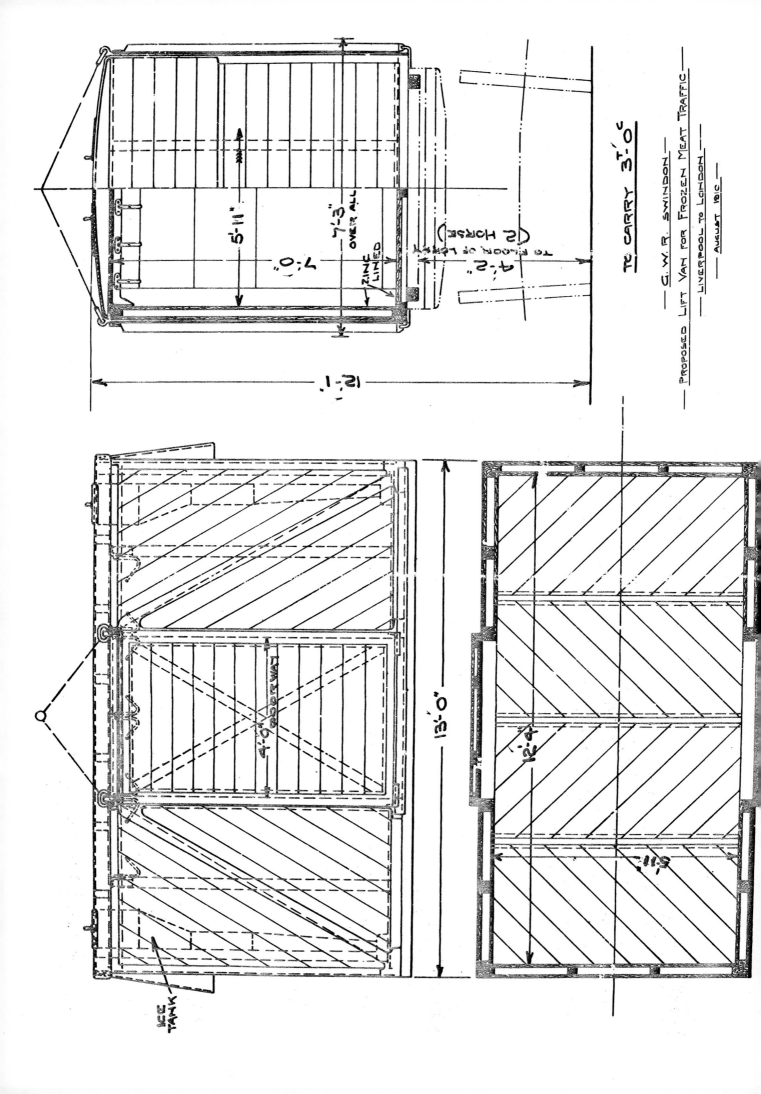

TO CARRY 3'-0"

— G. W. R. SWINDON —

— PROPOSED LIFT VAN FOR FROZEN MEAT TRAFFIC —

— LIVERPOOL TO LONDON —

— AUGUST 1910 —

5'-11"

7'-0"

7'-3" OVER ALL

ZINC LINED

(2 HORSE)

4'-2" TO FLOOR OF LORRY

12'-1"

13'-0"

4'-0" DOORWAY

12'-4"

11'-9"

ICE TANK

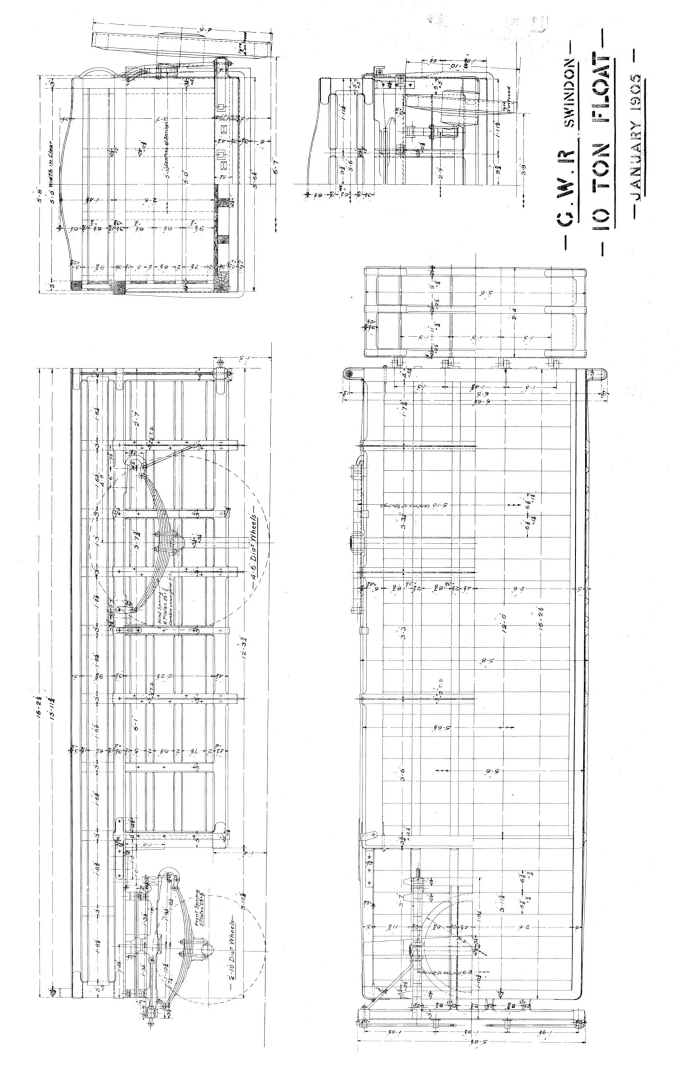

G.W.R. SWINDON

10 TON FLOAT

JANUARY 1905

Fig. 177

Fig. 177. The 10-ton float made at Swindon in 1905 had many uses, amongst which was the transport of cattle or other loads which could not be manhandled up the height of a normal wagon floor.

Fig. 178. A winch has been added to the photographed vehicle and also a small box for carrying the details of the cattle loaded on board. These vehicles were supplied for service in Exeter and Bristol in addition to those manufactured for the London area.

The traces were passed round the iron bar on the leading edge of the splinter bar and fastened back onto themselves when adjusted to the correct length. This vehicle was still in use in 1933. If a load needed to be covered, there was provision for hoops and a sheet to be added. The wheels and body of this vehicle would have been painted in milk chocolate brown, with a cream panel and black lettering.

Wheels for such a vehicle hardly came into the 'standard' category. They were specially manufactured at Swindon with the aid of scale drawings. On this 1905 diagram (*Fig. 179*, opposite) even the number of threads per inch is recorded.

For smaller items which needed a low centre of gravity the one horse float was also made at Swindon. *Fig. 180* (page 122) is a diagram of a float with stands, capable of carrying milk churns or other loads that could not be lifted far off the ground. The shafts are shaped and are fitted with metal brackets for a chain to pass over the back pad of the saddle. This design is dated May 1889 and may well have been the basis for the similar vehicles which were issued to country stations where it would double as a small parcels or goods cart.

Fig. 181. This photograph of a 2¼-ton one-horse float shows that it was intended to be a severely practical vehicle. There is no facility for a cover to be attached, or for the driver to sit on the vehicle. This float was destined for use in and around Manchester.

Fig. 178

Fig. 181

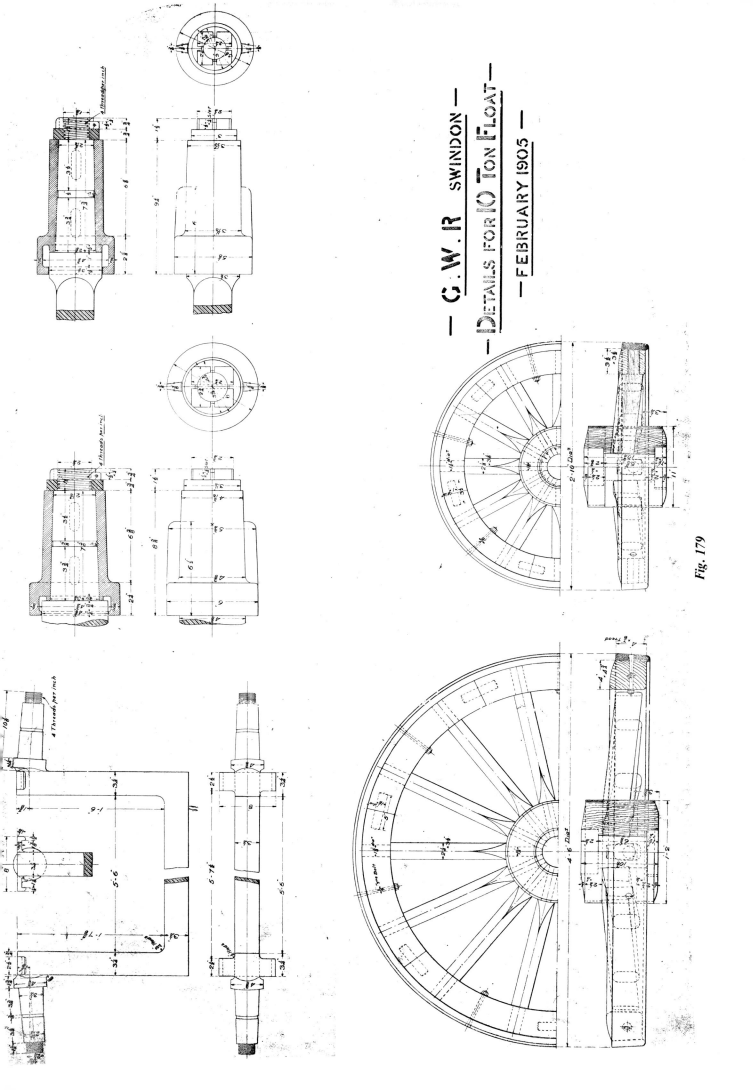

— G.W.R — SWINDON —

DETAILS FOR 10 TON FLOAT

— FEBRUARY 1905 —

Fig. 179

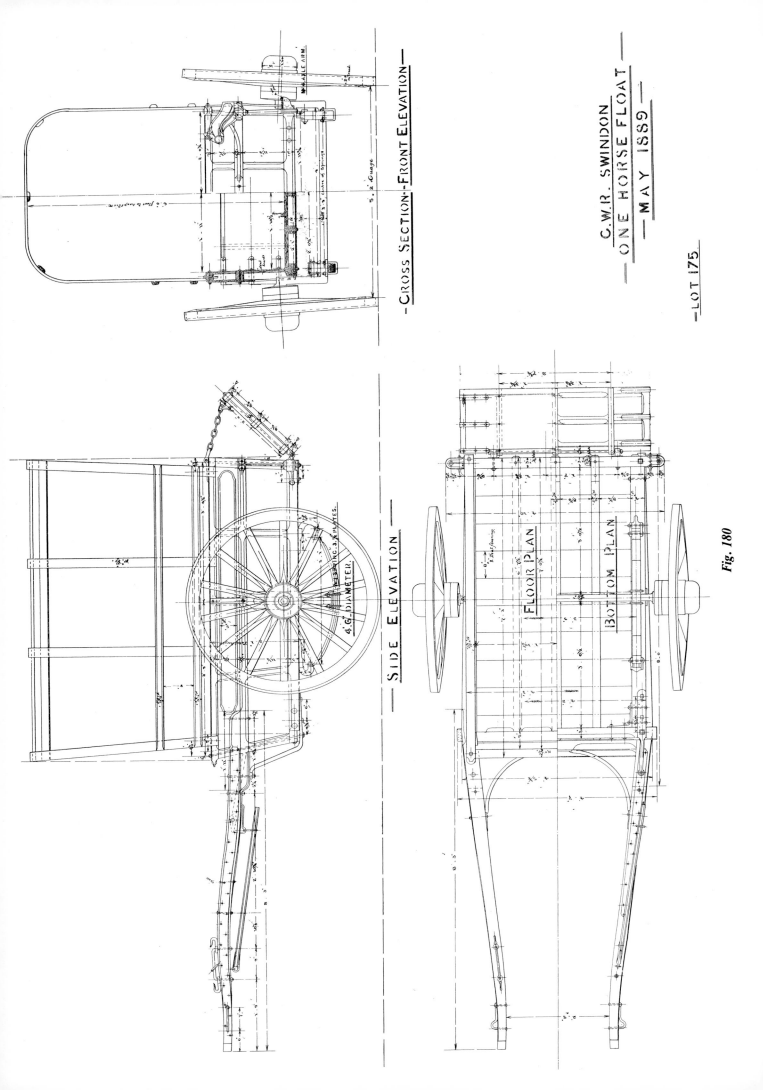

CROSS SECTION—FRONT ELEVATION

SIDE ELEVATION

FLOOR PLAN

BOTTOM PLAN

G.W.R. SWINDON
— ONE HORSE FLOAT —
— MAY 1889 —

=LOT 175=

Fig. 180

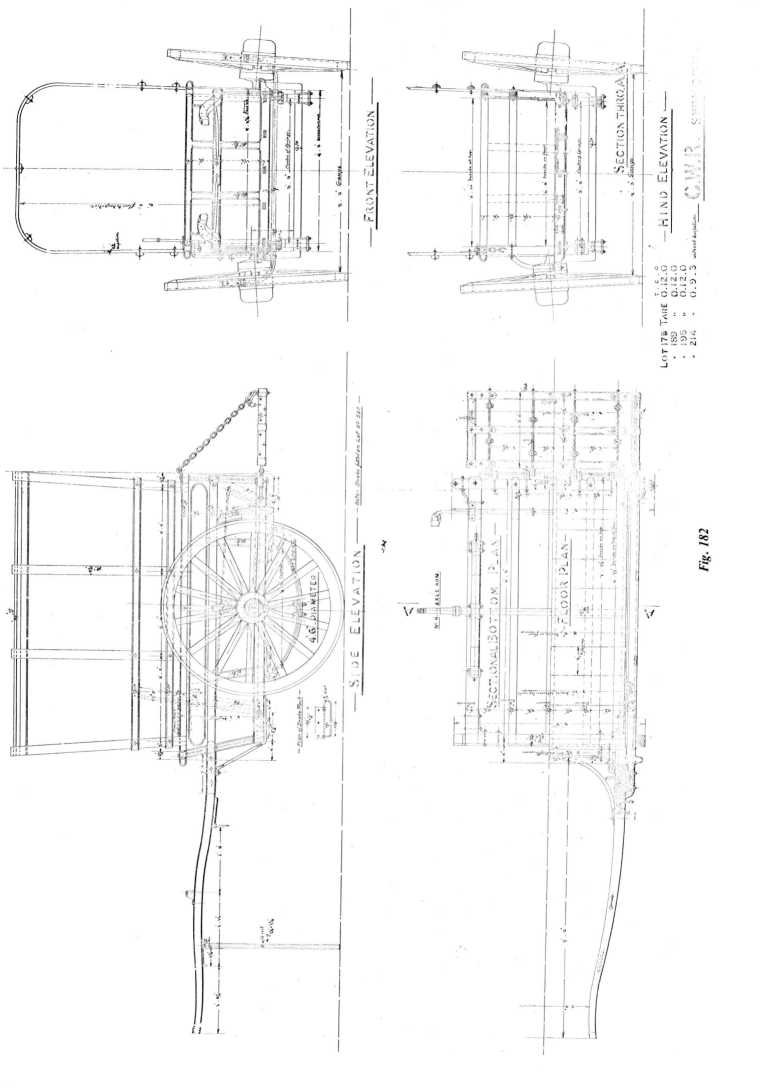

FRONT ELEVATION

HIND ELEVATION

SECTION THROA

SIDE ELEVATION

SECTIONAL BOTTOM PLAN

FLOOR PLAN

G.W.R.

4'6" DIAMETER

No. 4. AXLE ARM.

Note:- Brake fitted on Lot No 320.

5'3" Gauge

5'3" Gauge

Fig. 182

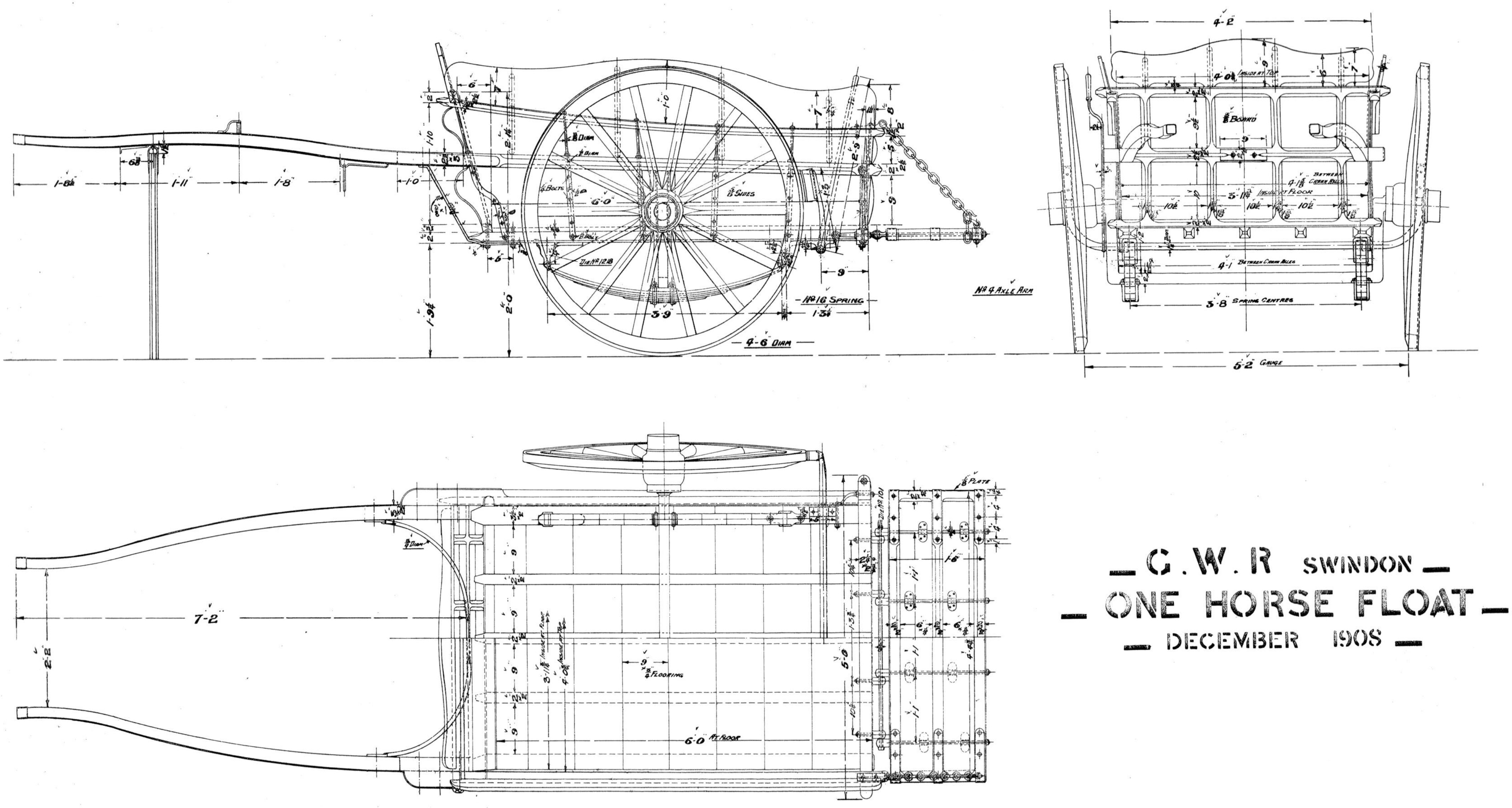

— G. W. R. SWINDON —
— ONE HORSE FLOAT —
— DECEMBER 1908 —

Fig. 183

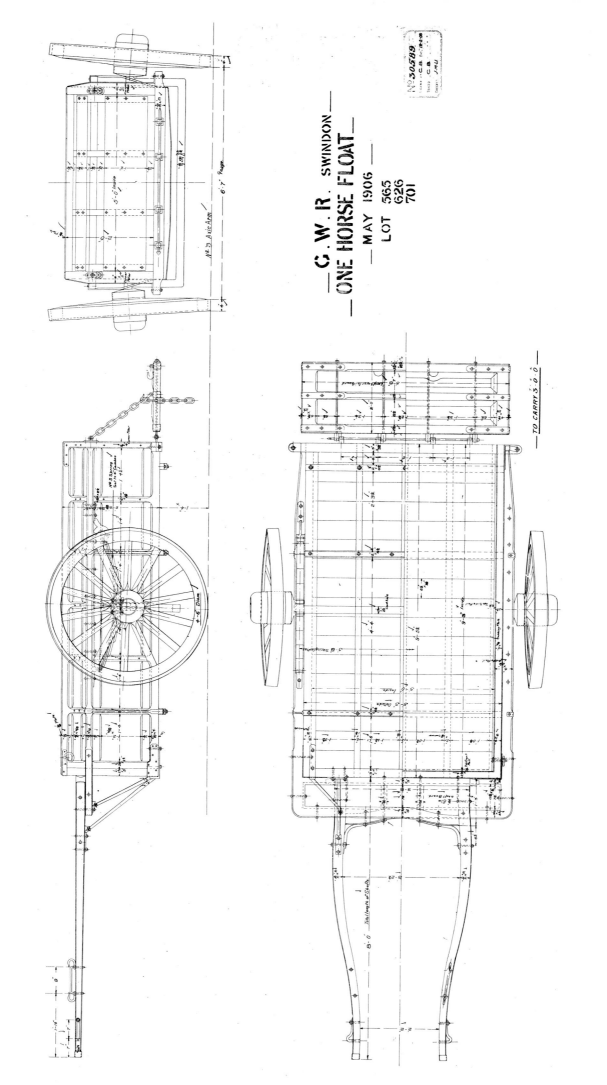

G.W.R. SWINDON

ONE HORSE FLOAT

MAY 1906

LOT 565
626
701

Fig. 184

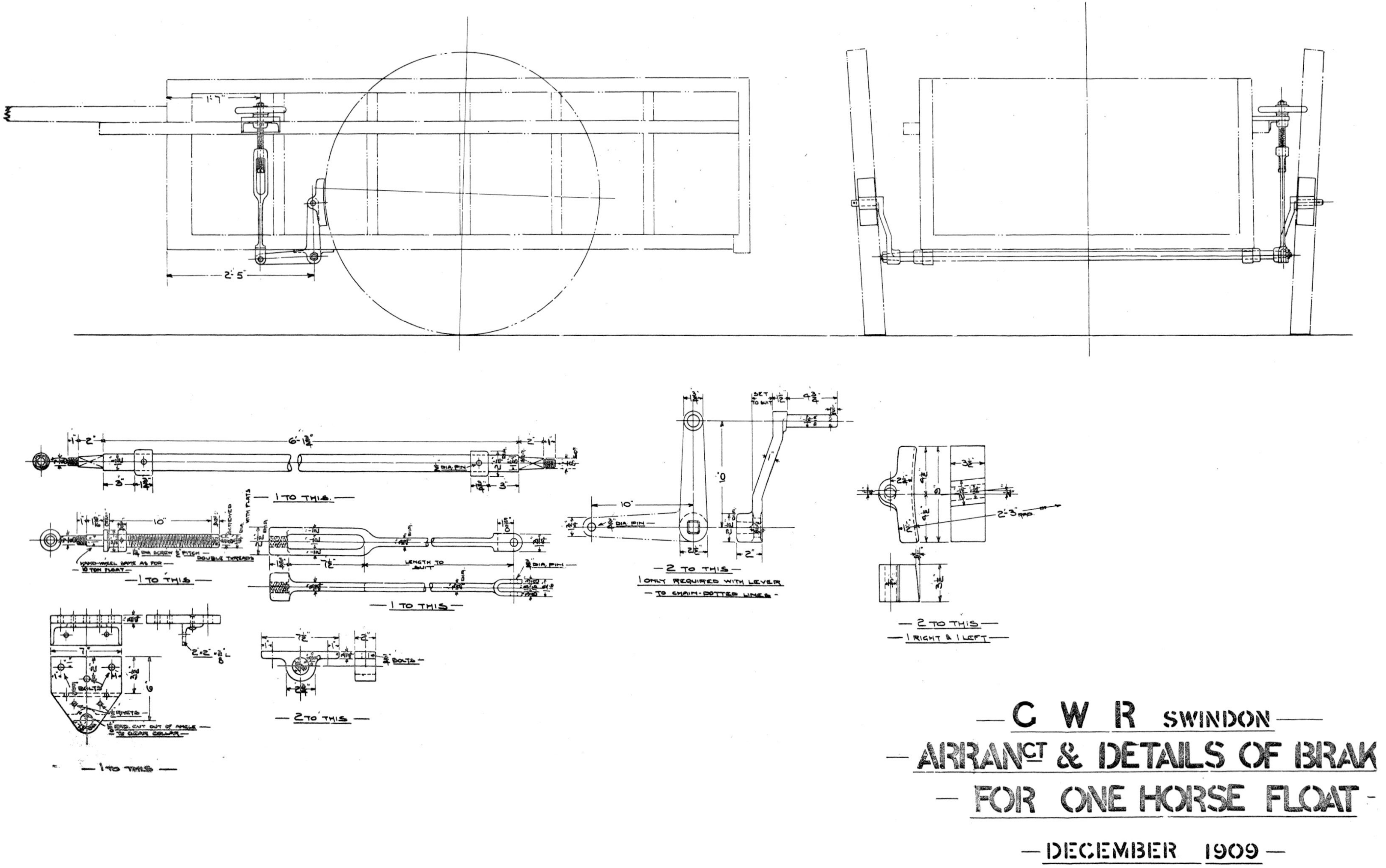

G W R SWINDON
— ARRANGᵗ & DETAILS OF BRAKE —
— FOR ONE HORSE FLOAT —
— DECEMBER 1909 —

Fig. 185

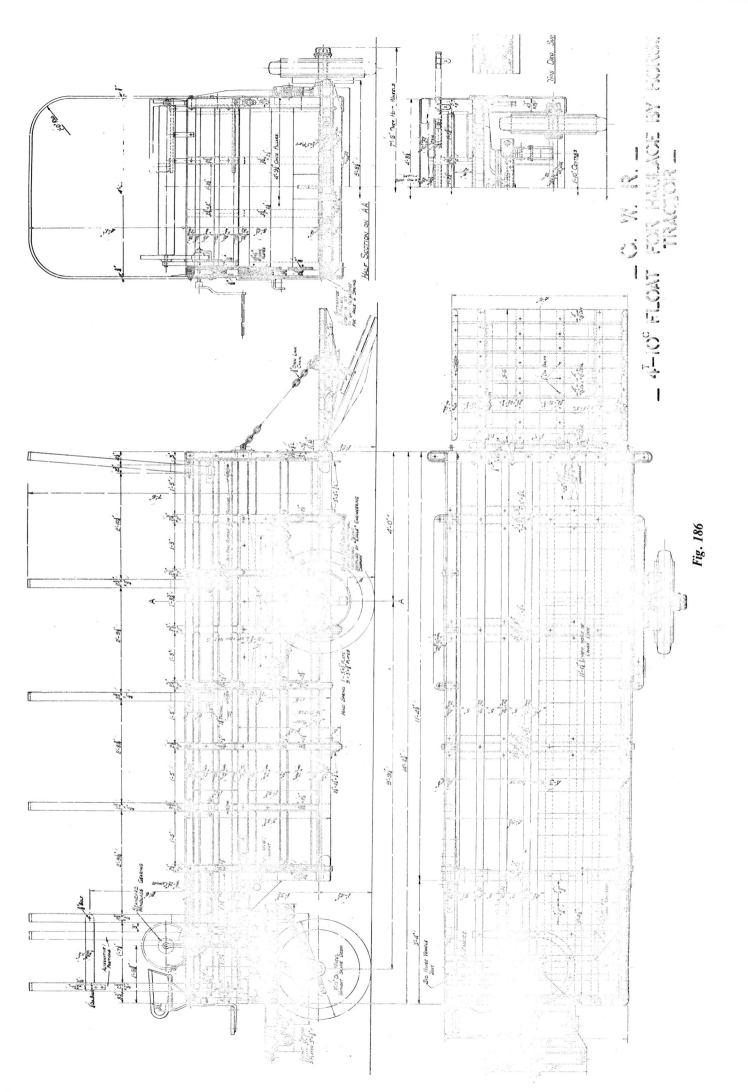

HALF SECTION ON AA

G. W. R.

4'-10" FLOAT FOR HAULAGE BY HORSES OR TRACTOR

Fig. 186

Fig. 182. Several one-horse floats were designed to carry a cover supported by hoopsticks. Such a vehicle was built for work at Chester and the same design was built to carry weights varying from 9 cwt to 12 cwt. A handbrake is provided to be operated by the driver from inside the vehicle, an unusual feature on two-wheeled vehicles.

A larger version was designed a few years earlier with an overall body length of 12 ft 6 in. It was capable of carrying 2 tons 5 cwt. A driver's seat was provided but no brake. The vehicle could be pulled by one or two horses, a second being added by the use of chains in front of the shaft horse. One of these vehicles was sent to West Bromwich to carry crates.

Fig. 183. The 1908 version has a more elaborately carved kicking board and side panels. The driver would probably have stood on the floor of the vehicle or sat on a box, but there does not appear to be a seat built into the design. Again, most unusual for a two-wheel vehicle however, is the provision of a brake operated by a lever connected by rods to the rim block.

Fig. 184. The less ornate 1906 one-horse float carried three tons but had no brake or any other refinements. One point of interest however is the way in which the shaft is joined to the vehicle by a curved piece of timber and two struts, instead of the shaft itself being connected directly to the body of the vehicle or as in some cases, carrying right through the bed of the cart.

Fig. 185. In 1909 a brake was considered to be necessary for a one-horse float and this scale drawing shows the detail required for GWR precision engineering at Swindon. Either a wheel or a handle was used to apply the brake, but in either case the driver would have had to dismount to operate it on the nearside of the float.

Fig. 186 illustrates a 4½-ton float with solid rubber tyres. It could be hauled by two horses or hitched to a motorised tractor unit. A winch was provided to assist

with heavy loads and struts above the vehicle supported a canvas hood for the protection of the freight, as seen in the accompanying photograph taken in December 1931. (*Fig. 187.*)

Fig. 188. A plate glass float designed in 1921 carried the same weight as the previous vehicle. Note that the brake acts on the leading edge of the rear wheel.

As mentioned earlier, the trolley was one of the most common vehicles used by the Great Western. They were rarely adorned by any carved boarding or kicking panels. This diagram, *Fig. 189*, is of a 7-ton trolley made in great numbers at Swindon in the late 1890s. The handbrake was operated manually by turning the wheel in front of the rear wheels and the wheel chain and skid or brake shoe has been dispensed with. The vehicle was intended to be pulled by one horse which by modern standards was a considerable load. Records show that a chain horse could be added by attaching chains to the 9 in 'D' rings on the shafts. In view of the fact that the driver would have had to put the reins down while attending to the brake, or send the van lad to apply it, this method of braking was discarded in favour of a foot or handbrake by the driver's seat on the vast majority of new vehicles by the turn of the century.

Fig. 190 is a 10-ton bogie trolley built specifically for moving heavy machinery in the Hockley area. The body of the vehicle has been reinforced by using cantilevered truss rods. Note that the width of the wheel gauge is 4 ft 5 in at the front and 4 ft 10 in at the rear. Built in 1897 the standard of workmanship and materials used in the construction would have ensured that its service life was considerable.

Fig. 191. Although probably slightly less than 10 tons in weight, this load required three horses to haul it on a heavy trolley. Two drivers attend the horses on the nearside but the reins have been coupled together for driving from the vehicle. This might have been done on

Fig. 187

Fig. 188

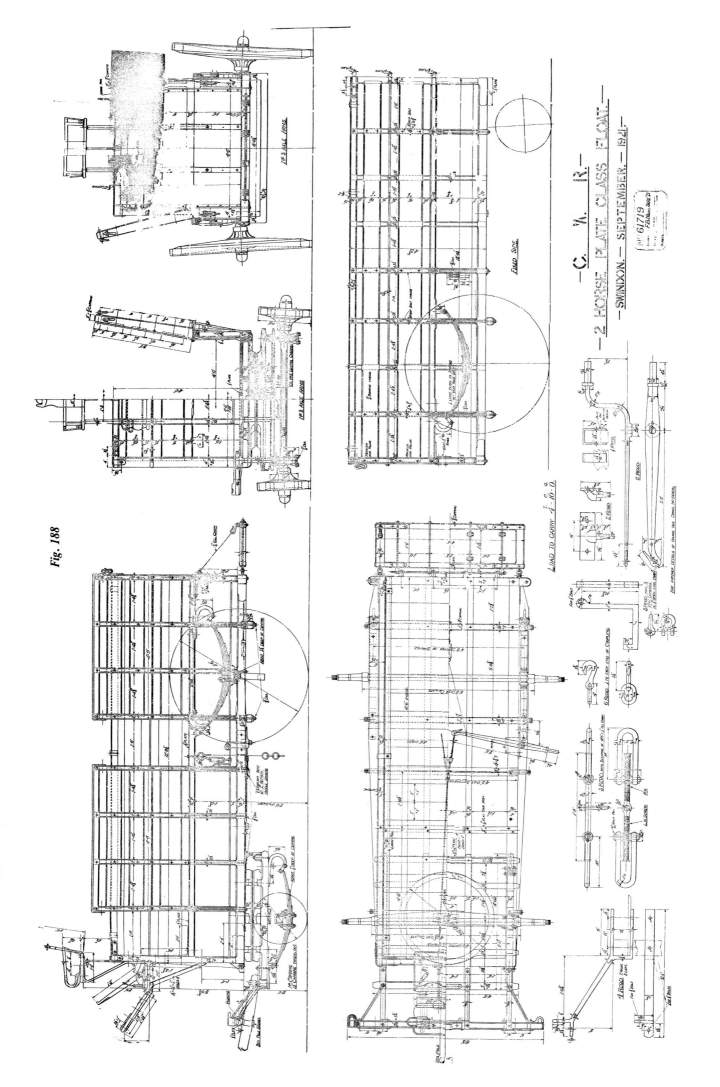

G. W. R.

2 HORSE PLATE CLASS FLOAT.

SWINDON. — SEPTEMBER. — 1921.

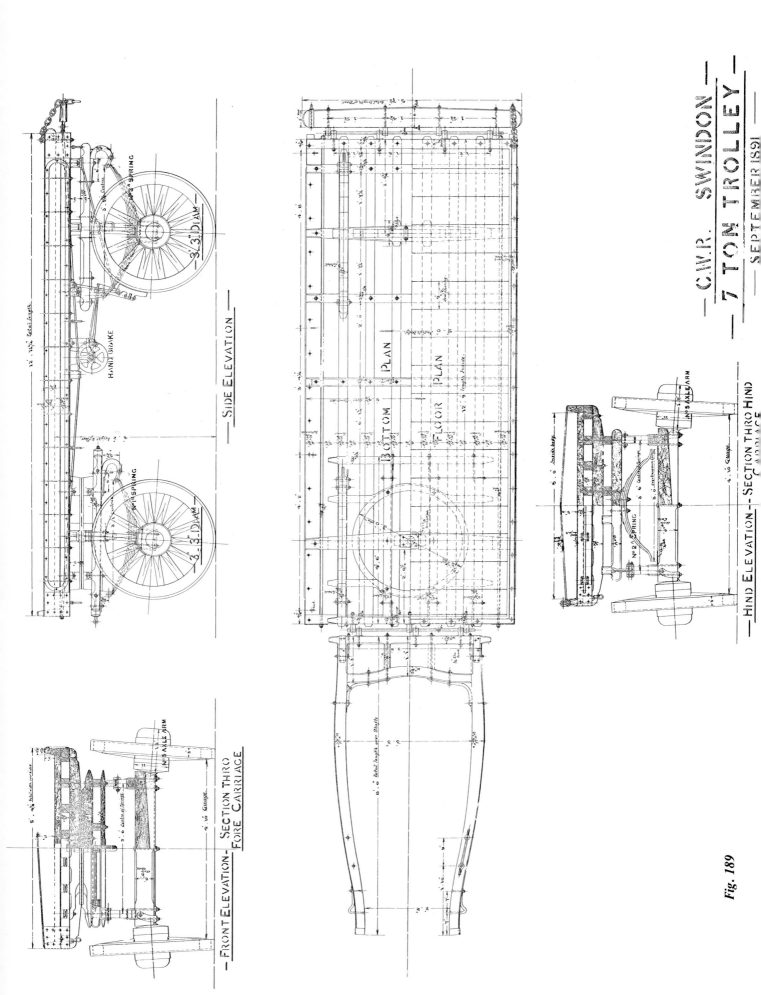

— G.W.R. SWINDON —

— 7 TON TROLLEY —

— SEPTEMBER 1891 —

— SIDE ELEVATION —

— BOTTOM PLAN —

— FLOOR PLAN —

— FRONT ELEVATION — SECTION THRO FORE CARRIAGE —

— HIND ELEVATION — SECTION THRO HIND CARRIAGE —

Fig. 189

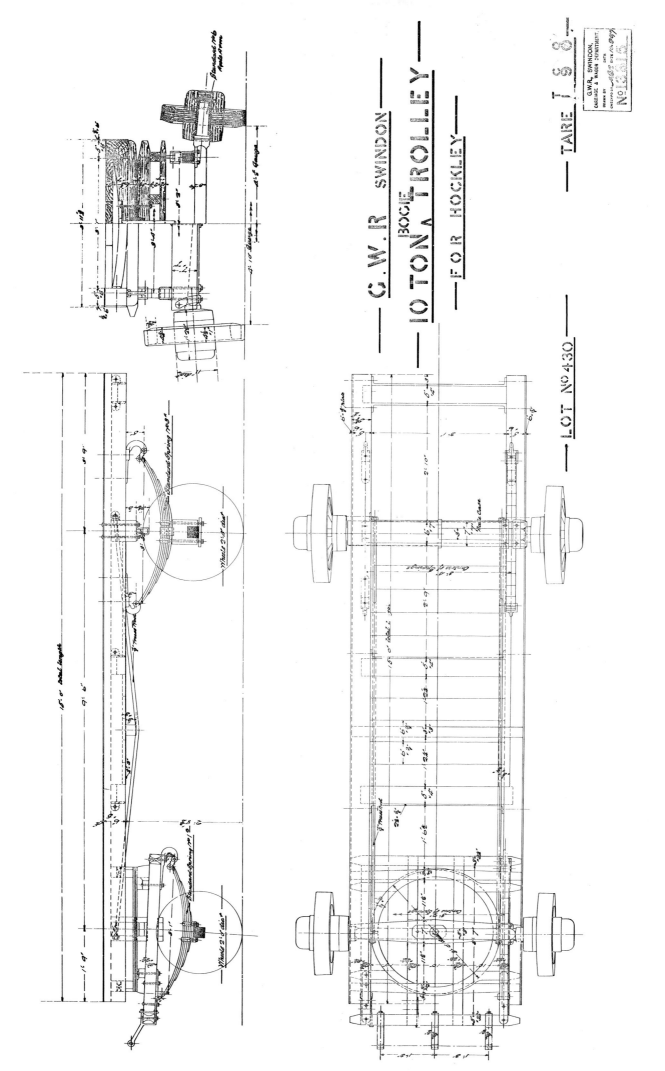

G.W.R SWINDON

BOGIE

10 TON A TROLLEY

FOR HOCKLEY

TARE 1 8 6

LOT No 430

Fig. 190

Fig. 191

the return journey when the vehicle would probably have been empty. The harness of the chain horse in front is very much lighter than the pair in the shafts. The back pad or saddle of the shaft horses could weigh up to 30 pounds and supported a chain from the brackets on the shafts in the groove. This supported some of the weight of the shafts. The chain horse had no back pad or saddle, just a simple broad leather strap with loops at either end through which the traces passed from the collar to the outside of the shafts where they were attached to a metal bracket.

In addition to the wheel-operated brake between the nearside wheels, a wheel chain is hanging down in front of the rear wheel. The submarine carried an inscription which reads:

Submarine Railway White City
J. Yetton & Co. Ltd. Contractors
Carr Street, Limehouse.

Fig. 192 (opposite). Boiler trolleys or lorries were built at Swindon to carry considerable loads. This 7-ton trolley designed in 1891, only had single shafts but the

brackets for a chain horse are shown clearly on the shafts. The chain traces were passed through the bracket and adjusted to the correct length before being hooked onto a link.

The drawing, *Fig. 193* (page 134), was designed in 1899 to take loads up to 40 tons. Together with the weight of the vehicle 7 ton 6 cwt 3 lb, three or four horses would have been required to haul a modest load and possibly six when the lorry was fully loaded. As the double shafts are connected to the drawboard beneath the floor of the vehicle, they were bent upward in order to fit the horse at a comfortable height. A screwbrake is operated on each of the rear wheels by brakewheels on either side. The purpose of the bogie was to make long loads a little more flexible and to enable a heavier load to be carried, spreading the load over three axles and six wheels. Excluding the chain linking the two parts together, the total length of the vehicle is 26 ft 6 in. Vehicles of this type were used at Wednesbury to carry steel. *Fig. 194* is of No. 1089 to this design.

Fig. 194

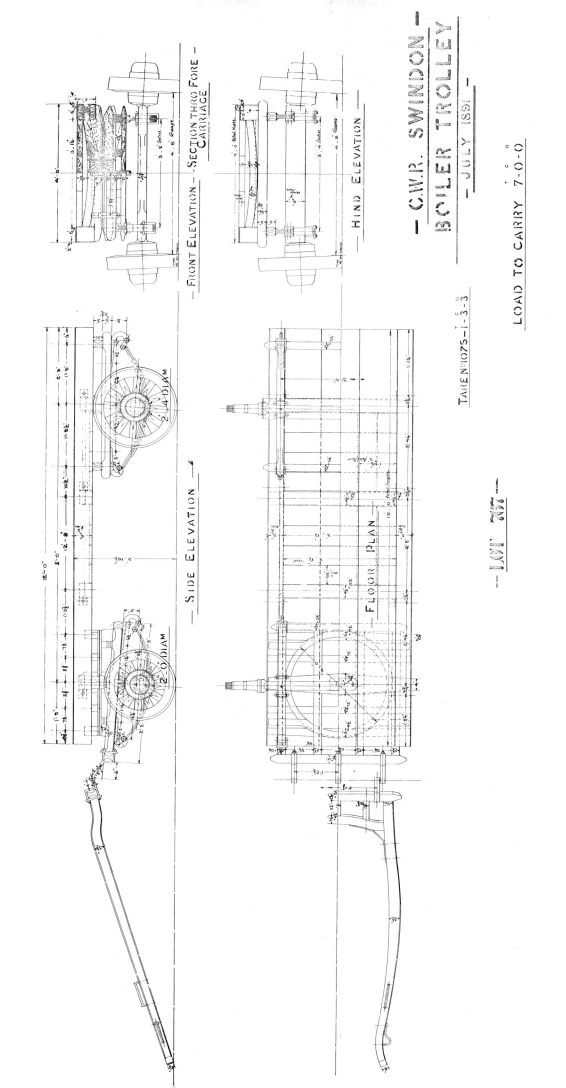

— G.W.R. SWINDON —

— BOILER TROLLEY —

— JULY 1891 —

TARE Nº 1075-1-3-3

LOAD TO CARRY 7-0-0

— FRONT ELEVATION — SECTION THRO FORE
CARRIAGE —

— HIND ELEVATION —

— SIDE ELEVATION —

— FLOOR PLAN —

— LOT 696 —

Fig. 192

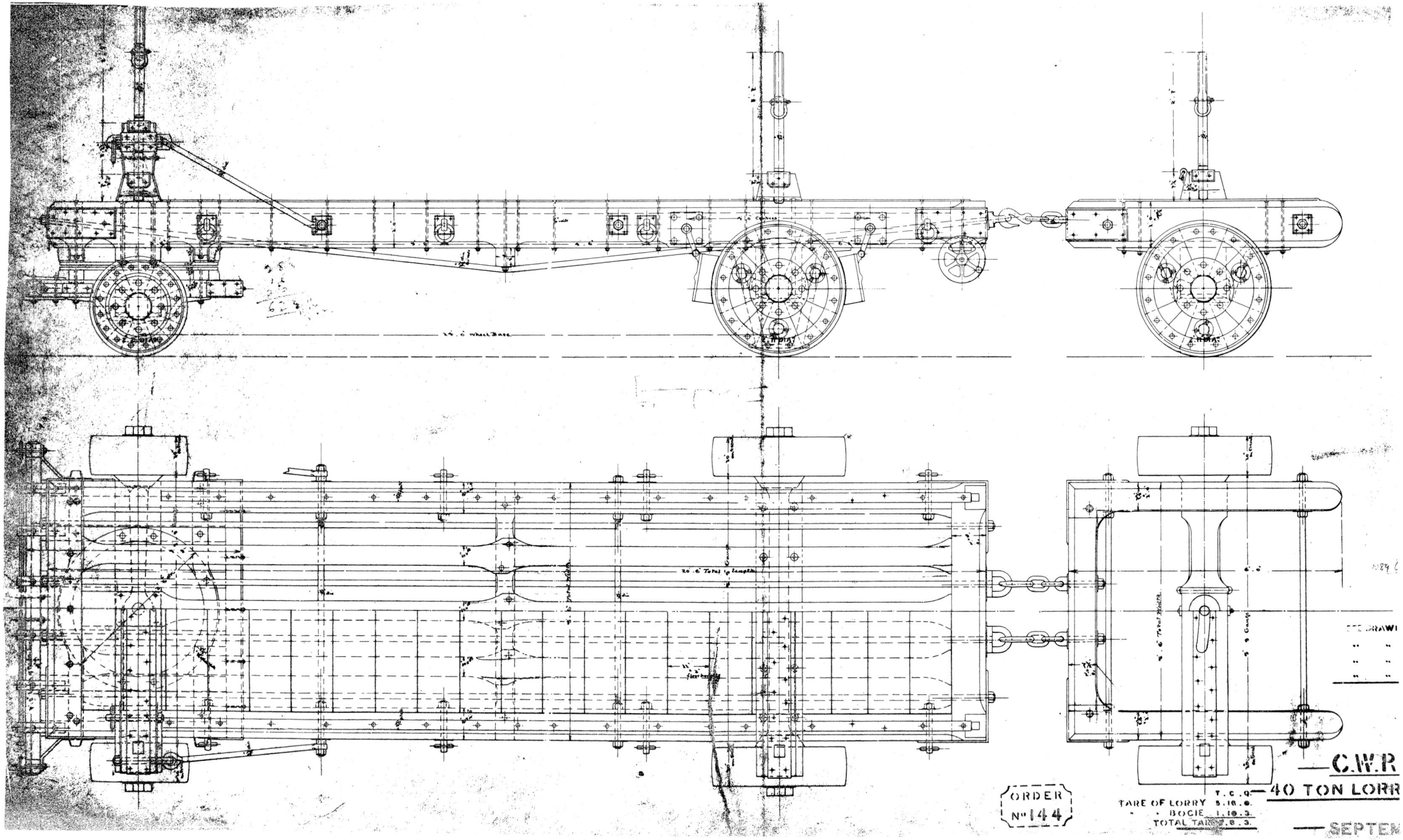

G.W.R

40 TON LORR

T.C. 9
TARE OF LORRY 5.18.8
DOCIE 1.19.3
TOTAL TARE 8.3

ORDER Nº 144

Fig. 193

Fig. 195

Fig. 196

Figs 195 and **196.** 1937 brought great changes to the design of the lighter trolley or lorry. Pneumatic tyres reduced the friction on the road so that the maximum load of 1 ton 10 cwt would not have been a heavy load for one horse to pull. The driver's comfort had also been improved with the provision of a padded seat. Note the strap attached to the back of the canopy which was for the van boy to hold on to unless the shape of the load allowed him to perch on it.

Two photographs taken in 1947 of a trolley for approximately 2½ tons. **Fig. 197** shows the turnout leaving Slough station. Note the ornate harness of the grey gelding which is certainly not workaday. The splinter-board or leading edge of the vehicle displays the number

of the vehicle, 1511, but there is no mention of the weight the vehicle should carry when loaded.

The photograph in **Fig. 198** was taken in the show ring at the Royal Windsor Horse Show. Note that the weight that the vehicle could carry has been painted on the front edge of the trolley. The vehicle would have been in the Trade-Heavy class.

Figs 199 and **200.** This chart of eight New London Cartage vehicles, was drawn in 1933 at the Derby Works of the London Midland & Scottish Railway under the direction of W. Stanier. They were very similar to those still being designed and built by the Great Western Railway despite the introduction of the petrol engine.

Fig. 197

Fig. 198

Fig. 199

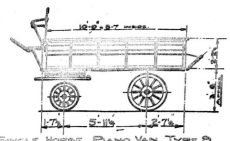

SINGLE HORSE PIANO VAN. TYPE 9.
TO CARRY 2½ TONS. TARE 19 0
DRG. N° 13/1098.A. TILT ARRGT. 15/1229.
FRONT WHEELS 2'-9" DIA. N° 3A. SPRING N° 3.
HIND WHEELS 3'-3" DIA. N° 5. SPRING N° 4.
SHAFTS PATT. N° 5.

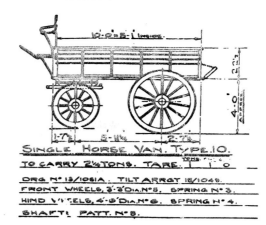

SINGLE HORSE VAN. TYPE 10.
TO CARRY 2½ TONS. TARE 1 1 0
DRG. N° 13/1061A. TILT ARRGT 15/1048.
FRONT WHEELS 3'-3" DIA. N° 5. SPRING N° 3.
HIND WHEELS 4'-0" DIA. N° 6. SPRING N° 4.
SHAFTS PATT. N° 5.

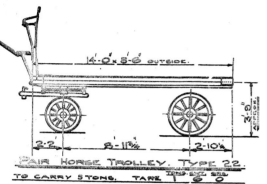

PAIR HORSE TROLLEY. TYPE 22.
TO CARRY 5 TONS. TARE 1 6 0
DRG N° 13/1130.
FRONT WHEELS 3'-0" DIA. N° 4A. SPRING N° 5.
HIND WHEELS 3'-0" DIA. N° 4. SPRING N° 6.
POLE ARRGT. DRG N° 13/989.

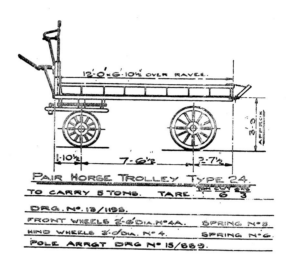

PAIR HORSE TROLLEY TYPE 24.
TO CARRY 5 TONS. TARE 1 6 3
DRG. N° 13/1199.
FRONT WHEELS 3'-0" DIA. N° 4A. SPRING N° 5.
HIND WHEELS 3'-0" DIA. N° 4. SPRING N° 6.
POLE ARRGT DRG N° 13/989.

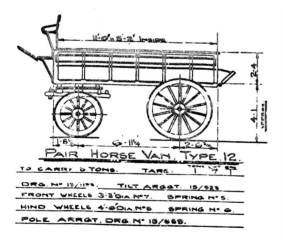

PAIR HORSE VAN. TYPE 12.
TO CARRY 5 TONS. TARE 1 7
DRG. N° 13/1139. TILT ARRGT. 15/923.
FRONT WHEELS 3'-3" DIA. N° 7. SPRING N° 5.
HIND WHEELS 4'-0" DIA. N° 6. SPRING N° 6.
POLE ARRGT. DRG. N° 13/989.

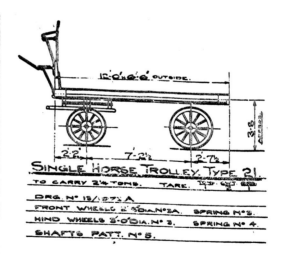

SINGLE HORSE TROLLEY. TYPE 21.
TO CARRY 2½ TONS. TARE 13 0
DRG. N° 13/973 A
FRONT WHEELS 3'-0" DIA. N° 3A. SPRING N° 3.
HIND WHEELS 3'-0" DIA. N° 3. SPRING N° 4.
SHAFTS PATT. N° 5.

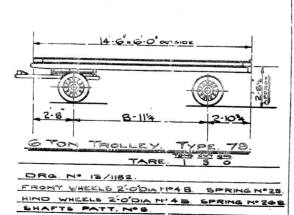

6 TON TROLLEY. TYPE 79.
TARE 1 5 0
DRG. N° 13/1182.
FRONT WHEELS 2'-0" DIA. N° 4B. SPRING N° 25.
HIND WHEELS 2'-0" DIA. N° 4B. SPRING N° 24B.
SHAFTS PATT. N° 8.

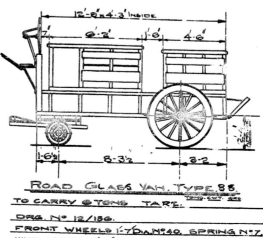

ROAD GLASS VAN. TYPE 85.
TO CARRY 2 TONS. TARE
DRG. N° 12/136.
FRONT WHEELS 1'-7" DIA. N° 40. SPRING N° 7.
HIND WHEELS 4'-6" DIA. N° 49. SPRING N° 5.
SHAFTS PATT. N° 8.

Fig. 200

Fig. 201. When a quantity of timber was to be cut and transported by rail the initial haulage from the woods to the timber wagon was often carried out by single horses pulling a sled-like vehicle on the end of a chain attached to the traces, similar to shunting horse harness. The mare in this photograph has little need of blinkers and would have been led by a boy.

Timber wagons shown in the photograph, *Fig. 202*, and the diagram, *Fig. 203*, of 1890 could be pulled by two horses in shafts or two horses either side of a pole. Both types of hauling gear were detachable by removing a pin, and extra horses could be added when necessary by clipping the chain trace for the leading horse onto the bracket on the shafts or on the pole.

As the wheels were wider than usual (6 in) special dragshoes had to be made to slow the vehicle down on steep hills. There was also a rear brake operated by turning the wheel at the rear of the vehicle.

The centre pole of the vehicle is 21 ft in length and was strengthened by metal plates in places where the major stress occurred and further secured by using a pin. The length of the vehicle was adjusted to the size of the timber to be carried and the pin could be dropped through pre-drilled holes in the pole which could be pushed through the metal plate on the rear portion.

The photograph shows the wagon shortened in this fashion.

Fig. 204. The 1912 timber wagon shown in this diagram is even longer, but was of simpler construction, with a slanting drawbar to raise the standard shafts or pole to the practical draught level for the horses.

Fig. 201

Fig. 202

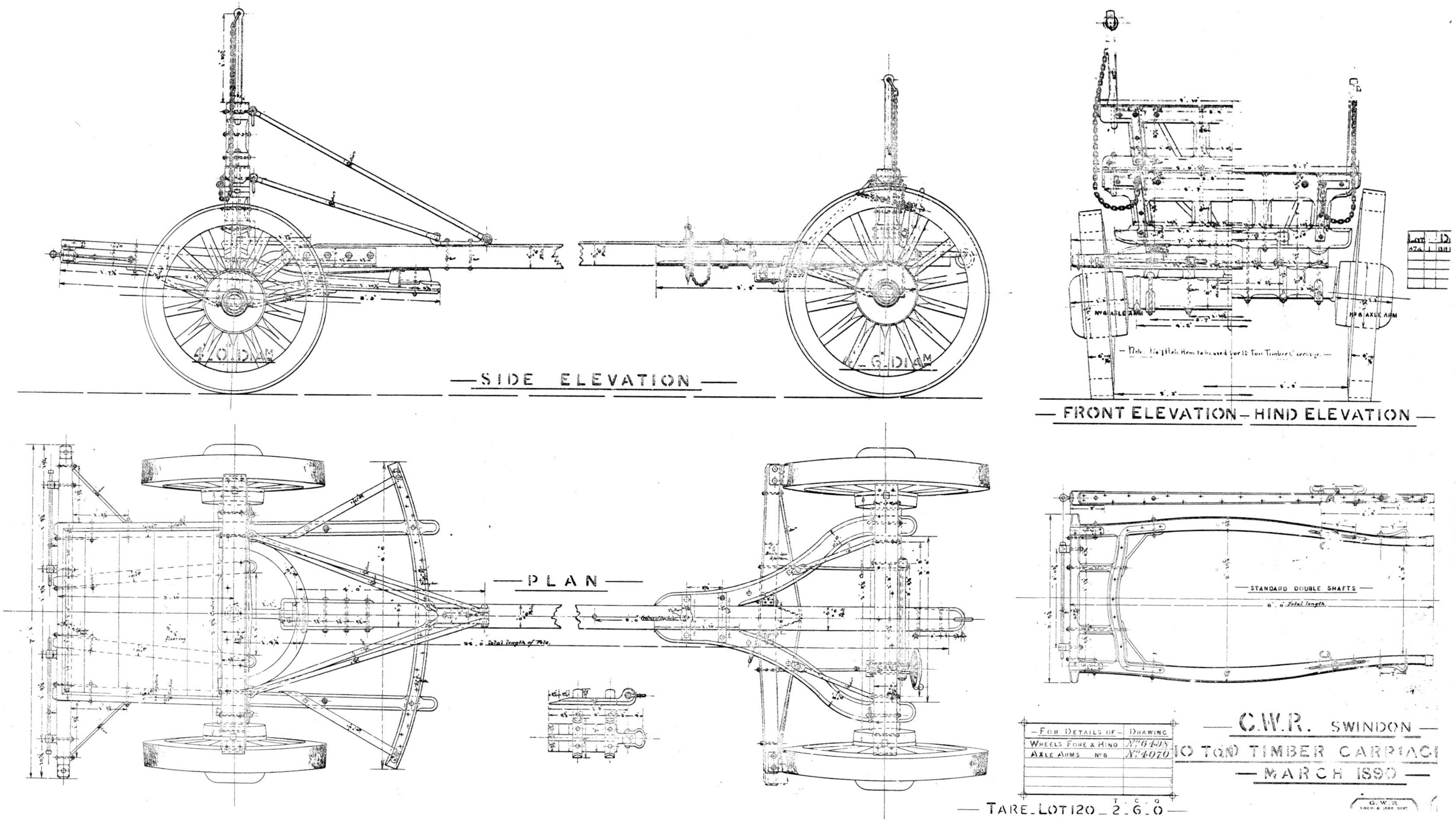
SIDE ELEVATION
FRONT ELEVATION - HIND ELEVATION
PLAN
STANDARD DOUBLE SHAFTS
8' 0" Total length
4' 6" DIAM
4' 6" DIAM
No 6 AXLE ARM
No 6 AXLE ARM
FOR DETAILS OF - DRAWING
WHEELS FORE & HIND No 6498
AXLE ARMS No 6 No 4070
G.W.R. SWINDON
10 TON TIMBER CARRIAGE
MARCH 1890
TARE LOT 120 2 6 0
G.W.R. LOCO. & CARR. DEPT.

Fig. 203

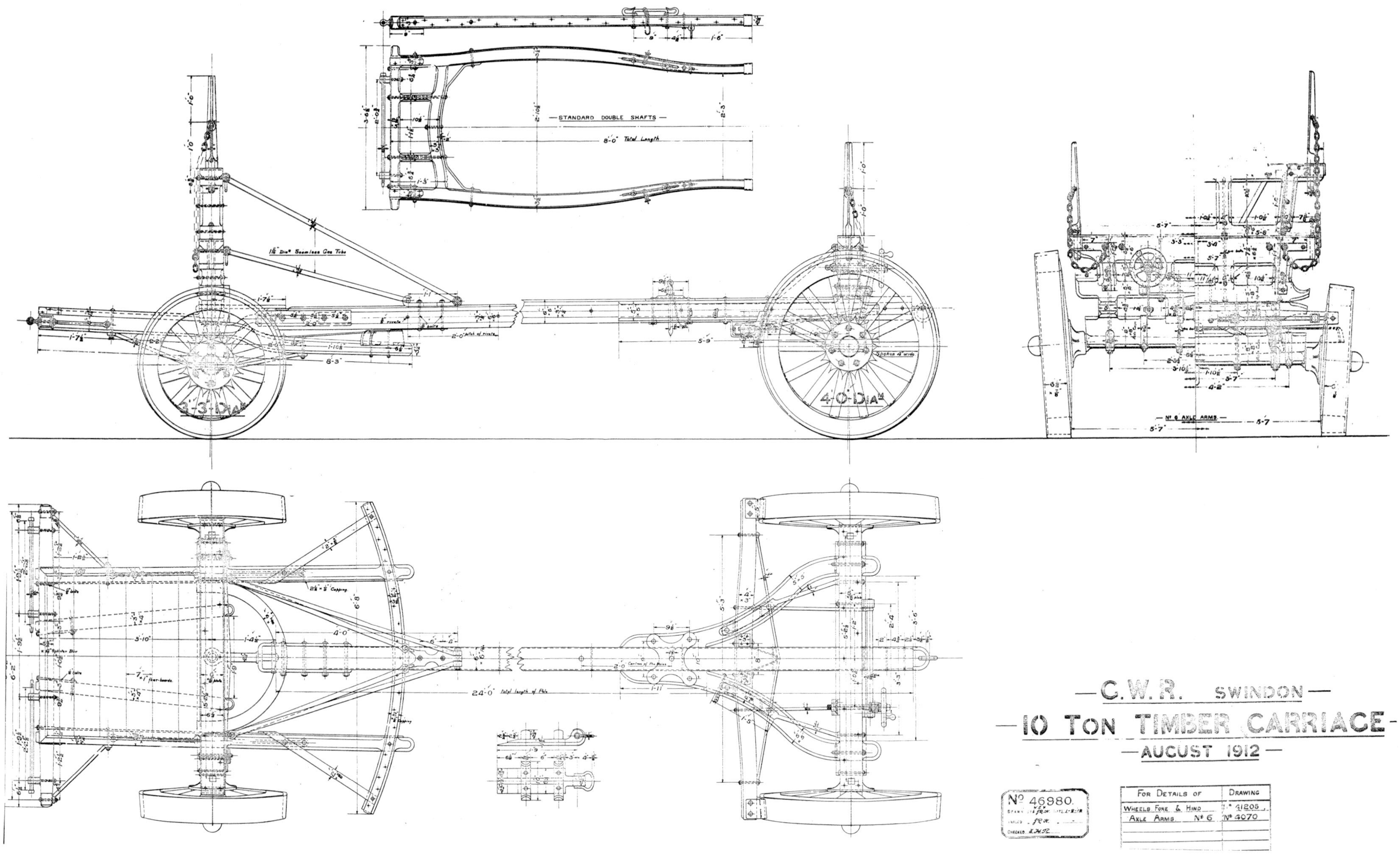
STANDARD DOUBLE SHAFTS
8'-0" Total Length
1½" Dia. Seamless Gas Tube
4'-0" DIAM.
4'-3" DIAM.
Spokes 4" wide
No 6 AXLE ARMS
24'-0" total length of Pole
— G.W.R. SWINDON —
— 10 TON TIMBER CARRIAGE —
— AUGUST 1912 —
No 46980.
FOR DETAILS OF
DRAWING
WHEELS FORE & HIND
No 41205
AXLE ARMS No 6
No 4070

Fig. 204

Fig. 205

Fig. 205. This photograph is of a lighter version at a yard where the road sets have been 'ribbed' to give better grip for the horses' shoes. Lengths of rail were carried short distances on this type of vehicle, together with any other long loads.

Fig. 206. This shortened timber wagon of a fairly early design is being used as a makeshift converted trolley. Single shafts have been fitted for this comparatively light load. The skid or drag shoe is shown clearly but the chain does not look long enough to reach the back wheels of the timber wagon. The rim blocks of the brake are also visible although the operating wheel at the rear of the vehicle is hidden.

Fig. 207 is a drawing of a converted timber carriage similar to the previous photograph. Some timber carriages were adapted for carrying containers of stone, the pole being shortened to just over 8 ft. Yeovil, Bath and Frome each had one of these vehicles. The securing pin and the reinforcing metal plates are clearly shown on the diagram of the side elevation.

Fig. 206

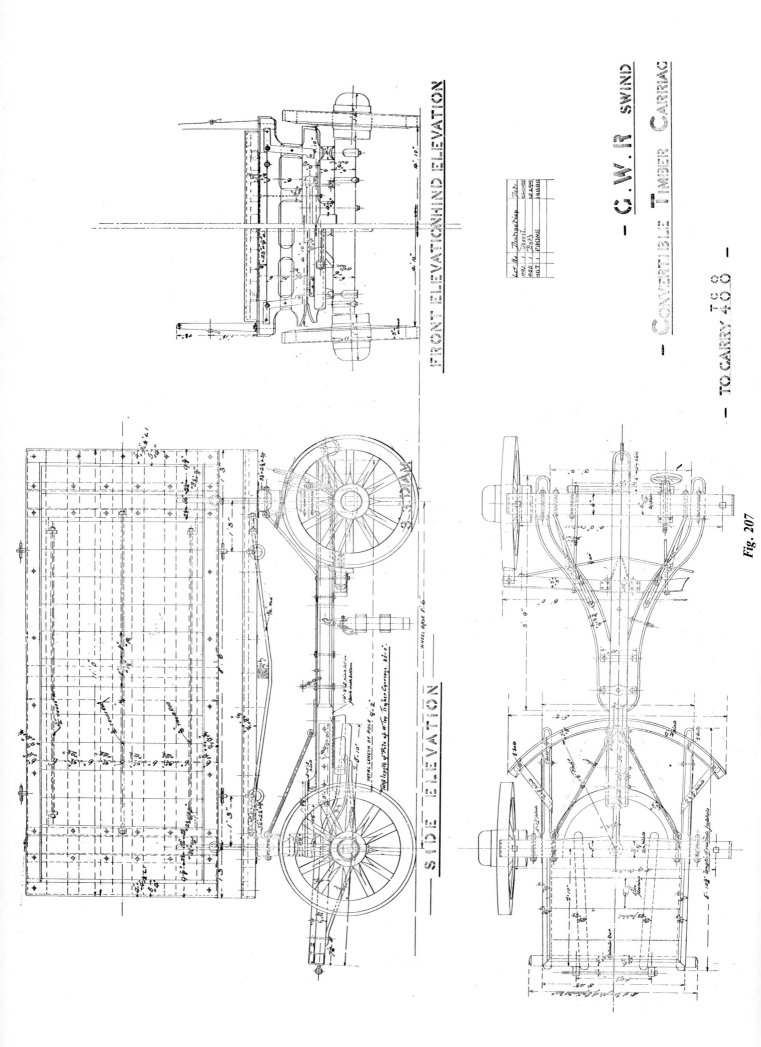

FRONT ELEVATION   HIND ELEVATION

SIDE ELEVATION

— G.W.R SWIND
— CONVERTIBLE TIMBER CARRIAG
— TO CARRY 40 0 —

Fig. 207

Fig. 208

Fig. 209

Fig. 208 depicts a rather unusual vehicle for carrying boats. Stations such as Brentford, Plymouth, Kingswear and Bristol had a trolley for this purpose, usually pulled by one shaft horse with additional chain horses as required. This boat trolley was built in 1894.

The Great Western had rights over several canals. *Fig. 209* is of a barge horse on the Neath & Brecon Canal. While a horse could haul up to 10 tons given good conditions on a road, barge horses pulled loads of up to 70 tons along the waterways.

Fig. 210 illustrates the traffic on the waterways of 1840. On the left can be seen a lad leading two tired horses. A tow horse could be hired for a number of stages and then he was returned, either by working down, or by being led back to the stable at the end of the day. The skew bridge is one of Brunel's architectural achievements, and crossed the Kennet & Avon Canal at Bath.

Fig. 211. Pianos became the vogue in the early 1900s and the Great Western Railway was quick to appreciate the potential traffic and probable profit to the Company. This low level van with a tarpaulin cover of 1908 had rather better springs than the normal van for carrying items of a similar weight, an additional pair of springs being situated across the rear axle.

The driver had a brake acting on the rim of the disc wheels and sat over seven feet off the ground.

Fig. 212. The 1895 photograph of a pianoforte van without the hoops in position. The lettering on the side of the vehicle is somewhat disjointed owing to the brackets for holding the hoops and tarpaulin in place.

Furniture removals were also a steady occupation for some drivers and their teams. The Great Western Railway undertook complete household and farm removals, packing the contents into large horse-drawn road vehicles, transferring the load onto rail wagons and back into another road vehicle at the station nearest the destination of the furniture, etc. Two horses were used to haul the vehicle which was built on the lines of a float with a bent axle to enable the body and loading ramp to be as near the ground as possible. The driver sat 8 ft 6 in off the ground!

Fig. 213. This photograph of vehicle No. 583 was taken in 1894. There is no brake except the wheel chains for both front and back wheels. These would not have been used for stopping the wheels turning when taking the vehicle downhill as the wheel tyres would have been worn out very quickly without a skid shoe. They were more likely to have been used to hold the vehicle still when it was parked beside a house or station. The van lad would have stood beside the horses' heads at such a time when he was not required to assist with loading. While the vehicle was in motion the van lad either walked beside the horses, or if there was room in the rear of the van, he may have perched on the lower door to prevent theft from the vehicle, this being one of his duties. Although the vehicle weighed over two tons, the load it carried was not much more than this judging from the strength of the rear springs. Note the 'snap box' behind the rear wheel which was for the driver's lunch.

Fig. 214 shows a simplified diagram of the construction of such a furniture van, drawn in 1926. The bent axle of the rear wheel is clearly evident in the rear view.

Fig. 215. This second photograph of vehicle No. 583 was taken in 1920. Various alterations have been made to enable the vehicle to carry a greater load. The size of the wheels has been reduced but it is not clear if the springs of the rear wheels have also been changed for a stronger version. The snap box has been removed, a skid shoe of fairly substantial proportions has been provided and also a foot brake. The vehicle now weighs 1 ton 18 cwt but apart from the change of wheels it is difficult to see where the tare reduction has been made. Chain horses could be added to pull the vehicle up hills and double shafts could be used instead of a pole if the driver preferred.

Fig. 210

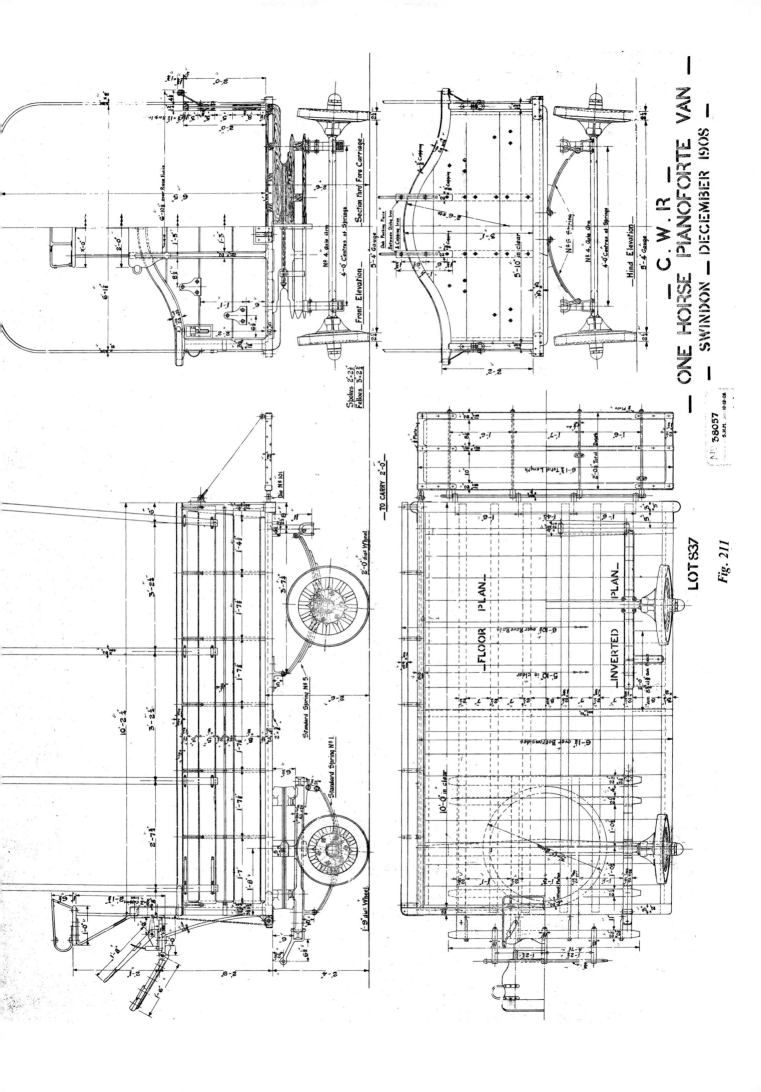

— G. W. R —
ONE HORSE PIANOFORTE VAN
— SWINDON — DECEMBER 1908 —

LOT 837

Fig. 211

Fig. 212

Fig. 213

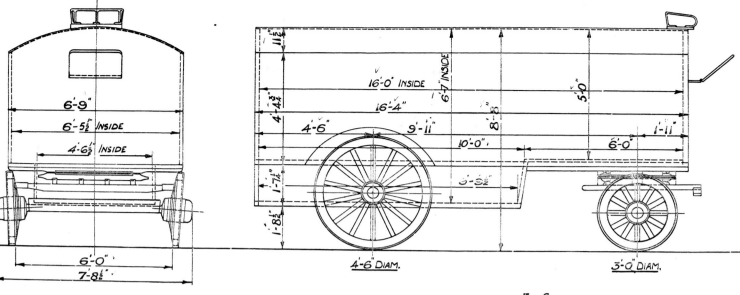

TARE WEIGHT 2-4

Fig. 214

Fig. 215

Fig 216. Although this drawing is dated June 1919, some furniture removal vans were still being made to the previous design shown in *Fig. 213*. This vehicle was 14 ft 7 in long and over 8 ft high. Again, it could be drawn by two horses harnessed alongside a pole or by two horses side by side in double shafts. There does not appear to be any provision for carrying water buckets or nosebags for the horses and it is mentioned in one or two stable records that relays of horses were used when a long journey was unavoidable. It does not however say that the driver was relieved – only the horses!

Fig. 217. This photograph is of a farm removal after loading onto rail wagons and containers. Assorted vehicles including the two-wheel cart advertising the dairy produce are secured onto flat wagons while the

household contents have been packed into containers advertising the Great Western Railway facility of 'door to door transport of household removals and merchandise'.

Figs 218, 219 and **220.** Three photographs taken in the late 1890s of competitors' vehicles made by the Gloucester Railway Carriage & Wagon Company. They were highly decorated and more 'box-like' than those built at Swindon for the Great Western Railway, although two of these have in fact got bent axles for the rear wheels. The ornate lettering and beautiful lining out make the railway company's more utilitarian vehicles look almost dull in comparison. All three vehicles worked in the GWR area, and would have been seen at stations in the West Midlands.

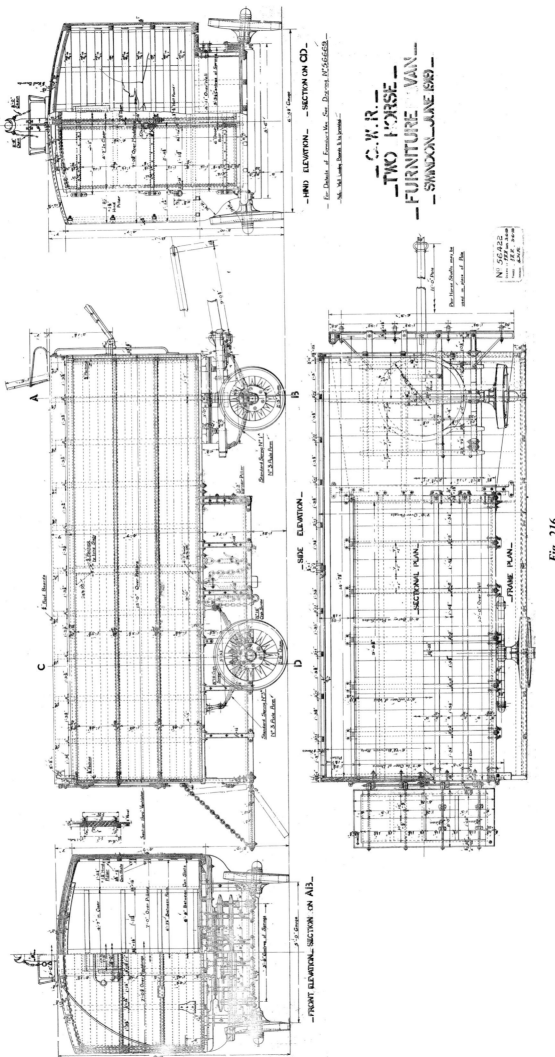

Fig. 216

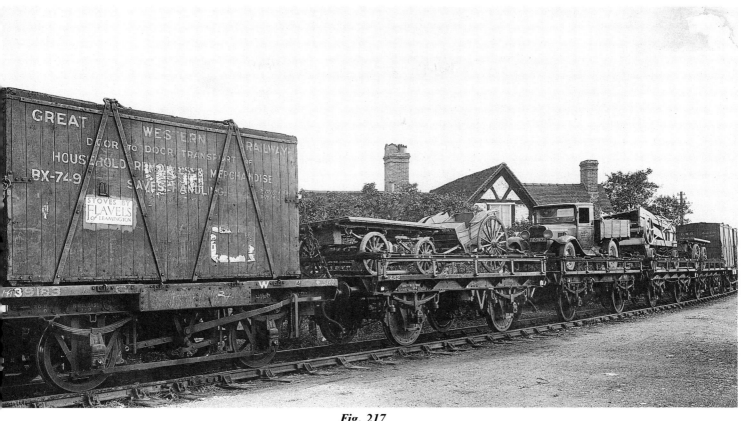

Fig. 217

Fig. 218

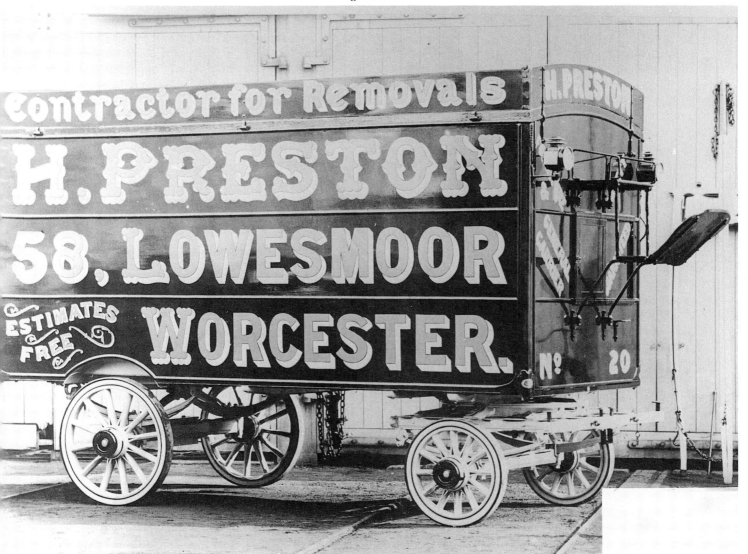

Fig. 219

Fig. 220

Fig. 221. This photograph dated 31st May 1942 shows the wide variety of vehicles used to remove the furniture and effects belonging to the well-known girls school, Malvern College, out of Blenheim Palace, their war-time home. 140 tons of chattels were removed to several different addresses in Malvern, which H.M. Office of Works had decided was a sufficiently safe place for the school to return. While the majority of vehicles were Thornycroft motorised vehicles, a light one-horse trolley is parked at the end of the line awaiting its share of the load which was divided between some 76 vehicles.

In 1921 the volume of cocoa traffic from the docks had increased to such an extent that a specialised vehicle was made in Swindon to be drawn by two horses pulling a load of seven tons. This diagram, **Fig. 222**, was dual-purpose being adaptable for carrying curved loads, perhaps of pre-formed iron, which required a bolster or centre support. Similar to the piano lorries, extra springs were positioned transversely above the rear axle. The pole slotted into a socket beneath the floor of the vehicle and although not shown, the traces would have also been attached to the drawbar, probably fastened back onto themselves after passing round the leading edge.

Fig. 223. This photograph of a cocoa lorry with the pole slotted through the axles out of the way, shows the lashing points for the ropes which held the 7-ton load securely in place. The rear board shown in the previous diagram has been removed, and a handbrake has been added.

Great Western staff received their wages from the senior man in charge of their station, or in the case of large establishments, from the pay clerk. The money was collected from banks and takings transported to the banks by cash trolleys stowed inside an adapted omni-bus. This Great Eastern Railway vehicle, **Fig. 224** (page 154), was almost identical to that used by the Great Western Railway for which no records of reproducible vehicles were available at the time of writing. Money, bullion and other valuables were also carried for companies wishing to use the railway service. The low floor and drop-down lower portion of the door enables loading to be carried out with the minimum of delay. Despite the weight that could be involved, only single shafts would have fitted the vehicle which had a drawbar only 3 ft 2 in wide.

Spring carts were almost exclusively provided at country stations for the movement of small quantities of goods. They were fast, light vehicles drawn by a pony or a light weight horse. Although the two vehicles photographed here **Figs 225**, and **226** were built in consecutive years, 1895 and 1896, the style of writing or lettering is very different. It was standard practice at the factory at Swindon for each part to be stamped with the number of the vehicle. The shafts of the vehicle numbered 1288, although not detachable from the cart, are stamped with the same number. Shaft stands are provided to support the cart when empty or idle.

Fig. 227. The light crank axle cart was not provided with shaft stands but had a 'V' strut under the leading edge of the body which supported the cart when empty or idle. The shafts are not usually strong enough to support a vehicle if the weight is thrown forward onto the tapered and shaped fore-end. This vehicle was made in considerable numbers in 1900 for use at small stations where it was a multi-purpose cart used for moving small quantities of goods which required a modicum of cover. Although the exact locations are not recorded, the vehicles were numbered individually.

Fig. 221

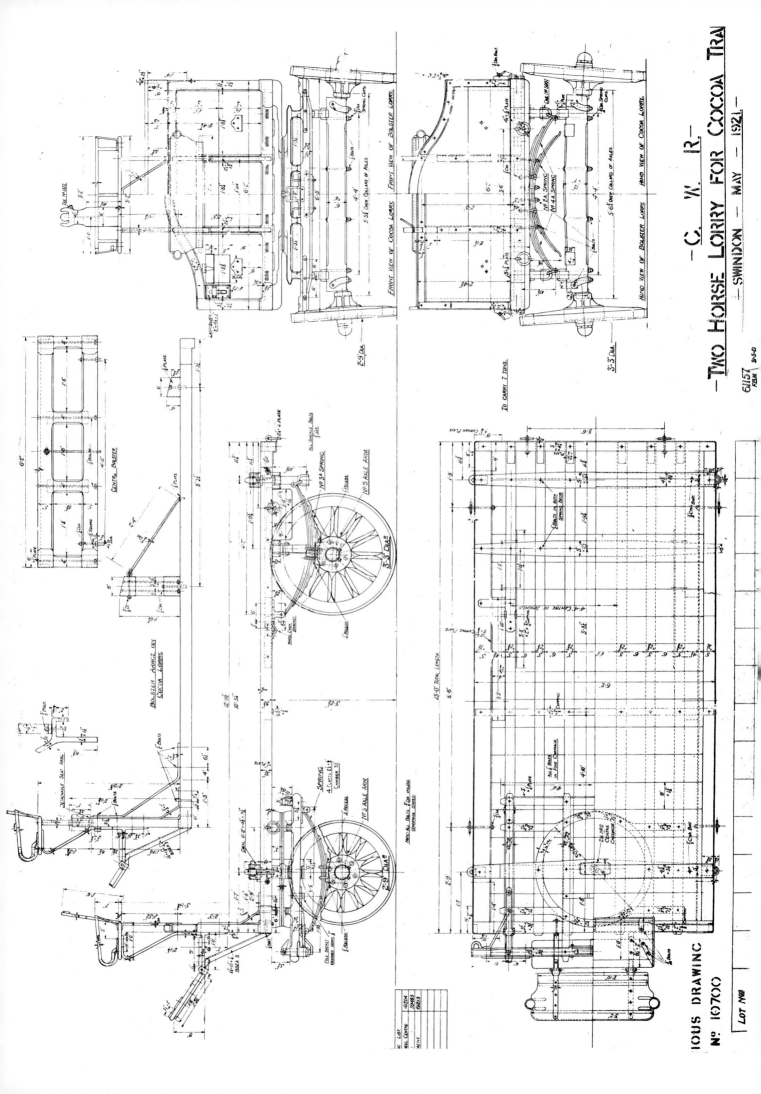

- G. W. R. -

TWO HORSE LORRY FOR COCOA TRAFFIC

- SWINDON - MAY - 1921 -

To CARRY 7 TONS.

Fig. 223

Fig. 225

Fig. 226

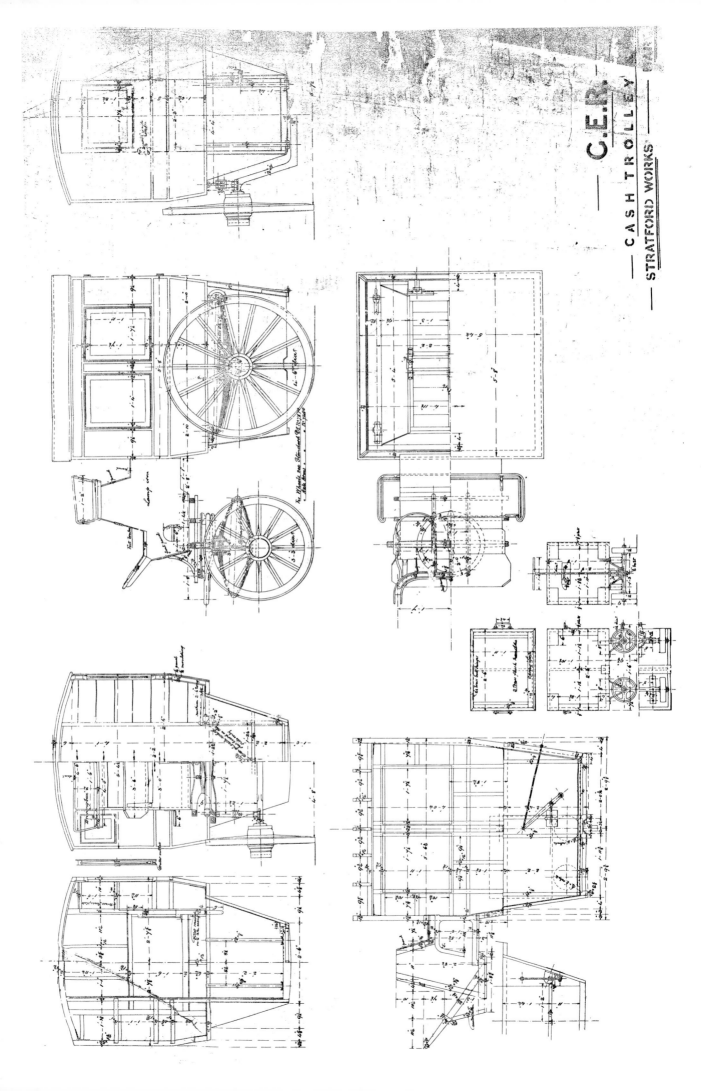

C.E.R.
CASH TROLLEY
STRATFORD WORKS

Fig. 224

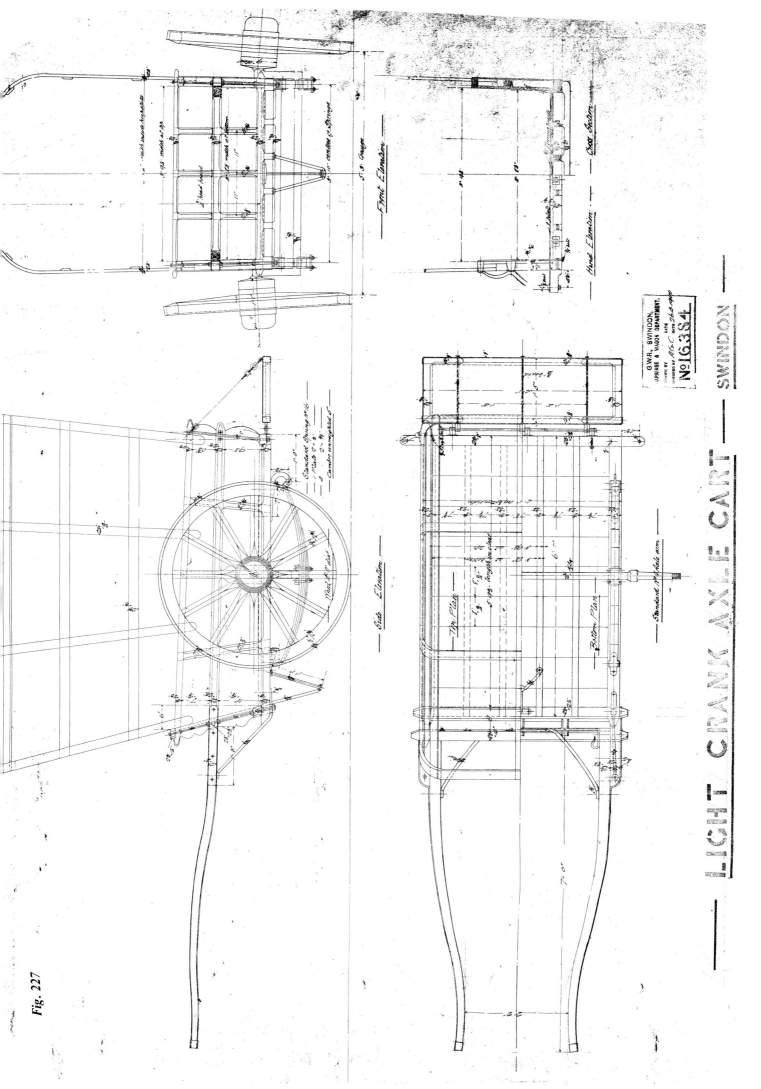

Fig. 227

LIGHT CRANK AXLE CART ——— SWINDON ———

Company Horses

The scene at a horse fair in Mid Wales, 1909. (*Fig. 228.*) At the station, horses intended for use by the Great Western Railway Company are being loaded into a train of cattle wagons. The price of such horses at this time was approximately £50 each.

The small boys in the foreground appear to be more than willing to assist with the loading should a horse resist when being led up the ramp!

The large two-wheeled contraption on the left of the picture is a timber wagon. The pole is pulled down manually and the log which is held in the chain and iron loop is lifted off the ground. It was not intended to be pulled by horses and would probably have only been used to move logs in a confined space.

The Great Northern Railway spent an average of £44 10s (£44.50) on their horses, but the Great Western inspectors justified their greater expense by purchasing horses of superior condition. The average working life of the horses on the GWR was five to nine years, and many lasted even longer. Most of the other major users of horse power reported a length of service of between four to seven years. Between 1854 and 1869, 308 horses were purchased by the Great Western directly from two main suppliers with that number supplemented by purchases from sales such as those held at Lampeter and Welsh farming centres similar to that shown in the photograph (*Fig. 228*).

When purchasing horses from a private vendor, the Chief Horse Inspector visited the farm personally and selected the animals he wished to purchase. These were usually five to six years old, when the age of a horse is easy to determine from its teeth, and already broken to harness. The records only denote 'M' for male horse and 'F' for a mare or female horse. It is unlikely however that stallions were purchased for draught work as in general the temperament of a stallion would have caused friction in the stables at certain times of the year.

The horses were taken direct to Hockley where they were further inspected, given a number which was branded onto the hoof, and given a trial by an experienced driver. Horses which were found to be unsatisfactory, either from the work point of view, or because they proved to be older than the certified invoice stated, were returned to the vendor. Until these horses had been tested and proved free from vice and sickness, they were kept apart from the regular Hockley stud of working horses. When this stud was originally established it housed 114 horses increased to 134 by 1869 when the Chief Horse Inspector carried out one of the best documented and detailed inspections of all the horses owned by the Great Western Railway Company.

Extracts from that report made to the General Horse Committee:

Of the 190 horses at Hockley and its 'outlying stations', the condition of the animals was reported as follows:

79	Good condition
15	Fair
39	Suffering sore shoulders
23	Lame
20	Bad
7	Greasy heels
6	Spavin
1	Blind
1	Bad wind
2	Bad side bones
1	Lazy
12	Condemned

Fig. 228

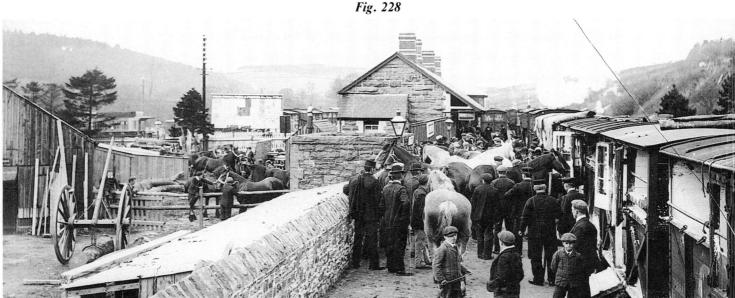

The 'outlying' stations under the overall supervision of Mr Bell at Hockley were:

	No. of horses
Stourbridge	4
Brettle Lane	3
Worcester	7
Birkenhead	13
Liverpool	4
Saltney	5
Warrington	1
Chester	6
Shrewsbury	7
Reading	1

The stables, shoeing facilities and harness were also inspected and the report considered at the meeting of the Horse Committee held at Paddington under the Board Chairman.

The farrier at Hockley was criticised because his shoes did not last as long as those provided by smiths contracted to supply the 'out' stations.

Collars were reported to be in poor condition which had resulted in the high percentage of horses suffering from sore shoulders. (See list on condition of horses.)

Horses which were no longer suitable for use by the Company, either because they had come to the end of their working life or because of persistent sickness or injury, were sold at auction and the sum paid noted by the accountants against the detailed record kept on each horse. Such records were kept on all horses in all the Great Western Railway stables. Its sex, identifying marks, age and number, together with its current value were all noted. In 1870 the initial cost was depreciated by 6d (2½p) per week.

Over the years even the reason for a horse being destroyed was mentioned and discussed in detail. At one monthly meeting held in 1876 it was noted that horse No. 723, purchased for use at Paddington in 1875, was destroyed due to puncture of the coffin joint. Similarly No. 738, purchased in November 1867, was destroyed due to injury to the fetlock joint and No. 86, purchased the previous year was put down due to inflammation of the intestines.

In addition to Hockley being the location for the largest Great Western stud at this time, and therefore the centre for the records, there were also facilities for sick and resting or reserve horses to be cared for in separate premises surrounded by fields.

The horse keeper received a salary of £100 and a Company house immediately adjacent to the stud buildings. A stableman earned 30s (£1.50) per week and worked under the supervision of a foreman stableman.

In addition to being the central stable or stud of the GWR system, Hockley was also the main goods depot for the Birmingham area. The photograph (*Fig. 229*) taken in about 1922 shows a wide variety of loads on various vehicles. The load nearest the camera was glass carboys inside a crate which was packed with hay or straw for protection. Most of the vehicles are pulled by one horse and many more can be seen in the background under the loading bay. The diversity of the goods passing through this goods yard was typical of any of the larger stations. Bearing in mind that the goods on the trolley weigh at least 36 cwt, the fastenings with which they have been secured to the vehicle appear to be extremely fine!

Fig. 230. Birmingham Moor Street also used the horses stabled at Hockley. This scene in the early 1920s primarily shows a locomotive on the traverser (the unique 4-4-2T, No. 4600), but in the background is a selection of horsedrawn vehicles, some of which have already been loaded with pipes.

Fig. 229

Fig. 230

Mint Stables, Paddington

The London horse stud relied on rented stable accommodation or elderly stalls at Smithfield and Poplar from which the horses had to be led before starting a day's work from Paddington station, a task carried out by the van lads. It was therefore proposed in 1875 that new stables for 120 horses should be erected as near Smithfield as possible, the stalls to be arranged in rows of ten. Accommodation was also to be provided for any sick horses in a building with 15 looseboxes adjacent to a paddock. This new stable was to have a forge, harness room and a day room for the staff. The latter was considered an unnecessary luxury by many of the critics at the time, but an office for the vet was accepted without demur.

This architect's drawing, (*Fig. 231*) of part of a typical Great Western stable, shows the detail which was required when constructing new stable accommodation. Any exposed edges were rounded, screws countersunk, and a three inch fall provided on the blue brick floor to provide good drainage.

This second drawing, (*Fig. 232*) is specifically of the elevation of the mangers or feeding receptacles. These were manufactured in bulk at Swindon out of $\frac{1}{4}$ in steel. Two hooks are visible above the manger. Great Western horses were often secured by two halters or ropes, particularly when travelling in a horsebox. The main restraining rope was attached to the ring of the head-collar under the horse's jaw, while the second rope was only necessary if the horse was in the habit of backing towards the staff or had any vice like biting. The rope was either tied round the horse's neck, behind the ears, and knotted firmly, or a leather collar, similar to that worn by a dog was buckled round its neck and the rope looped over the hook high above the manger.

The other diagram, *Fig. 233*, is of a row of six stalls in a medium size stable. The width available has been divided fairly to give as much room as possible for each horse. Great Western stalls were nearly always two or three inches wider than those provided by commercial concerns of the period, and indeed, those of other railway companies.

Fig. 234. This picture is an official photograph but without identification. Obviously it is the upper story of a large stable having roof lights and has only just been completed. Indeed, through the doorway at the far end can be seen a workman's ladder still erected. Odd pieces of wood are stacked against the left-hand wall and one manger is either excess to requirements or has not yet been fitted. If this was a ground floor, there would be small trap doors in the left-hand wall at floor level for easy removal of solid waste. Whether it is in fact a view of the upper storey of the Mint stables added in 1910, is open to question. Note the harness brackets on the left-hand wall which have been shaped to support the harness of each horse opposite its own stall. Collars were kept in the drying room and rarely inside the stable itself.

Paddington stables were built adjacent to the Mint Tavern at a cost of £25,300. They were intended to accommodate 288 horses, that being the number which was hired at a cost of £103 per annum per horse. Initially it had been suggested that the public house itself be converted into stables, but the remaining 57 years of its lease would have cost a further £7–£8,000 and would have provided stalls for only 50 more horses.

Horses were to be purchased for both the new Smithfield and Paddington stables, and a corresponding number of sets of harness made. The horses were expected to cost £63 each and the harness, which was to be made by the eight harness makers at Hockley, a total of £1,573 8s. When this project was complete, the projected London Stud would boast 288 horses stabled at Paddington and 146 at the City stables, the latter including 18 stabled at Crutched Friars and also used for City cartage work.

By 1877 the cost of hiring the necessary horses for the Paddington area had increased again and completion of the new stabling accommodation became of the utmost urgency. A new provender store at Didcot was in operation by this time and supplies purchased for distribution under the supervision of the Chief Horse Superintendent of Paddington, the Manager of the Horse Department.

The horses were purchased and branded numerically, starting with No. 1. They were to be worked in the following categories:

Paddington

	Working	Resting	Total
Chain horses	5	1	6
1 Horse teams	31	16	47
2 Horse teams × 63	126	41	167
			220

Smithfield

	Working	Resting	Total
Chain Horses	3	—	3
1 Horse teams	29	8	37
2 Horse teams × 38	76	12	88
			128

Crutched Friars

	Working	Resting	Total
1 Horse teams × 12	11	3	14
2 Horse teams × 2	4	—	4
			18

Thirty-five horses working at Poplar Goods Yard used stables leased from the North London Railway Company at a cost of £80 per year. Fifteen reserve horses were purchased to carry out the work which was then per-

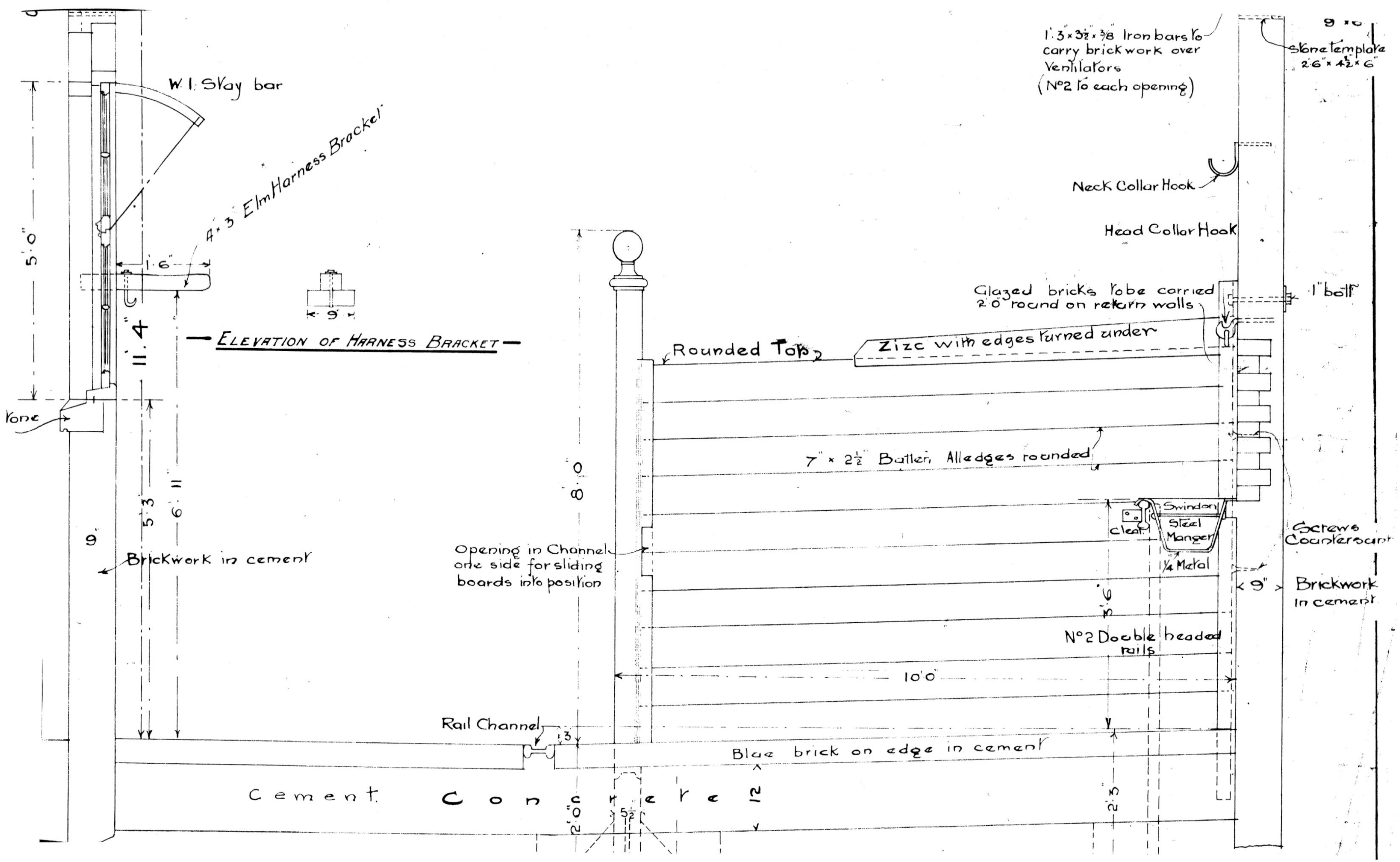

Fig. 231

Stone template
2'6" × 4½" × 6"

9" × 9"

1'3" × 3½" × ⅜" Iron bars to carry brickwork over Ventilators (No 2 to each opening)

1" bolt

Screws Countersunk

Brickwork in cement

Neck Collar Hook

Head Collar Hook

Glazed bricks to be carried 2'0 round on return walls

Rounded Top

Zinc with edges turned under

7" × 2½" Battens All edges rounded

Swindon Steel Cleat

Steel Manger ¼ Metal

No 2 Double headed rails

9'0

10'0

2'0

5'2

Blue brick on edge in cement

Opening in Channel one side for sliding boards into position

8'0

Rail Channel

Cement Concrete

1'3

Brickwork in cement

6'9

5'3

6'9

ELEVATION OF HARNESS BRACKET

W I Stay bar

4" × 3 Elm Harness Bracket

9"

5'0"

1'6"

11' 4"

Yoke

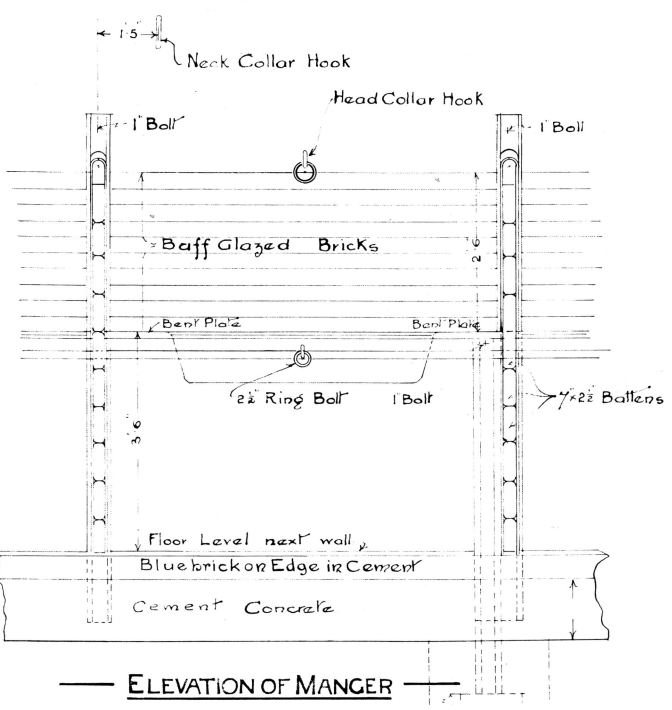

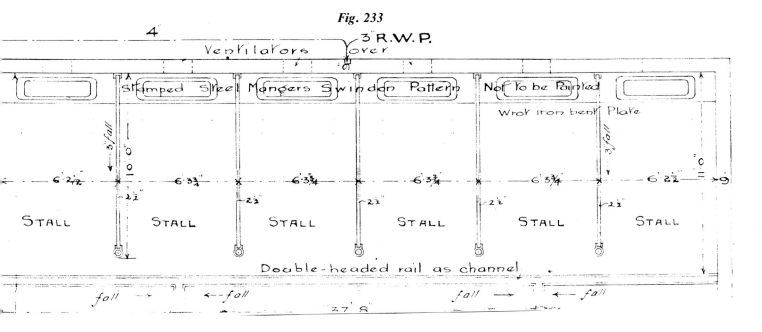

ELEVATION OF MANGER

Fig. 232

Fig. 233

Fig. 234

formed by freelance drivers and 'tonnage' horses. The driver was paid 2s 7½d (13p) per ton for most local journeys and 3s 6d (17½p) per ton for journeys taking him beyond Albert Docks or Victoria Docks.

Few of the other stables owned or operated by the Great Western Railway were of a standard comparable to the newly constructed block at Paddington. Further additions to the building in the early 1880s provided a total of 204 stalls on the ground floor and 178 on the 'one pair' or first floor. The building work was finally completed in 1884 and was the pride of the Horse Department.

At the same time as the stalls and looseboxes were built for the horses, the opportunity was taken to make provision within the building for a farrier's shop, harness room, vet's dispensary, a messroom for the men, an engine room and a number of offices for the clerical staff. A provender store was built in the centre of the complex. This building was designed to store the food and bedding requirements for about 400 horses for two weeks.

The number of staff employed at the Paddington Mint stable in 1883 was 51, and 20 at Smithfield.

1883 Paddington stable staff

2 Clerks
2 Stable foremen
34 Stablemen
1 Foreman smith
2 Night watchmen
2 Firemen
6 doormen
2 Collar makers

A harness maker was employed the following year at a cost of 30s (£1.50) a week.

1883 Smithfield stable staff

1 Horse foreman
14 Stablemen
1 Day stableman
1 Night watchman
1 Fireman
2 Doormen

The number of men increased gradually over the next six years as the stables were filled and the Company was

able to use its own horses to carry out all the work which had previously been done by extra hired horses or regular contractors. Wages increased too, but hardly in proportion to the increase in work. The 50 horsekeepers or stablemen at Paddington had a rise which took their wages to 26s (£1.30) per week, with an additional 1s (5p) after six months' service. If required, long service staff were permitted to take their whole year's wages in a lump sum in advance.

Detailed records were kept by the horsekeeper as to the amount of goods hauled by each horse or team. The figures for 1887 were reported to the Horse Committee when questions were raised as to the bonus payments the drivers were receiving. Each horse or team was required to haul certain quantities of freight during the working day.

1 horse	1 ton 10 cwt at 6 mph 20 miles per day	12 hrs
2-horse team	3 ton 10 cwt at 6 mph 20 miles per day	12 hrs
3-horse team	5 ton at 6 mph 20 miles per day	12 hrs
4-horse trolley	7 ton walking 20 miles per day	12 hrs

The Paddington horses hauled an average of two tons each per working day. Those from the Smithfield stables, being the heavier horses, hauled an average of 4 tons 1 cwt and 14 lbs. Those from the Poplar stables moved a total of 37,301 tons between the 41 horses, which is an average of 3 tons per horse per working day. Only 559 tons were carried by hired contractors during the winter months of that year. A bonus was paid to drivers who fulfilled more than their quota, thus reducing the amount that had to be hauled by hired horses and drivers. The Company saved thousands of pounds by encouraging the drivers to work their horses hard.

The routes drivers or carmen were to take between the stations and various delivery and collection points were laid down very precisely. Horses being driven from Paddington to Smithfield passed along South Wharf Road, Praed Street, Marble Arch, New Oxford Street, Holborn, Holborn Viaduct, Burr Street and finally Coutts. One reason for the use of these particular streets was that they were well policed and also frequented by the Great Western Railway company's own police force to prevent crimes and robbery.

By 1890 the remaining tonnage horses and their private contractor drivers had been replaced by Company horses. The extra horses were stabled at Paddington and Smithfield and the five extra vehicles accommodated in the carriage sheds. The contractors' horses had been stabled under the arches of the railway bridges but it was not felt that this practice could be continued indefinitely by the railway company. Eighty horses were purchased for Paddington, stabled in bale stalls, looseboxes and possibly even in the smithy. Sixty would work at any one time while the remainder were rested. A further eleven horses had to be purchased for the Smithfield stable and were primarily used to cope with the ever increasing market deliveries. In 1894 records show that the GWR owned 1,839 horses, while the Midland Railway owned 4,346.

In 1910 the Paddington stud needed to expand yet again and a fourth floor was added to the entire stable building in order to house the estimated 200 extra horses required to haul the freight which was now being conveyed by rail. All the new doors and windows were replicas of the existing openings so that the external appearance of the building retained a uniform appearance.

The selection of drawings reproduced here give a good

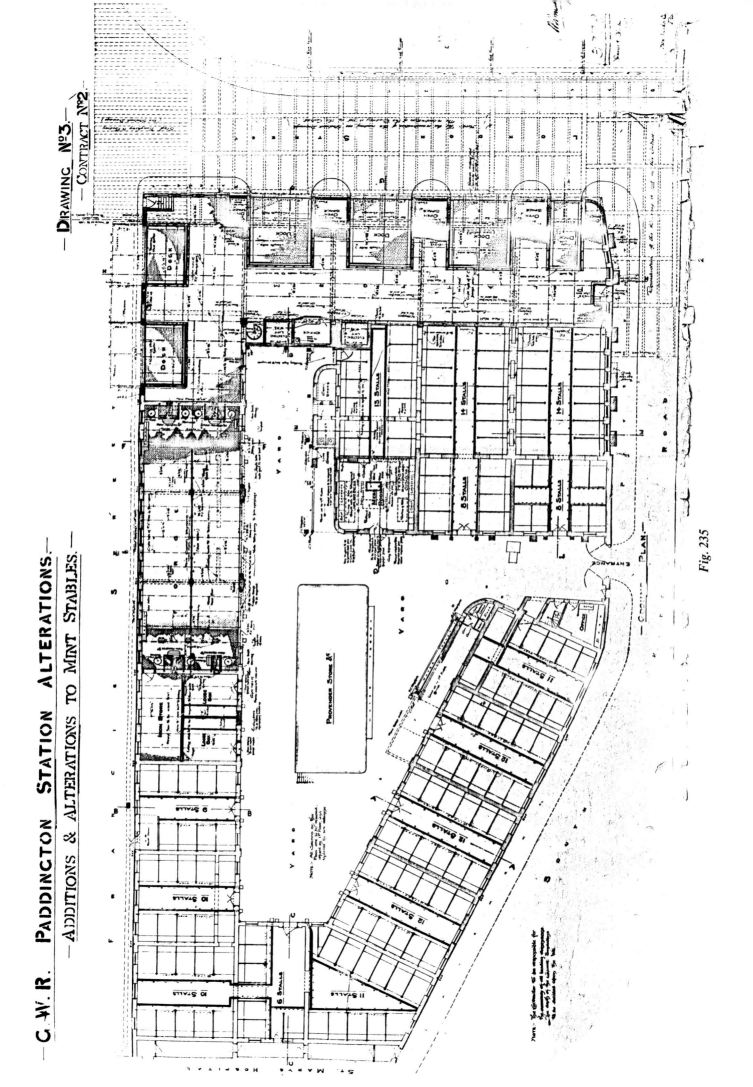

G.W.R. PADDINGTON STATION ALTERATIONS.
—ADDITIONS & ALTERATIONS TO MINT STABLES.—

DRAWING N° 3.
— CONTRACT N° 2.—

GROUND PLAN.

Fig. 235.

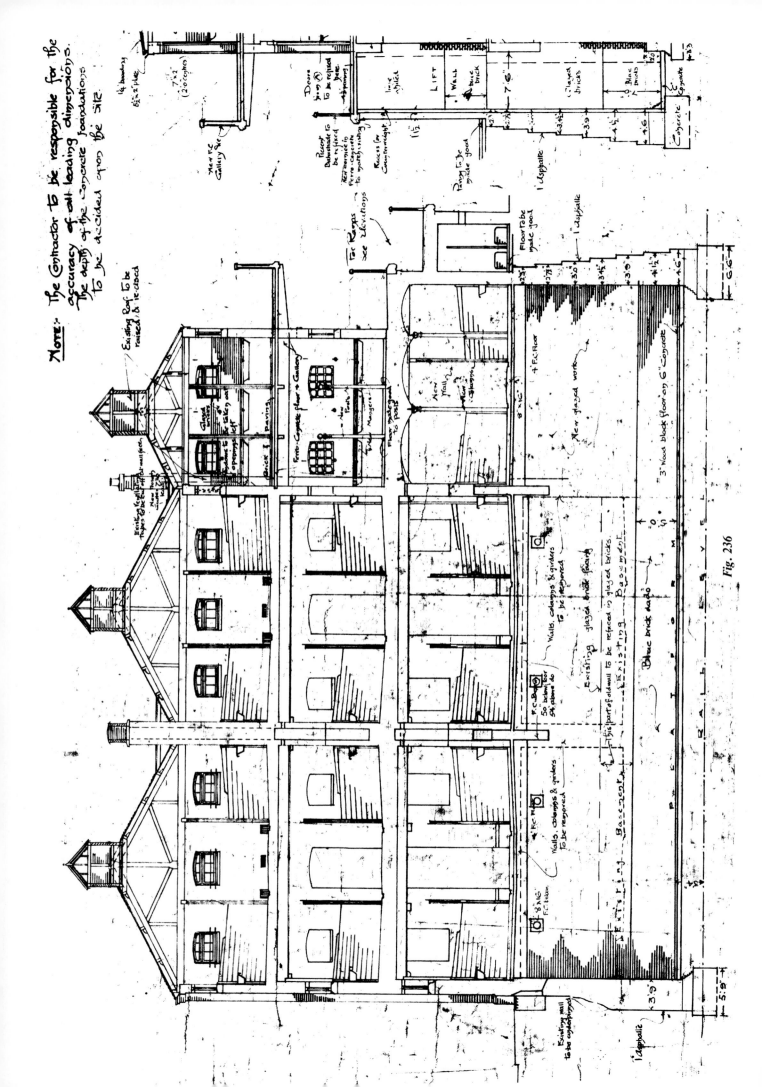

Fig. 236

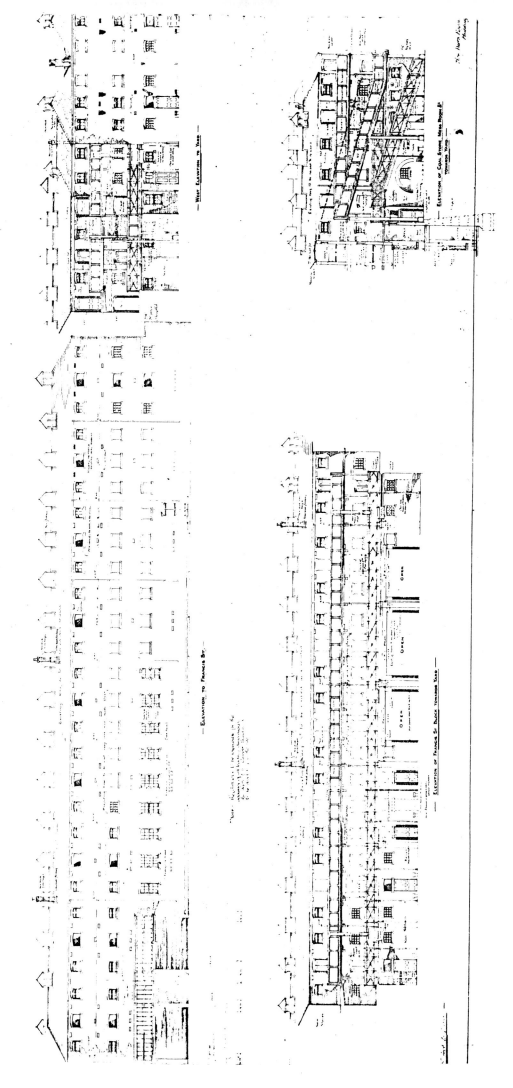

PADDINGTON STATION ALTERATIONS.

— ADDITIONS & ALTERATIONS TO MINT STABLES. —

DRAWING № 7

— CONTRACT №2. —

— WEST ELEVATION TO YARD —

— ELEVATION TO FRANCIS ST. —

— ELEVATION OF COAL STORE, MESS ROOM &c TOWARDS YARD —

— ELEVATION OF FRANCIS ST BLOCK TOWARDS YARD —

Fig. 237

— G.W.R. PADDINGTON STATION ALTERATIONS. —
— ADDITIONS & ALTERATIONS TO MINT STABLES. —

— DRAWING Nº 8 —

— CONTRACT Nº 2. —

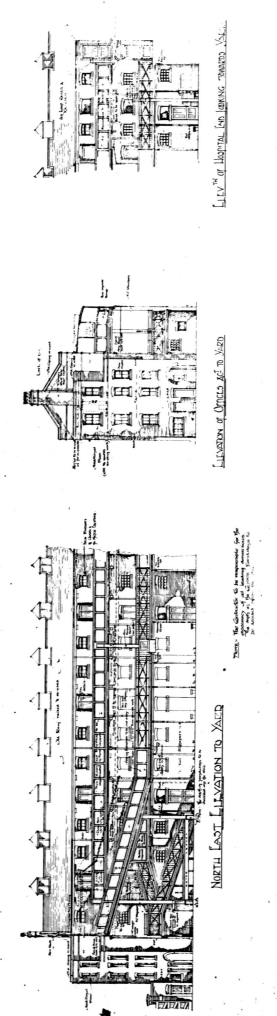

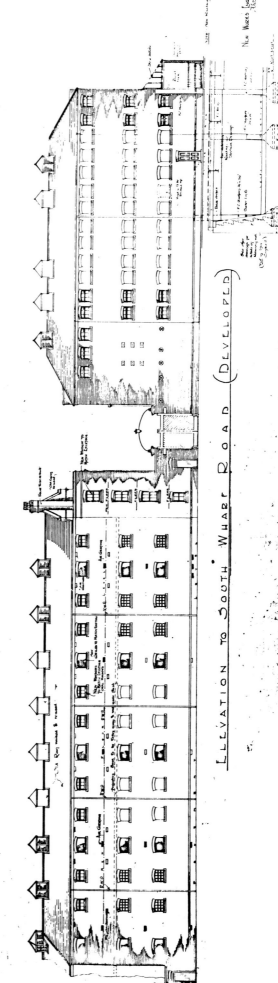

Fig. 238

Fig. 239

idea of the extent and the standard of workmanship involved in these alterations which were carried out prior to the First World War.

The ground floor plan, part of which is shown in *Fig. 235*, now only had accommodation for 150 horses in blocks of stalls, plus two looseboxes, in addition to the six loading docks, a mess room, provender store, iron store, forge, offices, coal store, electric lifts, w.c.s and stair wells.

Fig. 236 shows a Section E – E diagram from South Wharf Road on the left of the drawing to the ramp going up to the first floor on the right-hand side. Note the range of implicit instructions given by the New Works

Dept. Paddington to the contractor. The stables were built to the highest standards of the times, measuring 10 ft in length and approximately 6 ft 2 in in width. Every possible precaution was taken to avoid injury to the occupants. The edges of the bales or boards between the stalls were all rounded at the top, the newel post was topped with a ball and the steel manger set in a frame-work of wood fastened to the wall with countersunk screws.

The newel post was used to secure the horse when he had been harnessed and turned to face outwards ready for work. Short reins fastened to the animal's bit (*Fig. 234* shows this well), and prevented him/her from turning round or from 'adjusting' a piece of harness when the stableman's back was turned!

The Francis Street block of the Mint stable complex (**Fig. 237**) shown in this architect's drawing can be located on the plan of the entire building – see **Fig. 235**. Two of the ground floor doors led into the two loose-boxes while those on the left gave access to two sets of stalls. Note the instruction to the contractor – "Existing roof to be raised and re-used". No waste was allowed during the carefully checked building process.

Fig. 238 is of the opposite side of the complex, looking out on the busy South Wharf Road. The huge entrance gates on the right of the photograph, **Fig. 239**, remained open during most of the day as there was so much activity, but were closed at night when the night staff and watchman had taken over responsibility for the safety and care of the horses.

The ramp had to be extended to reach the new floor and was built of ferro-concrete. Detail is shown in **Fig. 240** (opposite). Note the instruction to fill the spaces between the timber treads with gravel so that the horses would have a good surface to go up and down to their stables on the upper floors.

Fig. 241. This picture was taken just before the conversion took place, and only went up to the 'pair' or upper storey. Each of the upper storey windows was in a stall to provide light and ventilation for the occupant.

Two views taken in the 1920s show the horses being led up and down the ramps. The new gravel surface can be clearly seen. In **Fig. 242** a farrier is doing a repair job on the shoe of a horse. It is not harnessed so presumably, unlike those coming down the ramp, it is not intended to work that day.

The carts in **Fig. 243** were drawn by two horses. The pole can be seen under the nearest vehicle while the cover is folded on the floor of the vehicle. These carts were used to carry baskets of fruit or other items which would be stacked two or three high and then covered.

Fig. 244. Another architect's drawing in the series – the loading bays at station level facing London Street. The ramp represented by the dotted lines on the elevation is to be removed and the sliding door bricked up. The new ramps to gain access to the upper floors were built on the station side of the complex.

Fig. 245. Photographed through the girders of the new Paddington Goods Yard, built just after the First World War, the Mint Stables can be seen in its finished state. The two-storey ramps are clearly shown.

Fig. 246. Horses require ventilation without draughts. The air ducting therefore was carefully planned and additional air flues and controls extended upwards so that the top floor was supplied with fresh air.

Fig. 241

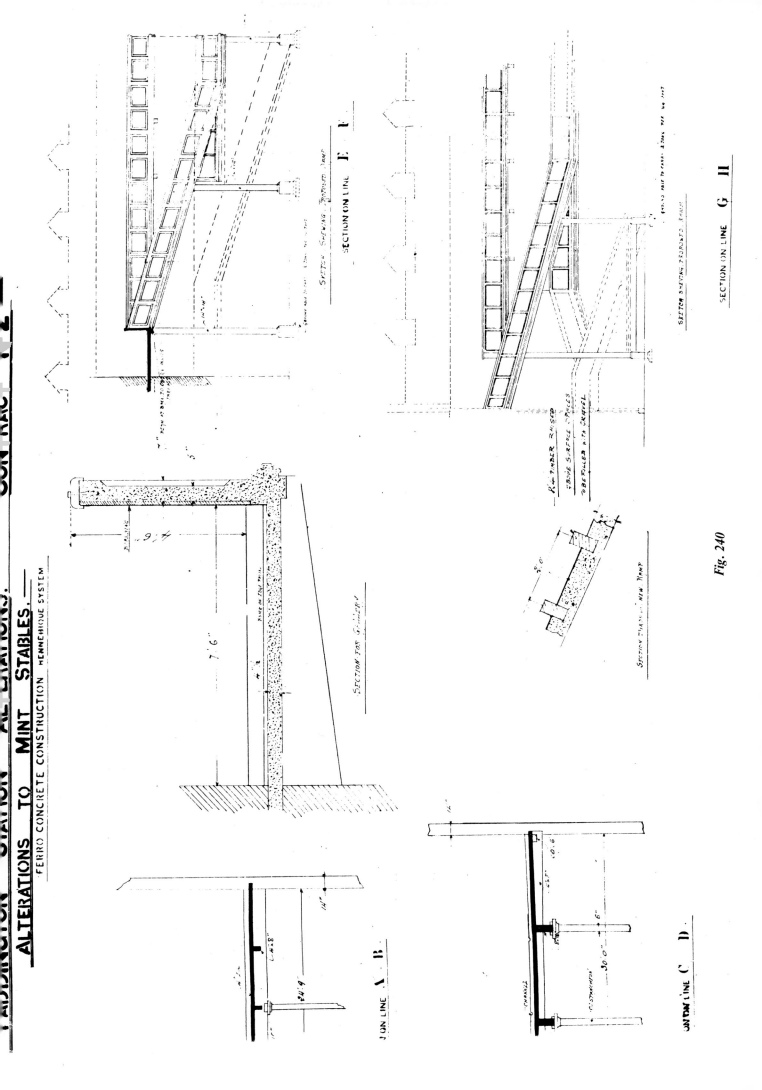

Fig. 240

Fig. 242

Fig. 243

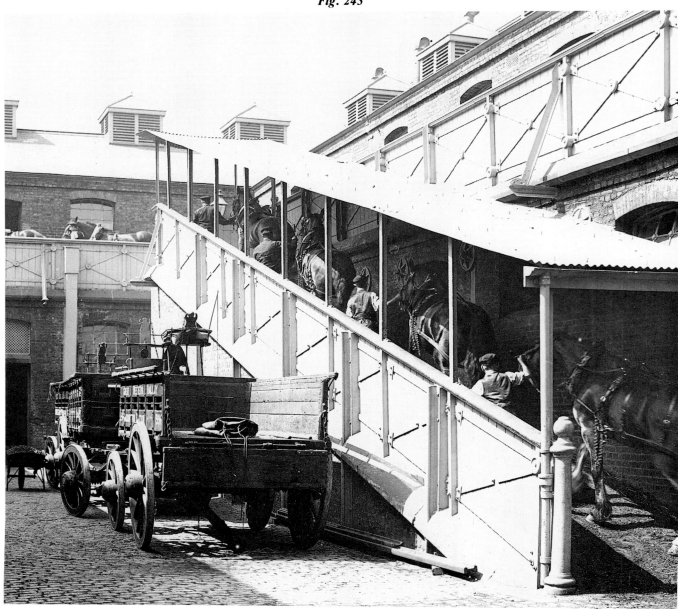

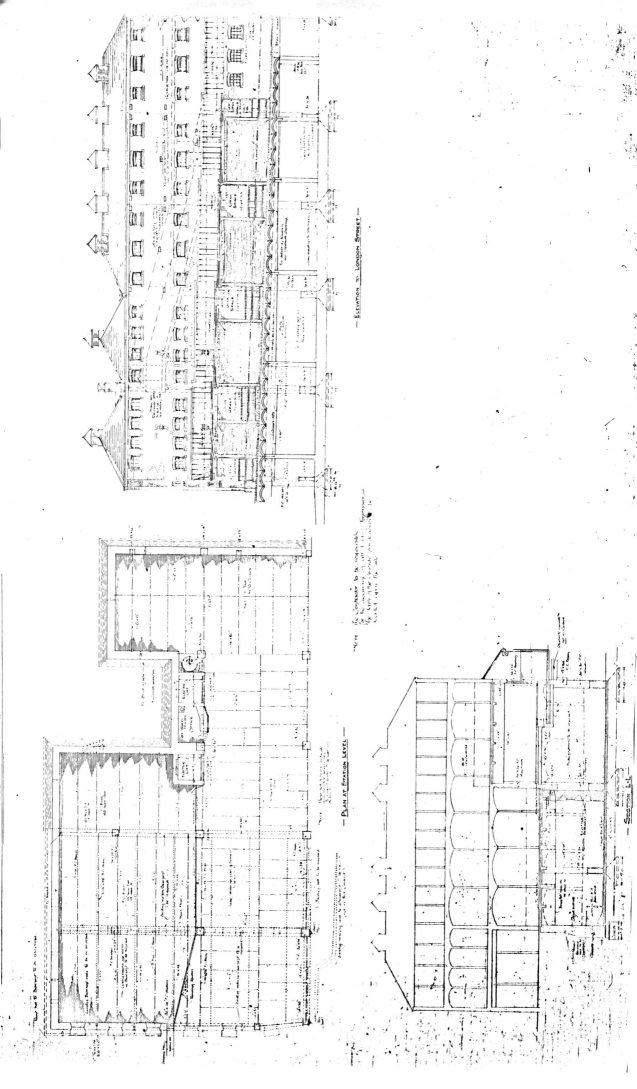

PADDINGTON STATION ALTERATIONS.
— ADDITIONS & ALTERATIONS TO MINT STABLES. —

— DRAWING Nº 2 —
— CONTRACT Nº 2 —

— ELEVATION TO LONDON STREET —

— PLAN AT STATION LEVEL —

— SECTION I-I —

Fig. 244

Fig. 245

Fig. 247. The smithy was greatly enlarged to employ six farriers. Note the use of old railway rails at the back of the hearths and also above the furnaces.

Fig. 248. The photograph of the interior of the smithy, taken some years after the alterations, shows three of the smiths shoeing some of the heavily built horses. The grey nearest the camera has a docked tail while the half clipped horse, the middle of the three horses, has a fully grown tail. In the background one of the twin hearth forges can be seen with two men, one of whom is also wearing the leather apron of a smith, standing beside it.

Fig. 249. The stableman in the smithy is probably standing by the horse's head to control it if required, but otherwise would do very little apart from leading the animal back to its stable when the shoeing operation was complete.

Fig. 250 is of the same farrier preparing a red-hot shoe on the anvil. The anvil on the far left of the photograph would have been used by a farrier using the other hearth.

Figs 251 and *252.* Not all horses were shod with the ease depicted in the previous photographs! This animal clearly has an aversion to having new shoes applied and was therefore forcibly restrained in a frame designed specifically for the purpose. An assortment of ropes and straps prevented the horse from bucking, rearing and kicking out at the farrier and his assistant who may well on this occasion have been another fully qualified farrier. The horse has put his ears back, signifying his dislike of the treatment but apart from the hatred of being shod, the horse is probably a good worker, with no other vices.

The Great Western were primarily concerned with the amount of work that could be satisfactorily performed by a horse, not with the amount of trouble shoeing caused the farriers. It was also the job of the farrier to burn the number allocated to each horse onto a forehoof as soon as it arrived at the stable.

Shortly after the final building works at Paddington Mint stables had been completed, the 'London Stud' of the Great Western Railway numbered almost 1,000 horses.

Paddington

72	Parcel
485	Cartage (goods)
32	Shunting
10	Hill and G.A.
1	Trap
87	Sick
38	Resting

725

Poplar

49	Cartage
3	Hill, G.A.
3	Sick
5	Resting

60

Smithfield

141	Cartage (goods)
9	Shunting
4	Hill, G.A.
9	Sick
8	Resting

171

The horses listed as sick were suffering from a variety of ailments, documented in the Minutes of the Horse Department after an inspection of the Stables in 1912.

3	Catarrh	57	Lame
7	Debility	1	Pneumonia
7	Fever	15	At grass
8	Galls		

Those horses which needed long term veterinary treatment were taken to one of the Great Western's own hospitals for sick horses. Looseboxes for 30 horses were available at Westbourne Park Road, Paddington and slightly fewer at West Ealing. The drawing of Westbourne Park Road shows the alterations carried out to increase the number of sick horses that could be accommodated *Fig. 253.* Note the small sliding doors along the ground level adjacent to the ventilation grille. This was the opening through which dirty straw etc., could be taken out of the stable.

Fig. 254 shows some of the 24 single-storey looseboxes at West Ealing. Adjoining fields permitted 40 horses to be cared for during the summer. Pure water has been brought into the stable complex in a water cart and is used to fill the water trough behind the cart. The driver's seat looks somewhat precarious atop the barrel, but no doubt better that than walking beside the horse.

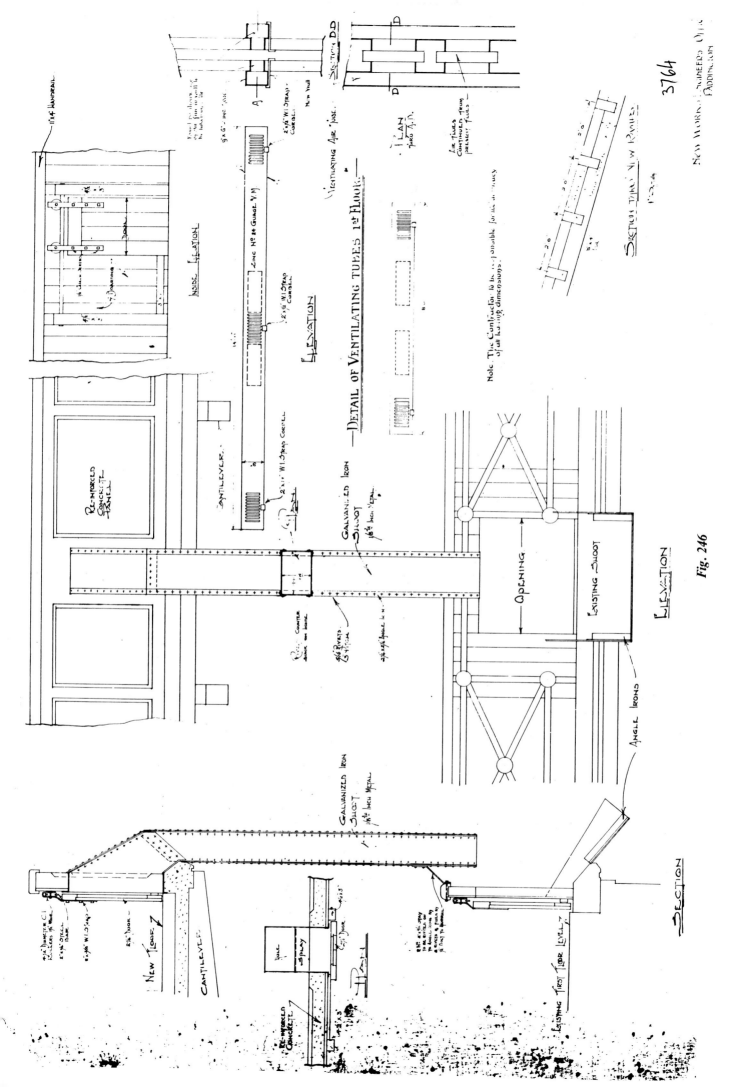

DETAIL OF VENTILATING TUBES 1st FLOOR.

Fig. 246

G. W. R. — PADDINGTON STATION ALTERATIONS. —

— ADDITIONS & ALTERATIONS TO MINT STABLES. —

— DETAIL OF SMITHY. —

DRAWING No 14
CONTRACT No 2

Fig. 248

Fig. 249

Fig. 250

Fig. 251

Fig. 252

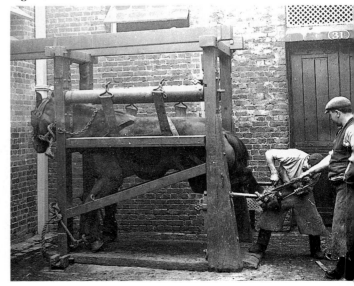

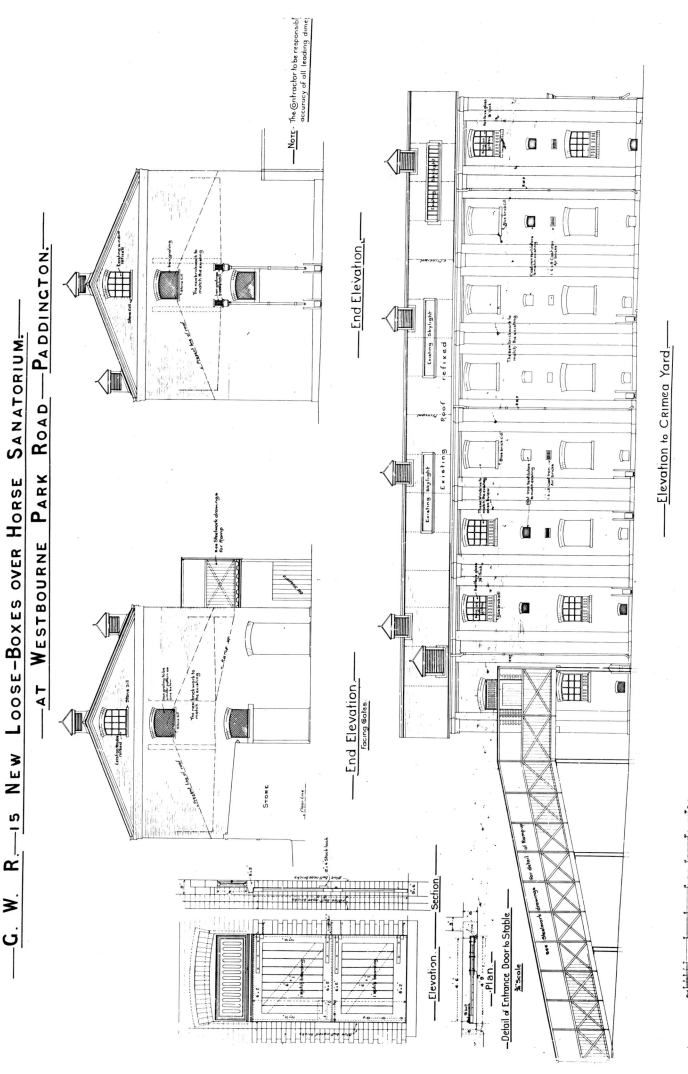

G. W. R.—15 New Loose-Boxes over Horse Sanatorium.

—at Westbourne Park Road—Paddington.—

End Elevation.

End Elevation.
Facing Gates.

Elevation to Crimea Yard.

Store

Detail of Entrance Door to Stable

Section.

Elevation.

Plan.

Fig. 253

Fig. 254

For an overall picture of the complexities of the cartage department at Paddington station I cannot improve on the following excerpt from the Great Western Railway magazine under the title of "A Day's Work at Paddington Goods Station". It was printed in March 1908.

"... after the invoices which accompany the goods have been checked as to their charges by experts on the night clerical staff, they are passed to another staff, who prepare a carman's delivery sheet for each entry, and thence to the unloading gangs in the shed, the checkers of which certify whether the goods have been actually received by checking each entry in blue lead. Meanwhile the delivery sheets are being passed out as rapidly as possible to the cartage foremen, who sort them into district order and judge by experience what is a fair load within the compass of a delivery van, at the same time deciding whether the goods have actually arrived or not. The sheets are then passed through the sheet register and handed to the carman told off for delivery to the particular district, whose duty is then to load his van in proper order for delivery, i.e., the articles for delivery last are placed first on the van, and so on, and are checked by the carman as he places them on his van and the sheets initialled by him. The latter are then checked back from the carman with the register, and all sheets bearing money items are again passed through a special register, by means of which a settlement of all moneys collected is made at the end of the day, and the billheads of all items which for any reason have not been secured are demanded by the settling clerk before the carman is released.

We are responsible for the delivery of all fish, poultry, meat, flowers, etc., received by passenger train for market, and for this purpose have a staff of 72 teams and one 5 ton capacity motor coming on at 2 am. After the passenger department have been served the residue of this staff is available for the delivery of our own market and perishable goods, and the exhaustion of this staff necessitates our sending out callers up, who secure the services of the requisite number of regular day men (at busy periods totalling up to 80 or 100 men), who are granted a special allowance for this extra service.

The normal order of coming on duty, however, may be placed at: 68 men and boys at 2 am, drawing regular market allowance; 22 at 5 am; 71 up to 7.30 am; 218 at 8 am; and 26 at 9 am; totalling up to an authorised number of 405 carmen, and the same number of vanguards, or a grand total for the whole cartage staff of nearly 1,000 men and boys.

The number of carmen's delivery sheets average a daily total of about 2,000, and it will be readily conceded that the preparation of such a number and the daily audit of and checking out and in, is a work of some magnitude, and, as the number of sheets lost is comparatively insignificant, it speaks well for the care and skill exercised.

The system of bonus payments, as applied to carmen, may be understood by reference to the following table of minimum weights to be moved per team, viz.:—

4 horse teams 60 tons per week
3   ,,   ,,   50 and 58 tons per week
2   ,,   ,,   24, 27, 30, 33 tons per week
1   ,,   ,,   12 and 15 tons per week

after which, bonus is paid at the rate of 10d. per ton to carmen and 3d per ton to vanguards, and to indicate the nature of its success, I need only say that between 80 and 90 per cent of the men get it, and that we have saved upwards of £15,000 in hire and reduced our cost by 8d. per ton.

The allowances are now calculated on a daily basis, e.g., a wagon team moving 15 tons on one day would be entitled to 5 tons bonus at 10d., that being the excess weight over and above the 10 tons per day required of the team. The varying weights required per team are paid according to the nature of the traffic dealt with, district or distance covered.

I need hardly say that the position of Cartage Superintendent is one of great trust, and only a long apprenticeship can give the necessary grasp of the intricate details that go to make up the daily routine of his duties and those of his assistants, and give confidence in that ready decision so necessary to deal efficiently with the numerous questions and difficulties that daily arise.

The following information may also be of interest in the consideration of the cartage work of this station. There are 670 horses in daily use at Paddington, but we are responsible for the work done by 693 horses, the remainder being attached to depôts and offices, with a reserve of 259 horses. The number of vehicles attached to Paddington Goods is 577. All these vehicles have to be washed and kept clean by the goods staff. Lamps have to be given out to all carmen each day, also buckets, rope sacks, sheets, etc.

Fig. 255. A typical two-horse goods vehicle.

Fig. 256. A general view of the Yard and Old Offices.

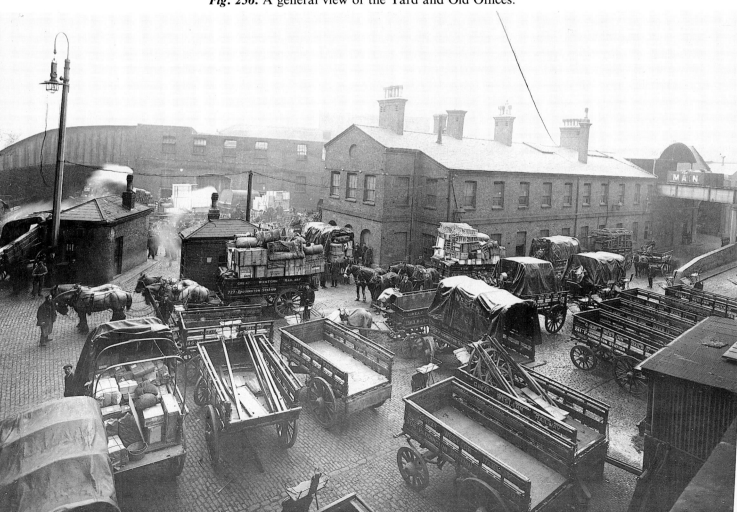

The Company have three very fine 4 horse wagons teams, a somewhat rare class of team in London. They have great drawing power, and are most useful for heavy boilers and machinery, requiring a dozen horses some times. The horses in these teams being trained to pull together, can move weights that twice as many horses, not so trained, would havea difficulty in doing. At one time the four horse teams were harnessed tandem fashion, that is in line, a quite unique style, and one that would be very troublesome now in London streets with their congested crossings and rapidly moving motor traffic. Goods motors will probably replace the horsed vehicles in the future, near or far, but at present they have not proved a commercial success.

For many years the clerical staff had outgrown the accommodation provided, necessitating a scattering into every hole and corner that could be utilised, amid conditions that became insanitary and unhealthy, and I desire to record the grateful thanks of the staff to the Directors and officers for the handsome, commodious, and completely appointed offices now provided for their use and occupation.

It may be of interest to record that the old goods offices in the yard, now in course of demolition, were once the chief offices of the Company. The Chief Goods Manager occupied the room latterly used by the Goods Superintendent.

Among the many up-to-date appointments in the various offices—and those who have seen the desks, racks, labatory fittings, and general furnishing of the new building will readily follow me—the arrangements made to meet the modern requirements of the telephone service are deserving of special mention. From one solitary instrument in use in the old offices in the year 1898, the number now in use has risen to no less than 47, for public and private use. A switchboard has been erected in connection with the National Telephone system, carrying five trunk lines and 11 extensions, introducing into the offices what is practically a small telephone exchange, and it was with no small amount of gratification that a remark was received during a recent visit of a number of other Companies' officials, who were visiting the London termini to enquire into the telephone arrangements, that ours was by far the best installation they had inspected.

In proceeding to a description of the organisation of the clerical staff of Paddington Goods Station, I wish to interpolate the explanation that the division of the work into the numerous sections shown in the accompanying chart, may not seem so necessary to those who have had experience of comparatively small stations only, as it appeals to those who are more intimately acquainted with the enormous detail connected with the miscellaneous character of the traffic dealt with at Paddington, and I will ask them to try and realise that the ordinary divisions of traffic working, with which they are familiar require a subdividion here to bring them within the scope of a day's work, and as multiplicity is more productive of possible error, so the balancing and correctness of the parts are necessary before the component whole can be evolved. The chart now introduced conveys, in graphic form, the arrangement of the staff of clerks, each of whom, in one way or another, is connected with the operations of "A Day's work at Paddington Goods Station".

Fig. 257 shows an overall view of Paddington Goods Yard, in 1919 during the middle of the day. Various vehicles have already been loaded, while more carts are under the canopy being attended to by the porters and van guards. When a horse was brought in with an empty cart, having dropped the goods at the despatch side, he would be unhitched from it at the loading bay and taken over to one of the full carts in the centre of the yard, hitched up and driven over to the weighbridge. The weighbridge office is the small building in the left foreground. As mentioned in the selection of Rules quoted earlier, each vehicle had to be weighed on leaving and returning to the station. The amount carried each trip was added up to produce the driver's weekly total and the possibility of a bonus. The two vehicles on the approach road (right hand side of the picture) seem to be overloaded by modern standards.

Fig. 257

ORGANIZATION OF OFFICE STAFF AT PADDINGTON GOODS STATION, 1908.

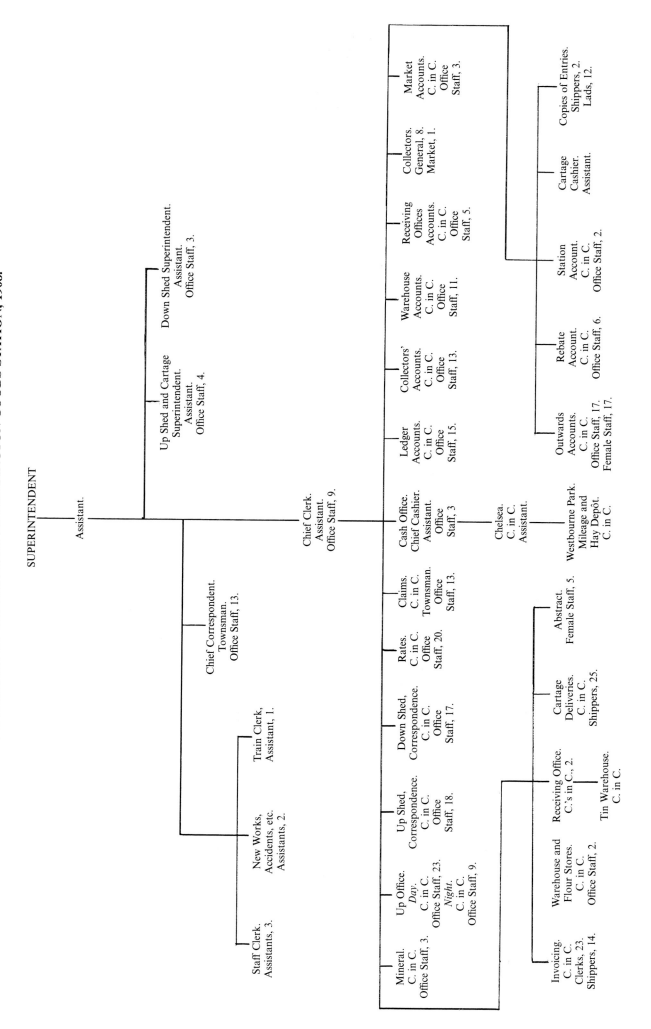

TOTAL OFFICE STAFF: 364.

SUPERINTENDENT

Assistant.

Up Shed and Cartage Superintendent. Assistant. Office Staff, 4.

Down Shed Superintendent. Assistant. Office Staff, 3.

Chief Correspondent. Townsman. Office Staff, 13.

Staff Clerk. Assistants, 3.

New Works, Accidents, etc. Assistants, 2.

Train Clerk, Assistant, 1.

Chief Clerk. Assistant. Office Staff, 9.

Cash Office. Chief Cashier. Assistant. Office Staff, 3

Chelsea. C. in C. Assistant.

Westbourne Park. Mileage and Hay Depôt. C. in C.

Claims. C. in C. Townsman. Office Staff, 13.

Rates. C. in C. Office Staff, 20.

Down Shed, Correspondence. C. in C. Office Staff, 17.

Up Shed, Correspondence. C. in C. Office Staff, 18.

Mineral. C. in C. Office Staff, 3.
Up Office. *Day.* C. in C. Office Staff, 23. *Night.* C. in C. Office Staff, 9.

Ledger Accounts. C. in C. Office Staff, 15.

Collectors' Accounts. C. in C. Office Staff, 13.

Warehouse Accounts. C. in C. Office Staff, 11.

Receiving Offices Accounts. C. in C. Office Staff, 5.

Collectors. General, 8. Market, 1.

Market Accounts. C. in C. Office Staff, 3.

Outwards Accounts. C. in C. Office Staff, 17. Female Staff, 17.

Rebate Account. C. in C. Office Staff, 6.

Station Account. C. in C. Office Staff, 2.

Cartage Cashier. Assistant.

Copies of Entries. Shippers, 2. Lads, 12.

Abstract. Female Staff, 5.

Cartage Deliveries. C. in C. Shippers, 25.

Receiving Office. C.'s in C., 2.

Tin Warehouse. C. in C.

Warehouse and Flour Stores. C. in C. Office Staff, 2.

Invoicing. C. in C. Clerks, 23. Shippers, 14.

Fig. 258. This picture of the arrivals side of Paddington station taken in 1912, shows a diversity of vehicles. Traffic is being transported by both motor lorry and by horse and cart, while passengers leave the station in the familiar omnibus, or rather daringly, in a motor car.

Fig. 259. The office wall chart in the Goods Manager's office at Paddington gives details of those areas in 1945 which still used horses, the numbers actually working, resting or sick. Twelve large stations plus parts of central Wales were still employing horses to deliver goods and parcels or perform other functions such as shunting. (As the data on the chart is very small and almost indecipherable in the photograph this is summarised in the accompanying table.)

The last cartage horse left Paddington Station in 1947 but one old mare was kept to pull a small refuse cart round the station precincts. Known to many as "Maisie", she continued her duties until the mid 1960s when she was officially retired to a grassy field.

	District Stud		Reserve		
	Working	*Spare*	*Working*	*Resting*	*Sick*
London	195	6	—	11	30
Bristol	169	—	6	1	10
Exeter	18	1	—	1	—
Plymouth	36	2	—	4	1
Newport	29	—	—	2	—
Cardiff	108	—	3	7	3
Swansea	39	—	—	2	—
Gloucester	29	1	—	—	—
Worcester	23	—	—	—	—
Birmingham	193	7	—	32	13
Shrewsbury	3	1	—	1	—
Central Wales	14	—	1	1	—
Liverpool	15	—	—	—	—
	871	18	10	62	57

Total: 1,018 horses.

Fig. 258

Fig. 259

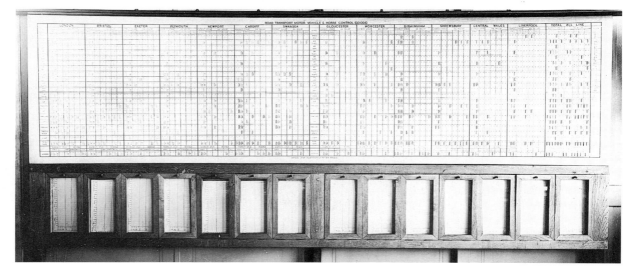

Goods Yards

Other goods yards around the GWR system were run according to the same system as Paddington. Goods arriving at the station were checked before being loaded onto the trolleys and carts across the platform. This scene at Hockley Goods Inward shed (*Fig. 260*) must have been taken during the winter as there is snow on the tarpaulins and the roofs of the goods wagons. Packages of every description are being unloaded, some to be placed immediately on to the waiting carts while others have been stacked on the floor. A railway police-man is checking the contents of one van which may have been sealed during transit to prevent theft.

Fig. 261. Cardiff Newtown Goods Yard is also busy but perhaps a little less well ordered than the previous scene. Vehicles seem to be moving in all directions regardless of whether they are laden or not. In the background of this 1924 picture are two new GWR Express Cartage motor vehicles. However, horse power still predominates as there are no less than 16 carts, trolleys and vans pulled by one or two horse teams in the photograph. The Company still owned almost 3,000 horses at this time.

Fig. 262. This picture taken in the same year shows the exit at Bristol Temple Meads Goods Depot. Again a mixture of horse and motor transport, all carrying far more staff than was normal so it is presumed the photograph was posed deliberately to show as many employees as possible. It was unusual for a coloured horse to be employed but it appears to be a useful sort of cob which is being driven without blinkers, as are several

Fig. 260

Fig. 261

of the other horses. Many readers will no doubt notice the poor condition of the horses' legs which probably points to the amount of heavy work done by these horses, but the condition of their coats belies any thought of ill-treatment of an intentional nature. It was a constant cause of trouble to all draught horses, the pounding of their hooves on the settes and hard surfaces of roads as they moved their loads.

Fig. 263. A typical scene at a loading bay of a fairly large station. Two pole wagons, each with a pair of well matched horses, one pair blinkered while those with white blazes are being driven without. Work has stopped while the photograph is taken and once again all available staff have gathered to be recorded for posterity! The driver of the wagon nearest the camera has a rather individual style of whip above the company issue driving apron. That of his companion appears to be less ostentatious.

Fig. 264. Although the location is unidentified, this scene portrays the loading of freight that has been brought to the shed by returning carts and wagons. The baskets are empty and so probably is the crate of Danish eggs upended in the foreground on the left of the picture. The covered cart in the background is drawn by two horses either side of the pole. Only one appears to be in position at the time of the photograph. Another covered van is partly hidden beneath the crate that is being moved by the crane operator.

Fig. 262

Fig. 263

Fig. 264

Provender Stores

Until 1884 provender for the railway horses was stored at Handsworth in a converted goods shed. It was loaded onto rail wagons and distributed to all the stables on the system without charge. Individual stables only kept one week's supply in hand at their limited stores, perhaps an outside shed or spare stall. The horses were fed on a mixture of oats, beans, bran, linseed, indian corn, hay and straw. The proportions were mixed in accordance with the type of work the horses were expected to perform. Maize was substituted for oats in 1869 when the cost of the latter rose sharply. Nutritionally the calorific value of both oats and maize was about the same, but maize is cheaper and was more readily available. Yearly feeding costs for each horse were £22 0s 9d in 1871 and £23 6s 8d in 1872. This sum included the cost of the stable straw which was used as bedding.

In winter two pounds of extra beans were added to the daily food rations of:

```
16 lb hay
 8 lb oats
 6 lb maize
 3 lb beans
 2 lb bran
 ——
35 lb
 ==
```

In 1882 the Great Western board considered the possibility of having a second provender store in the original stable complex at Paddington. The suggestion was rejected on financial grounds. Only one set of machinery was required to process the feed required for the 500 horses employed at the time and the cost of buying or building a suitable store, machinery and wages would have far outweighed the cost of transporting the provender from the present store or indeed from Didcot, which had just been selected as the most suitable site for a new store. Didcot was central to the Great Western system and a store could be built on land already owned by the railway. Labour costs at Handsworth had risen to £12 per week and much of the machinery had become obsolete.

The new store was to be built within the Didcot station precincts, and together with the machinery was to cost "not more than £16,000". Two staff houses were to be constructed nearby at a cost of "not more than £450", but do not appear on this plan (*Fig. 265.*)

The four-storey building, of an imposing appearance (*Fig. 266*) was operational in 1884 and coped with the increase in the number of horses used on the system without difficulty. Each stable still stored one week's supply on their premises and the new delivery arrived by rail according to a pre-arranged routine.

The following article by W. H. Stanier was printed in the *Great Western Magazine* in October 1906 and gives a graphic description of the functions of a provender store catering for the majority of the railway horses currently in the Company's ownership.

Horse Provender Stores, Didcot
By W. H. Stanier.

The large building at Didcot on the up side of the main line has often been a puzzle to travellers. Some have supposed it to be a prison, or a workhouse, or a lunatic asylum. It stands, however, on railway land, and the only connection which railways have with such institutions is to pay a large and, as we think, an undue, share of the rates for their support. The building is, in fact, the store in which the provender for the Company's horses—nearly 3,000 in number—is collected, the hay cut into chaff, the corn crushed, and the whole cleaned and mixed in due proportions and sent out as forage to various stations throughout the system.

Fig. 267. General view of Didcot Horse Provender Stores.

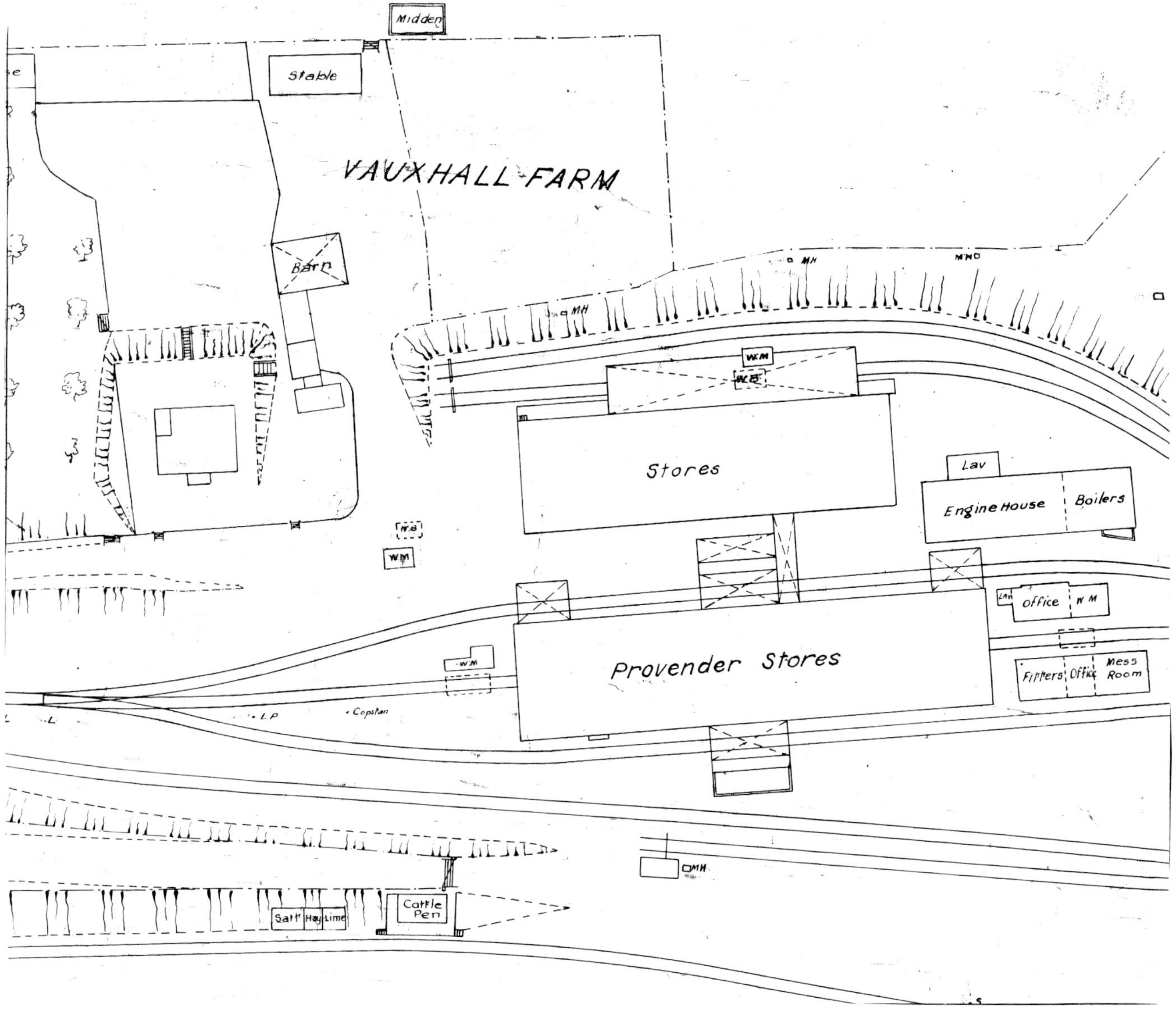
Midden
Stable
VAUXHALL FARM
Barn
MH
Stores
Lav
Engine House
Boilers
Office
W M
Provender Stores
Fitters' Office
Mess Room
Copstan
Cattle Pen
Salt
Hay
Lime
MH

Fig. 265

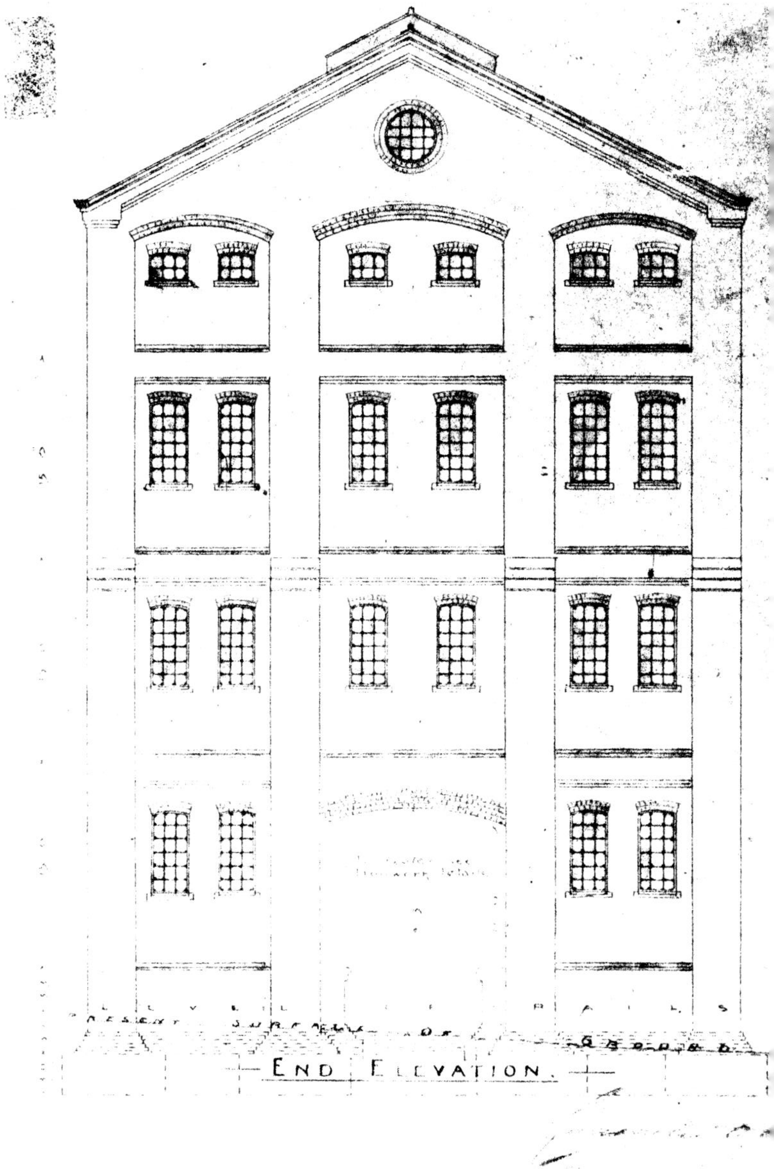
END ELEVATION

Fig. 266

Prior to 1884 the Company's Provender Depot was at Handsworth, but the increase in the number of horses, and the necessity for more up-to-date methods have necessitated the new premises, situated at a more convenient centre for distribution, to be provided. Didcot was chosen as the site for the new store, and is admirably adapted for the purpose. Not only is it a most convenient point for distribution, but it is the centre of a large horse-forage growing district. In addition to it now supplying constant work for about forty men, it has been of great advantage to the agricultural industry in Berkshire and the adjoining counties.

It may be interesting to note that about eight years ago the Directors, desiring to assist the agricultural interest in the districts through which the railway passed, determined, if possible, to purchase English instead of foreign oats. At first there was some little difficulty in obtaining adequate supplies, but since 1899 English oats only have been used. It is estimated that an area of approximately 9,000 acres is now utilised for the growth of the hay, oats and beans required for the Didcot Store.

The main building of the store is an imposing brick-built fireproof structure, about 202 feet long and 40 feet wide, flanked on each side by a high tower carrying a large water tank, these forming a conspicuous land-mark visible for many miles around. The building, as shown on the accompanying sectional drawing, is divided into four floors. In the preparation of the provender the whole of the hay and corn is first conveyed to the top of the building. The upper floor is used for the storage of corn and for the chaff-cutting machinery, the next floor for hay sifters and corn mills, the floor below for the mixers, and the ground floor for receiving from the mixers the prepared forage to be put into sacks and loaded into wagons. On each floor, space is provided for storage, but it was found that the accommodation was insufficient to provide for an adequate reserve of hay and straw and a separate hay barn was erected providing accommodation for 300 tons of hay and straw. This barn has special facilities for unloading the hay from either railway trucks or road vehicles, and, as shown in the illustrations, is provided with a power elevator which delivers trusses of hay and oat-straw to the top floor of the main building at the rate of 600 trusses per hour when required.

The machinery in the store was formerly driven by steam power, a vertical shaft, running from top to bottom of the building, being connected with horizontal shafting on each floor by means of mitre gearing. In 1901 the whole of the main shafting was dispensed with, and a large saving of power effected by the substitution of electric driving. The electrical power house is situated near to the hay barn and contains two 100 horse-power dynamos supplying current to sixteen motors distributed about the premises. Current is also supplied to the pumping station at Appleford one and a half miles away, and, as recently noticed in the *Magazine*, to the newly installed system of power operation of points and signals at Didcot. There is also a hydraulic plant for supplying power to the lifts and capstans, a pump for feeding the station water cranes, and another for picking up the Appleford water and sending it to the village reservoir which supplies both Didcot and North Hagbourne. Near the main building are the fitters' shop and stores, the storekeeper's office, and a well appointed mess-room in which the men, many of whom necessarily reside some distance from the store, may have their food cooked and take their meals in comfort.

The contracts for the purchase of the provender are placed by the Directors every three months and involve the expenditure of approximately £20,000 per annum. The hay, oat-straw, oats, beans and maize, which are the finished products of the agriculturist, are the raw material of the provender store, and have to pass through what may almost be described as a manufacturing process before being sent out as mixed forage ready for use. Arrangements are made with the contractors for the supply, as far as possible, of regular weekly quantities of the various kinds of provender – the present weekly rquirements being 1,000 sacks of oats, 220 sacks of beans, 480 sacks of maize, 110 tons of hay, 16 tons of oat-straw, 18 tons of bran, and 40 or 50 tons of straw, a large portion of the latter being used for packing purposes in the goods warehouses. It is one of the most important duties of the storekeeper to see that materials are of the best quality and in perfect condition. The stringency of the inspection is, in fact, sometimes resented by contractors who have not had previous experience of the requirements, but it is now generally recognised that it is useless to send to Didcot any hay or corn which is not of the highest quality, and very little difficulty is experienced in meeting the requirements.

The quantity of provender to be supplied per horse, and the proportion of the different ingredients in the various feeds, are determined by the Veterinary Department, requisitions being sent to the storekeeper by the Horse Superintendent. The usual mixture for the country horses is as follows:

Oats	$22\frac{1}{2}$	per cent
Beans	10	,,
Maize	20	,,
Hay	$41\frac{1}{2}$	,,
Oat-straw	6	,,

Fig. 268. Diagram showing arrangement of machinery.

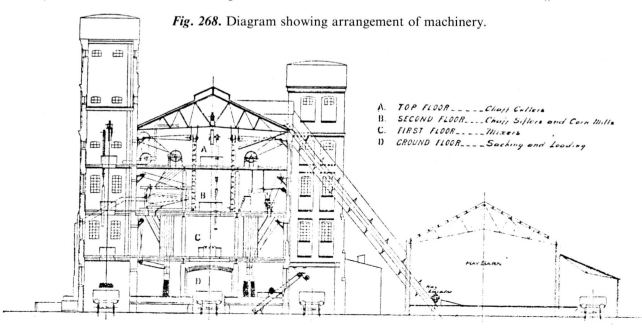

A. TOP FLOOR _____ Chaff Cutters
B. SECOND FLOOR ____ Chaff Sifters and Corn Mills
C. FIRST FLOOR _____ Mixers
D. GROUND FLOOR ____ Sacking and Loading

HAY BARN

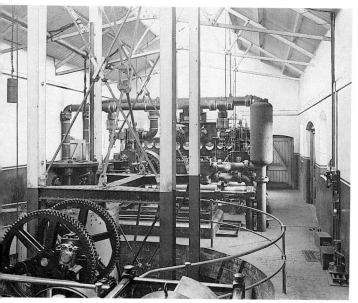

Fig. 269. Power House, Didcot Provender Stores.

The London horses have $2\frac{1}{2}$ per cent more oats and a correspondingly lower percentage of hay. During the winter months the proportion of beans is increased in some cases, and there are special mixtures for nose-bags and for sick horses. The daily net allowance of mixed provender per horse varies from 27 lbs to 32 lbs, in addition to bran and bedding straw.

Fig. 270. Interior of Hay Barn, showing elevator.

The deliveries having been inspected and approved, the hay and oat-straw is run into the hay barn siding, and by means of the elevator is quickly conveyed to the top floor of the main building. The trucks of corn are put into position at either of the two corn elevators on the ground floor, and the contents run out and shot into hoppers feeding direct into the elevator cups, which are fixed at intervals of ten inches on a rapidly travelling vertical belt, by which the corn is elevated to the top floor. Each elevator is capable of discharging fifty sacks an hour from the trucks on the ground floor into the bins on the top floor, a distance of sixty feet. The process of cleaning begins from the moment the stuff is first handled and continues to the time that the finished mixed provender is turned out. A powerful exhaust fan is fixed at the top of each elevator shaft, and as the corn is ascending a great deal of dust and light corns

are extracted. As the corn is delivered from the elevator it is passed over a suitably perforated surface, which removes small seeds etc, and then enters a conveyor and is discharged into any one of the ten bins as desired.

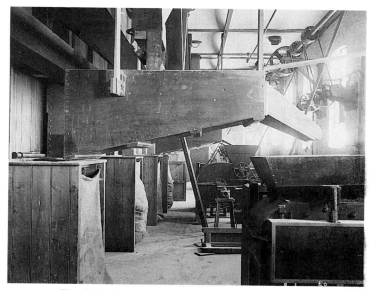

Fig. 271. Corn mills, showing shakers.

The trusses of hay and straw are raised from the hay barn and delivered by the elevator shoot on to the floor near the chaff cutters, of which there are six, working in pairs, one pair for each of three separate provender preparing plants. Two plants are generally working together. The trusses are quickly opened and forked up on to a small table and are directed into the feed box assisted by endless feed webbing towards the knives. The machines run at a speed of 480 revolutions per minute, and, having three cutting knives on the flywheel, quickly convert the hay into chaff. Each of the machines is fitted with Multiplex Safety Rollers which make it impossible for a man to get his hands as far as the knives.

Fig. 272. Grain bins and sacked oats.

The cut chaff falls on to a riddle on the floor below, and the cavings (long pieces) are returned back to the chaff cutter by means of an elevator. The wear on the knives is very great; although they are made of the best steel for the purpose, they will not, under the most favourable circumstances, turn out good work for longer than forty minutes at a time.

While the hay is being cut and passed to the sifters as chaff, the corn from the various bins is being let out by means of carefully adjusted slides to the creepers below. In transit it undergoes further cleansing, first by being passed over powerful magnets for the removal of the pieces of iron and steel which are frequently found in corn, and afterwards by being passed through a shaker, a box-like arrangement with a rapid sieve-like motion, which effectually cleanses it of all the remaining dust and delivers it into the mill-hoppers clean and bright. The oats, beans and maize, by carefully regulated adjustments and in the proper proportions, are now allowed to trickle out of the hoppers on to the crushing rollers. For oats, smooth steel rollers, are used which merely crush the corn; for beans and maize toothed rollers, working in pairs, are employed, these having the effect of cutting the separate grains.

Concurrently with the preparation and delivery of the corn, the chaff falls from the chaff cutters in a continuous and regular stream to the vibrating sifters, which have a top surface of perforated walnut wood, and an underneath surface of perforated zinc. As the chaff descends the sloping surface the long pieces find their way to the bottom and fall over into the elevator which takes them back to the chaff cutters. The short chaff falls through and travels over the zinc surface, and the heavier dust, inseparable from all descriptions of hay, falls through the perforations on to the floor, a fan in conjunction with the sifter materially assisting the process of cleaning. Great attention is paid to the very important matter of dust extraction and collection. Wherever possible, the provender is subjected to the action of exhaust fans in order to turn it out as free from injurious matter as possible. The dust occasioned by working is collected at every machine and finds its way by means of two main dust trunks into the dust rooms outside the building.

The crushed oats, beans and maize now pass to the floor below and enter a worm conveyor, where they are thoroughly mixed together by the time they reach the mixing chamber into which the chaff is falling. Here sets of arms working much like the beaters of the old-fashioned box churns ensure a uniform mixture passing into the sacks waiting to receive it on the bag spouts below. Nothing now remains but to weigh off each sack at the proper weight and load into trucks for despatch. The number of sacks required to contain one week's supply is over 6,000 and the total sacks in circulation is nearly 14,000.

The building is guarded against fire by the installation of 882 Grinnell Sprinklers supplied with water, in the first instance, from the tank on the top of the tower, and also by a pump in the power house pumping direct into the fire mains. By this arrangement, if a fire occurred, the sprinklers in the immediate vicinity would be automatically released, giving a heavy shower of water at that point and sounding an alarm which would bring prompt assistance. It is believed that these arrangements make it practically impossible for a fire of any magnitude to occur.

The Stores Department representative at Didcot, in charge of the store, is Mr. A. Campbell.

In 1909 the weekly food order for the 3,000 plus Great Western horses was as follows:

    1,000 sacks oats
      220 sacks beans
      480 sacks maize
      110 tons hay
       16 tons oat straw
       18 tons bran

The weekly bedding requirement was 40 to 50 tons of wheat straw. The weekly provender and bedding required for each stable was sent by rail on a particular day each week according to a set pattern.

Fig. 273. Chaff cutters, Didcot Provender Stores.

The Rule Book

Each railway company issued its own General Rule Book. In addition to the guide lines as to the required behaviour of an employee, the Great Western issued departmental rule books. The Cartage Department had a slim volume devoted to specialist orders.

The 1886 *Instructions to Cartage Foremen, Carmen, Loaders and others employed in London* sets out 69 rules covering many aspects. A selection of the more interesting rules are as follows:

'Carmen must see that their harness is kept clean and tidy by the vanguards, but the former to be ultimately responsible for its condition.'

'Collar must be dry.'

'Each Carman will be provided with a tarpaulin, rope and pouch. He will also be responsible for their good condition.'

'Uniform to be returned in a clean and tidy condition when leaving the Company's service, with the number badge perfect.'

'Chains or packing (used for securing loads) to be taken to the 'bought back' goods clerk on return to the depot.'

'The practice of watering the Company's horses at public watering troughs is strictly forbidden. Carmen engaging on a long journey will be given a GWR bucket and will ensure that their horses drink from no other source. The bucket when not in use to be slung under the vehicle.'

'No goods may be taken from the station without delivery sheets which must be entered in the register book. Carmen must check that the carriage notes agree with the "to pay" entries on their sheets.'

'Delivery sheets issued during the day must be returned the same night to the clerk appointed to receive them.'

'Starting horses hurriedly causes injuries. Horses must be brought quietly and steadily to draught.'

'Horses must be kept in firm control. If a horse is found to be difficult to drive due to kicking or any other vice, the Carman is to report this to the Cartage Superintendent. If horses are known to do well in the care of one particular carman, the circumstances will always be favourably considered on his behalf.' (ie He will be allowed to drive it whenever possible.)

'Although vanguards over 17 are permitted to drive horses between the depot and the station, (it is preferred that they be led) they must not tease or play with them as this makes them vicious. When practicable they may be coupled together but it is the carman's duty to put the horses to and to take them out of the vehicle before placing them in the charge of the vanguard for removal to the stables. They must not be left unattended when hitched to a vehicle.'

'Carmen must not frequent coffee houses etc. while on duty except where they have goods to deliver.'

'Vehicles to be weighed when leaving or going in to the station.'

'Boys (vanguards) under 17 not permitted to drive vehicle. Boys over that age may drive between depot and station or in empty streets under the supervision of the Carman.'

'Nosebags to be taken each day to the station by the vanguards.'

'Drivers of heavy teams must walk with the horses, not sit on the shafts or ride the horses.'

'Carmen provided with dickies (seat) must use them, not drive from inside the vehicle.'

'No shopping to be done while on duty.'

'No smoking on duty.'

'Carmen to report in and out for each journey and the time thereof.'

'If his horse falls sick away from the stable, the nearest veterinary help to be obtained and the vanguard to be sent back to the stables if telegraphing impractical.'

The Horse's Day

The life of a parcel horse at the turn of the century was somewhat less strenuous than that of the goods horse and a lighter type of horse was used.

The start of the day was identical with a first feed at approximately 6.30 am, according to how near the feed room the horse was stalled, followed by harnessing an hour later and being led out shortly afterwards. Most of the parcels were delivered to warehouses or city establishments but a small proportion were also delivered to individual households. Packages were also collected from collection points such as this depot in Middlesex (*Fig. 274*). The majority of the vehicles in the picture are

goods vehicles pulled by two horse teams but smaller items were taken by express parcel carts directly to the recipient if local, or to main line stations for onward journeys. Major reconstruction work is being carried out at the time of this photograph in the mid 1920s but it would appear that business is proceeding as usual.

Paddington parcel horses frequently collected parcels from collection points or from companies which had requested a collection and these were taken back to the station. Five to six hours work at one stretch were quite normal until the horses finally returned to the stables when tired. They very rarely used nosebags out on a

Fig. 274

round as their frequent return to the station meant that they were fed while the cart was being loaded for another delivery round.

Vanguards were employed to assist with carrying parcels from the cart to the premises of the addressee. They were usually boys aged between 14 and 18 who initially earned 10s (50p) to 12s (60p) a week. They were also responsible for cleaning the harness until the weight of the van loads increased to the extent where one driver used two or three horses during a day's work and the one lad could no longer cope with that quantity of harness. A full time harness cleaner and two junior assistants were

therefore employed at a total cost to the Company of just over £3 per week. In 1882 the harness is recorded as having cost £6 6s (£6.30) per set, but by the 1920s it cost double to replace.

Fig. 275. This express parcels cart was on its way to Plymouth, possibly after refurbishment at Swindon Works. It was unlikely that it was a new vehicle despite the number shown on the side and the absence of an advertisement on the side panel, as by 1947 most of the new parcel carts were motorised. Forty-three horses were still employed at Plymouth at this time as can be seen on the chart in the Goods Manager's office (*Fig. 259*).

Fig. 275

Shunting Horses

The skill of the shunter and his horse have long since passed into the realms of faded memories or possibly history. The horse was usually an animal of considerable size and strength whose task was to move goods wagons or passenger coaches from one place to another at the direction of his driver who walked beside him.

A locomotive drew a train of goods wagons into the station and backed those which were destined for that particular station, into the siding. Only half a dozen vehicles could be placed immediately adjacent to the loading bay at once, the remainder being parked in the other parallel tracks of the sidings. As the wagons were unloaded, so they were pulled away, two at a time, from the loading bay by the horse being shackled to the drawhook. He pulled them out onto the single line track towards the main line and then went back for two more. When the loading bay was empty, two full wagons from one of the other siding tracks was pulled out and manoeuvred into the loading bay, followed by the remaining trucks until the bay was once again full to capacity. The empty wagons were then pulled into the vacated siding. The process was repeated until all the wagons were empty.

The reverse occurred later in the day and also during the night so that full wagons were ready to be taken onto the main line for collection by the trains when required.

Some express trains included passenger carriages destined for small stations en route. A guard rode in the carriage to release the carriage from the train at the appointed place. Under its own momentum, the 'slip coach' then moved on towards the station platform where the passenges alighted. As soon as it was empty, a shunter and his horse got down onto the line and after attaching the harness to the drawhook, the horse pulled the coach into a siding to await a train going in the opposite direction which would return the coach to its point of departure.

The shunter was an experienced man, not only in knowing how and when to use his horse's strength, but also in marshalling the goods wagons and collecting passenger slip coaches at the appointed time.

Conditions of work for shunting horses and drivers in the mid 1800s were appalling. In winter they struggled knee deep through the mud and water between the 3 ft longitudinal rails which were little improved upon those used at the mines in 1830 and earlier. The rails or plates were made of cast iron laid on pieces of stone which gradually sank into the mire. The hours of work were set at 72 hours a week for both Company employees or contractors' staff. The only advantage of being a Company employee appears to have been the free issue every two years of an overcoat.

The work at both Paddington and Smithfield in 1880 is recorded as being heavy and accident prone. Many of the horses were therefore hired from a private contractor, Mr Younghusband. Thirty-one horses and drivers worked on the mixed gauge at Paddington and seven at Smithfield where the extremely poor lighting reduced the conditions to semi-darkness. The Company paid £3 a week for each horse and driver who worked without rest periods for 8-10 hours a day, five consecutive days, resting for one day before commencing the next shift.

By the late 1880s 115 horses were owned by the Company for shunting purposes. The horses cost an average of £55 18s (£55.90) each and were often well muscled geldings, standing about 16 hands high. Ninety-one drivers together with 44 slipper or chain boys were needed to work these horses. Although the Company wished ultimately to own all their own shunting horses over the system, the horses at Paddington and Smithfield were not replaced by Company-owned horses until July 1890 when 32 shunting horses were purchased and stabled at Paddington. A further nine were bought for the Smithfield work and were stabled in the arches beneath the bridge in the former contractor's stables, at a rent of £75 per annum. Poplar Goods Station already had hydraulic machines of a type which would eventually supersede shunting horses at other main line stations.

Two years later the Company owned 150 shunting horses requiring 120 drivers and 58 slipper or chain boys. Wages for a driver were approximately 24s (£1.20) a week with an extra 1s (5p) after six months satisfactory service, while the foreman shunter was paid £78 per annum. Seven days annual holiday was introduced with free rail passes for themselves and their immediate family.

Company-owned shunting horses were used at Oxford which had two horses and drivers, and also at Reading where four horses and drivers worked all day.

In 1882 two more shunting horses were purchased for work at West Bromwich and Great Bridge. The loads moved by the shunt horses at these two stations was recorded as follows:
Great Bridge – 12,000 tons in 1876, 20,000 tons in 1882.
West Bromwich – 31,000 tons in 1876, 54,000 tons in 1882.

At outlying stations where hired shunting horses and drivers were still used, strenuous efforts were made by the Horse Inspector to reduce the rates of hire. Competition for the work was fierce and many contractors accepted the reduced rates with as much grace as they could muster.

Taplow station used two horses and attendants for the rather risky work where frequent passenger trains had to be avoided. The price of £5 per week remained unaltered due to the dangerous nature of the work but the contractor at Oxford was not so lucky, his fee being reduced from five guineas per week to £4 15s (£4.75) which also had to include the task of watering the forecourt of the station.

The contractor at Thame fared no better when his fee was reduced by 10s (50p) a week to 50s (£2.50).

Other stations using hired horses were numerous, so I have selected some of the better known places which may be of interest.

Bath used two horses and drivers working eleven hours a day for 108s (£5.40) per week for the goods department while the passenger service used another horse for hauling slip coaches to the platform at a cost of 50s (£2.50) per week.

Westbury used two horses and drivers for shorter hours and paid 72s (£3.60) a week for their services. Bristol needed four heavy horses working in pairs with two drivers but the cost is not recorded. They apparently worked all day without stopping.

Hereford used two horses and a driver from 7.45 am to 7 pm at a cost of 80s (£4) per week. The Dorchester shunting horse was also required to pump the water for the station in addition to his normal duties. Bridgwater used seven shunting horses in the winter and eight in the summer taking goods vehicles from the station to the docks, a distance of some $3\frac{1}{2}$ miles, a practice which continued until the lines were renewed to enable locomotives to work right through.

Taunton's three horses with two drivers cost the Company £6 15s (£6.75) per week. Exeter had one horse and driver at a cost of 47s 6d (£2.37½p) while the shunt horse and driver at Plymouth was paid at an hourly rate of 2s (10p) before being forced to accept 15s (75p) per working day or lose the contract. Needless to say it was unlikely that the length of the working day was reduced in proportion to the reduction in the fee!

One horse and driver at Newton Abbot refused to accept a reduction in his payment of 48s (£2.40) per week and as there was no alternative supply, the Company was forced to continue with his services at the same rate.

Hale shunting team was used for the rough and heavy work similar to that at Stourport where the shunting horse often needed to be assisted by an additional or chain horse harnessed alongside. The hours of work were also strength sapping being from 7.30 am to 7 pm.

The horse at Warwick was renowned for his size and strength and it was generally reckoned that this horse performed the work of two if not three lesser horses. However, despite these capabilities, his driver was only paid 48s (£2.40) per week, a bargain price as far as the Company was concerned.

The Stratford upon Avon shunt horse was tragically killed by a passing train shortly after an increase in his hire fee had been arranged at 47s 6d (£2.37½p) per week. At Leamington Spa different rates were paid for passenger coach shunting which rated only 48s (£2.40) per week and goods vehicle movement which was paid at 60s (£3) per week. Lydney station provided rough and heavy work for which the contractor was paid 84s (£4.20) a week for his three shunt horses worked in turn, or as a team by a single driver.

The shunting horse at Hereford was jointly owned by the GWR and the London & North Western Railway, costs being divided equally between the two companies. Similarly at Newport the GWR and Monmouth Railway shared two shunt horses with a driver and divided the cost of 82s (4.10) per week between them.

The Horse Superintendents of Birmingham and London were responsible for the appointment or hire of all shunting horses and their drivers. The supervision of the work was carried out by the traffic managers or goods agent where no traffic manager was employed. In a publication issued by the GWR in 1888, 30 rules relating to the work and conduct of the shunting men was laid out in precise terms. Excerpts of the main points were as follows:

"The London and Birmingham Horse Superintendents are to appoint all shunting horse drivers and horse keepers.
Shunting horse drivers to be under traffic managers or goods agent where no traffic manager is employed at the particular station.
Report if horse appears sick.
Report condition of work harness or if harness has caused soreness.
Collars must be dry. Feet to be checked.
No sudden jerks and bring to draught gradually.
No-one else to drive their horse.
Ashes or grit to be spread when icy.
Hold horse's head when near a locomotive whether in harness or not.
Drivers without slipper boys must at all time have hold of their horse's head.
Shunting horse driver responsible for seeing that slipper boy is in his place at all times.
Any cruelty to horse will result in a fine and suspension from duty.
Horse must not draw more than one passenger coach, loaded or empty, or more than two loaded or empty goods wagons.
When practicable horses must be attached to the wagons so as to enable them to stay outside the rails.
Horses must not be used unshod or with shoes in a loose or broken state. Shoes must be made to fit the hoof and not applied hot.
A copy of these rules to be taken on duty with the driver and horse keeper."

The late Jim Russell's father, a GWR employee, was the shunt horse driver at Banbury station in the early 1920s. One story which has been passed down tells of his horse 'Jack'.

'Having watched the express train go through, the horse got down onto the line to await the regular slip coach. To the horror of watching passengers and staff a second relief train approached at speed. "Jack" leapt back onto the platform with the agility and grace of a young colt and so avoided a nasty accident!'

It is a sobering fact that the working life of a shunt horse was only four or five years.

Fig. 276

Fig. 276. This picture is of the last shunting horse at Paddington. It was taken in 1925 and still shows clearly the type of rail without sleepers that was prevalent throughout the system and which made the work heavy in winter months, because of the mud which developed in the path of the horse. The harness is simple and reminiscent of that used a century earlier by the horses which pulled the coal trains with the Dandy cart at the rear.

Horse Inspector and Stables

Before Paddington was developed as the foremost stable on the Great Western system, the principal Horse Inspector was attached to the stud at Hockley. It was his responsibility to purchase horses for each of the stables in his area according to the type of work to be carried out. He also had the less pleasant task of deciding which horses were no longer fit for service with the Company, either through sickness or through advancing years.

Records of every horse in Great Western stables were kept in the Horse Superintendent's office. Each horse was numbered on the hoof, and details of hours worked, loads carried, and time off sick were recorded in individual files. The details were reported each month at a meeting of the Horse Committee of the Board.

After Paddington Mint Stable had been enlarged to the extent that it was the largest on the system, the Chief Horse Inspector had his office there and presided at the monthly meeting when matters concerning horses were discussed.

The Horse Superintendents toured their 'territories' regularly checking the condition of the horses, the quality and quantity of the feed, the cleanliness of the harness, stable yards, vehicles and the efficiency of the staff at all levels.

The daily running of the stable was in the hands of the stable foreman. He was in charge of the stablemen who looked after the horses and was responsible to the Horse Inspector for recording the daily work schedule of each horse in his care and for ordering the feed and bedding requirements of his stable.

If a stableman felt that a horse was sick or injured, he reported the details to the foreman who had to make a decision as to whether the horse should just be rested for the day or ought to be seen by the vet. In either case, a 'resting' horse would be selected to replace the sick animal if necessary to make up the working quota. Horses worked five days and then had one rest day before commencing another period of duty.

The stablemen worked within the stable, feeding and watering the occupants, harnessing and unharnessing at each end of the working day. They also cleaned the stables and replaced the soiled straw. Many single storey stables had small trap doors in the wall which allowed manure to be pushed through and collected from outside to be stacked in the manure pit. The stablemen groomed the horses before they were harnessed and took them to the farrier when they needed to be shod.

In small stables, harness cleaning was also part of his duties, but staff were employed in larger establishments specifically to carry out this work. For a short period in the 1880s the GWR Board required that vanguards should clean the harness of horses that were driven by their drivers. This became impractical when a driver used

more than one horse or team. The van lads could not cope with cleaning more than one set which can involve seven or eight pieces of leather of various widths and thicknesses, plus a collar. Harness was cleaned at night in the Smithfield stable, immediately after use, and was generally in better condition than that used at Paddington which was cleaned the following morning, immediately prior to harnessing for the day's work. Collars were hung in the drying room after the hames had been removed, and were brushed to remove matted hair and mud before being used the following day.

The rest of the harness was hung on a peg immediately opposite the stall of the horse to whom it belonged. Broken harness was passed to the saddler or harness maker for repair and a note made that a particular piece of harness was out of commission. After the First World War many of the harness makers and repairers were ex-cavalry men and very skilled craftsmen. Army harness was made to a uniform pattern so that pieces could be exchanged with very little adjustment. Great Western harness, particularly the collar, was individually made for single, pair or four horse team work and marked with the number of the horse using it.

To give the reader some idea of the extent to which horses were used all over the Great Western system, I have included a brief description of some of the stations at which stable accommodation for parcel and/or goods horses was evident. However, the following list should not be considered to be a complete list of all the stations at which horses were employed. Many smaller depots were supplied with horsepower by a larger one having stable facilities, and the horse was walked, or possibly ridden if no inspector was around, to the station where his services were required, and returned to his stall at night.

Birmingham (Snow Hill)

One hundred and thirty horses were stabled here in 1867, 30 of them in rented stalls nearby. Eight to fifteen extra horses were hired each day for parcel collection and delivery so the stud was increased by 24 horses (20 working, four resting) and the staff increased accordingly. Twenty vehicles were ordered, ten carmen and ten vanguards joined the ranks in addition to two further stablemen or horse keepers and four clerks or checkers.

This station came into the limelight when it was closed on 9th August 1914 to normal passenger service in order to facilitate mobilisation of Territorial Army personnel and reservists.

Some of the railway horses were stabled in stalls built in tunnel sidings. These horses were used to shunt wagons around the fish platforms. When not in use the horses were tethered to pillars between the running lines. These horses were so well trained that there is no record of any horse ever having been hurt by moving into the path of an incoming train. It was claimed that when hauling the wagons, the horses knew what the signals meant as well as any railwayman and would actually refuse to move past a signal set at danger!

Birmingham (Moor Street)

Goods traffic accommodation was built on two levels. Beside the passenger station a high level yard was built and two low level yards underneath, now known as Shed A and Shed B. Access to the former was from Park Street and to the latter from Allison Street. Stabling for 67 horses was provided on this level together with provender and straw stores, looseboxes and a shoeing forge. Upon the opening of this depot in 1914, 24 horses were transferred from the Hockley Stud to fill the stables. More were added almost immediately as the local traders took advantage of the proximity of the new service. Moor Street was only 300 yards from the fruit, vegetable, fish and meat markets. Previously all their produce had to be carted the two miles from Hockley.

Birmingham (Hockley)

Hockley Stud boasted 190 horses in 1869, under the overall supervision of Mr Bell, Horse Superintendent. Two years later in an effort to cut down the wage bill, the goods horse drivers were asked to groom and harness their own horses before the day's work. Shunt horse drivers already cared for their own horses and used that same horse every day. Carmen requested that they should also choose their own horses and this was allowed in this particular stud but not encouraged on a network basis. However, the drivers refused to clean the harness so part of the saving of a stableman's wages was spent on employing lads to clean the harness.

The number of horses in the general stud was increased by 32 during the first six months of 1872. They cost £49 5s (£49.25) each and after checking, were sent out to stations under the control of the Hockley Horse Inspector – Kidderminster, Stourbridge, Brettle Lane, West Bromwich, Birkenhead and Cheltenham. Thirty-three had to be purchased at £48 to £54 each for use at Hockley and were branded Nos 941–972 inclusive, while 27 cast horses were disposed of at auction and five sent to the knacker. The local vet was paid a retainer for looking after the railway horses, his fees amounting to about £14 per month. Part of the stable accommodation was considered substandard and a new block was built in 1876 on the site of the forty-stall block. Ten of the occupants of this old block had been considered past their useful life to the Company and were taken to the auction at Wolverhampton. The new block had to have a new floor almost as soon as it was completed as the contractors had allowed too much fall or slope on the floor and the horses suffered from sore shoulders before they even went out to work. The swinging bails were not satisfactory and were changed in favour of stall partitions which the stablemen, whose wages had risen to 30s (£1.50) per week, preferred.

During another inspection carried out by the Board in 1879, all stable staff had to be present and the horses tethered on their pillar reins. Collars were to be hung inside out so that the linings could be seen, together with all available harness. Each department was scrutinised and a full report given at the monthly committee meeting as to the merits or faults found. It was mentioned during this report that horse No. 153, purchased in 1875, had fallen into a pond while out at grass on its rest day, but apart from that incident, the Board approved of the condition of the horses and stables.

The stud increased to 397 in 1882 and two saddlers or harness makers joined the staff at a cost of 20s (£1) per week per man. They made all the necessary harness for the proposed new intake of horses for the London Stud. These horses would be purchased by the Hockley Horse Inspector and tried out at Hockley before starting work in the city. All the Birmingham area parcel horses were moved to the new stable block at Hockley and more horses purchased to increase the stud to 402 in April of 1883.

There were still 245 horses working in the Birmingham and Hockley area in 1947.

Cardiff

There was stabling for 30 horses with a loft and granary above, when this station was first mentioned in the monthly Horse Committee report. There was also a smithy and a wheelwright's shop with a staff cottage adjoining the yard, but no mention was made of the occupant of the dwelling.

The staff amounted to 40, divided into the various categories:

Good – 6 clerks
      1 foreman
      4 assistant foremen
      25 carmen (drivers)
Passenger – 3 carmen
      1 shunting horse driver
Horse – 1 blacksmith
      1 striker
      1 horse keeper
      1 stableman
Road Wagon – 1 wheelwright.

There were five more stalls and two looseboxes which were leased out to a private contractor. Having recently been taken over by a new concern, the GWR asked if the owner would like to join their company to run the parcel collection and delivery department. The contractor opted to remain self-employed and assured the Company that his haulage business would not be in competition with the Great Western Railway. Other stalls and looseboxes had been rented to the previous contractor whose business was widespread. The horses and vehicles in these stalls and those in stables in Newport and the smaller hill stations of Bryn Mawr, Ebbw Vale and Risca were purchased from the estate of Mr Bond together with 67 vehicles. Those horses at Newport were added to the stud already established there by the Company.

Newport

Sixteen horses were kept in the stable here and Mr Bond's five were put in spare stalls near the station buildings. Staff included:

    5 clerks
    2 shunters
    14 carmen
    1 horse foreman at 35s (£1.75) per week
    1 horse keeper
    2 stablemen
    2 stable foremen
    1 wheelwright.

In addition to the Newport station stable, there was a further stable of 20 horses at the High Street station, and still more at Dock Street station. Shunting horses were hired at 82s (£4.10) per week for two horses and one driver when more help was needed to cope with the increase in dock traffic at both Cardiff and Newport.

In 1950–51 there were still more than 100 Company-

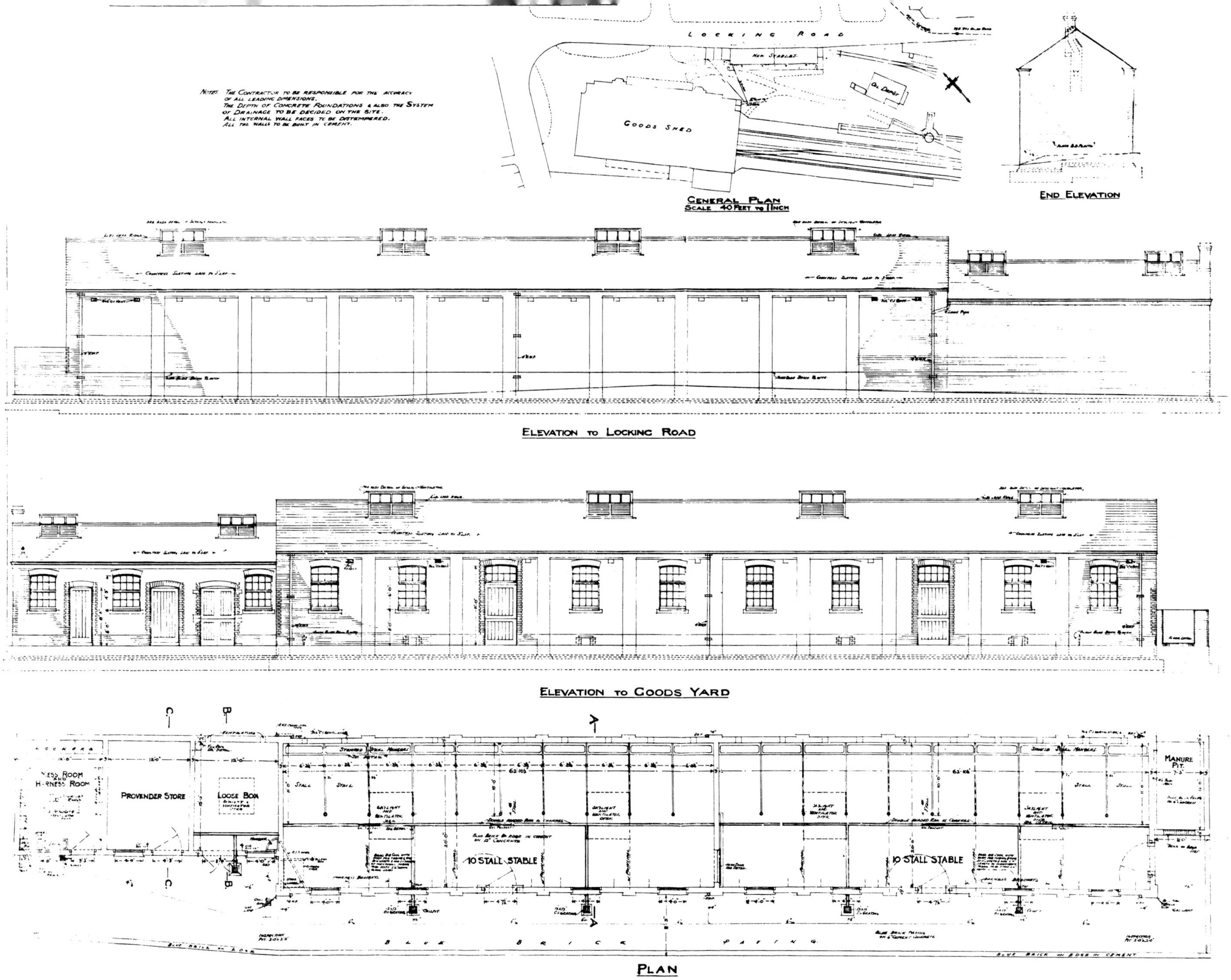

END ELEVATION

GENERAL PLAN
SCALE 40 FEET TO 1 INCH

NOTE: THE CONTRACTOR TO BE RESPONSIBLE FOR THE ACCURACY
OF ALL LEADING DIMENSIONS.
THE DEPTH OF CONCRETE FOUNDATIONS & ALSO THE SYSTEM
OF DRAINAGE TO BE DECIDED ON THE SITE.
ALL INTERNAL WALL FACES TO BE DISTEMPERED.
ALL THE WALLS TO BE BUILT IN CEMENT.

ELEVATION TO LOCKING ROAD

ELEVATION TO GOODS YARD

PLAN

Fig. 277

owned horses working at Cardiff, together with 200 contractors' animals and their drivers. Some of these horses were branded on the saddle patch or flank, but as this was not GWR practice, it is possible that they had been released after the war and purchased from the armed forces for railway work. Stabling at this time was in a three-storey building.

Weston-super-Mare

A 20-stall stable was built at Weston-super-Mare to accommodate the goods and parcel horses, ***Fig. 277***. The stalls were partitioned up to about 6 ft in height and topped with a zinc coping. The mangers were all of a standard design manufactured at Swindon. Hooks on the wall above the manger were for the two halter ropes, one from the head collar and when required an additional restraint around the neck, similar to that worn when travelling in a horse box by rail.

One loosebox, approximately 12 ft by 15 ft could be used for a sick horse, or a horse that was being rested for longer than usual. Next to the loosebox was a provender store which could store one week's supply. The harness room was also the men's mess or rest room. As the collars needed heat from the range fire to dry them, it was more than likely that this room was rather popular.

Despite the number of horses accommodated in this block, there does not appear to be any provision for a forge. It is therefore likely that there was a good local farrier who was contracted to make and fit shoes regularly.

Swindon

Large quantities of raw materials were delivered to the wagon shop here to produce the varied designs of vehicles required all over the system. In addition to this heavy haulage work, two coal wharves meant that there was a constant need for strong horses to pull the coal lorries. These horses were stabled near Mill Bank and the goods horses were stabled on the site of the present road where it passes under the railway lines. Horses were used inside the carriage works right up to the Second World War for shunting the vehicles under repair as they were cheaper than keeping a pilot locomotive in steam all day. One particular mare was a favourite of the driver of locomotive No. 101 who brought a piece of cake for her every lunch time, when she would present herself, unescorted, outside No. 17 shop!

The routine of the coal horses had hardly varied since the service of supplying company employees with a weekly amount of coal at cost had been introduced after the First World War.

In 1948 there were still four horses used for the coal rounds. Driver/Carman Fred Pretlove recalls that their day began at the Station Road stables under the arches when the first feed was taken round at 6.30 am in order to start work an hour later. Each horse was harnessed to a flat wagon which had been loaded during the night with 36 cwt of coal in strong sacks. These were taken to the houses of employees who had bought a ticket for two, four or six bags (***Fig. 278***). The coal was tipped by the driver into whatever receptacle was provided at the house, and the sack neatly stacked on the back of the lorry. Regardless of its sex, each six to ten-year old shire-type horse had to haul 8 tons 8 cwt per day before being returned to its stall at night. Five days work followed by one rest day was routine, so it is not surprising that the working life of these horses was comparatively short. It also follows, of course, that if the horses pulled that quantity during a day, the drivers, unassisted, lifted a

.... 456/99

.... 194......

Name ....

Residence ....

To Receive

FOUR Cwts. of Coal

4

Ticket No........................

....

Foreman.

This part to be given up to the Carter on delivery of the Coal

The quantity of Coal shewn on this Ticket must be delivered ONLY at the residence of the person mentioned hereon.

Any one found receiving Coal, or allowing it to be delivered in any way contrary to this regulation or selling or disposing of it in any way, *except for his own domestic use*, will be dealt with according to law.

Where Coal is delivered by means of a vehicle, the seller must deliver or send by post or otherwise to the purchaser or his servant, before any part of the Coal is unloaded, a Ticket or Note in this form.

Any seller of Coal who delivers a less quantity than is stated in this Ticket or Note is liable to a fine.

Any person attending on a vehicle used for the delivery of Coal who, having received a Ticket or Note for delivery to the purchaser, refuses or neglects to deliver it to the purchaser or his servant, is liable to a fine.

Fig. 278

corresponding weight during their working day. The driver cleaned his own horse and its stable, but the harness only received a cursory wipe over.

Many of the company houses were arranged on a back-to-back basis with a narrow lane running between the yards and it was down these that the coal cart passed so that whenever possible two houses could be 'coaled' during the same stop. The horses knew their routes and would pause for the driver without being guided all the time. The carman or driver provided his own jacket and a hat which was protected with a leather pad to support the sack when it was being carried.

In the summer, when coal deliveries were not required, the drivers were sometimes employed in dressing the sacks with a mixture of fish oil and coal tar to preserve them. No profit was made by the Company for this service to its employees so there were few complaints if the quality was doubtful and many Swindon employees took advantage of the facility until it ceased in the early 1960s. In contrast to the practice at London stations and stables, where grey horses were used for hauling fire-fighting equipment, two bay horses were reserved for pulling the Swindon fire engine until it was replaced with a motorised version.

A selection of smaller stations throughout the Great Western system which also had stables or access to the horses from a nearby stud follows:

Banbury had nine horses in its stables to haul the parcels lorries and goods which were the main traffic at the stations which were shared with the LMS. Each company was responsible for its own cartage of goods and parcel traffic. An additional horse was used for slip coaches and shunting work, looked after by the driver instead of by the stablemen who cared for all the goods and parcel horses in the stable.

Henley used a small stable which was hired. In 1892 there were three horses to haul the three single horse lorries together with a vehicle for boats. In addition to the three carmen there was one guard and a parcels porter to assist with the station's workload. Three years later the amount of work justified the building of a small stable block for four horses on land behind the station near the allotments, together with a carriage shed. Three years later yet another horse was required. In 1900 a four wheel single horse parcels van fitted with a handbrake was added to the wagon stock and another horse purchased. Presumably the last two horses were housed in the space allocated for harness opposite the four stalls.

The stables were extended in 1906 making it into a six stall building and two horses were bought to fill the spaces. The smallest of the horses, probably only a pony, was transferred to less onerous work at Bristol. More staff and another vehicle were added the same year. The steady increase in goods and parcel traffic up to 1920 was met with a corresponding rise in the numbers of staff and vehicles, but a sharp decline in the parcels traffic meant that it became uneconomic to retain so many company-owned horses and staff.

One driver and his horse "Sam" had been on the strength since 1916, calling at premises which displayed a card asking him to call. Mr Jones was transferred to Twyford as lampman, but no records show what happened to his horse.

In 1932 when the parcels service was re-introduced to Henley, only three horses remained in the stables. Two of them were heavy van horses, probably of Suffolk Punch or Shire cross breeding, as it was recorded that they stood almost 17 hands high, with feathered legs and wide muscular chests. The third horse was a lighter cob type and carried out all the parcels work. The driver or carman of the latter horse was a Mr W. Ayres who was later replaced by a motor vehicle driver when a motor van was introduced to collect the milk from the local farms, and the parcels delivery service was combined with the general goods delivery rounds. The two horse-drawn lorries remained in service at the station until after the Second World War.

Plymouth Millbay
The Company's stables were built into the granite and brick arches of the old South Devon Railway bridge, known locally as Union Street Arch, but the numbers involved are not recorded. Shunting horses were hired at 2s (10p) per hour for two horses used in tandem and led by one driver. In 1880 the rate was negotiated at 15s (75p) per day. In 1947 there were still 43 horses owned by the Company working from stables at Plymouth.

Tavistock
Originally belonging to the South Devon & Tavistock Railway, the line was absorbed by the Great Western Railway in 1878 and the small stable block used for company horses. A small workshop was added to the end of the stable block which was near the main station.

Tenby was absorbed in 1897 and also had stables near the station buildings but records do not show how many horses were involved.

Truro had a large stable on Richmond Hill, the approach road to the station but the work they performed is not described.

Winchester was a jointly-owned station which had no company-owned horses until 1932 when the goods and parcel delivery service was bought from the private contractor, Messrs White & Co. £154 10s was paid for the four horses, eight vehicles, harness and equipment. Private contractors continued to operate a horse-drawn cab service until the start of the First World War when most of the horses were requisitioned by the Army.

During an inspection carried out by the Chief Horse Inspector in 1879, it was noted that the stable accommodation at **Wolverhampton** was insufficient for the Company's needs. Two of the horses had to be stabled in the straw store while the straw was kept outside under a tarpaulin. Four of the Company's van horses were kept in miserable stables belonging to the West Midland Railway more than a mile away from Wolverhampton Low Level station where they worked. Six additional stalls were therefore added to the existing stable block at the GWR station, bringing the total number of horses that could be housed up to 36 in 1881. They were looked after by two stablemen and a foreman under the direction of a retired foreman from Hockley who was re-employed and promoted to Area Superintendent.

Bilston stables were inspected at the same time and found to be old, dark, and poorly ventilated. The number of horses kept there was not mentioned except for the two required for shunting traffic from Handsworth. Similarly, the stables at **Wednesbury** needed new floors and the drainage system appeared to be faulty.

West Bromwich stables housed 15 horses, but there was often too much work for them and two more horses were borrowed from Wednesbury station three miles away.

Other stables inspected were **Swan Village**, **Great Bridge**, **Dudley** and **Stourbridge**. These were all found to be satisfactory.

Kidderminster was also visited and the horses found to be in a healthy condition but stable facilities somewhat below the high standard expected by the Great Western Railway Company. Three horses were needed for shunting but there were only two stalls at the station. The other horse was stabled at a local public house at a cost of 1s 6d (7½p) per week. His stable was far better than the two at the station which was built against an embankment and hardly credited being called a stable. The Horse Inspector made the replacement of the 'hovel' an immediate priority task.

Hayle station stable had six stalls and was down a track leading off Station Approach Road. This undated drawing, *Fig. 279*, shows the plan for the six-stall stable to be built out of the best quality materials available. Blue brick was used in many smaller stables and the design of the ventilators was equally familiar. Details of the latter are shown on the second drawing, *Fig. 280*, together with the finer points of the interior fittings. One interesting detail is the provision of a number card frame above the manger. Presumably this card was more visible than the number on the front hoof of the horse.

Hayes, *Fig. 281*, shows the architect's drawing of the six-stall stable at this station. Some years later an additional five-stall stable block was built at an angle to the existing block. *Fig. 282*. The old manure pit was removed and a provender store created in the triangular space between the two rows of stalls. This undated general drawing of the Hayes & Harlington station stable gives details of the construction materials to be employed, together with a site plan on which the building was to be built.

Although fairly similar in size to the stables built at

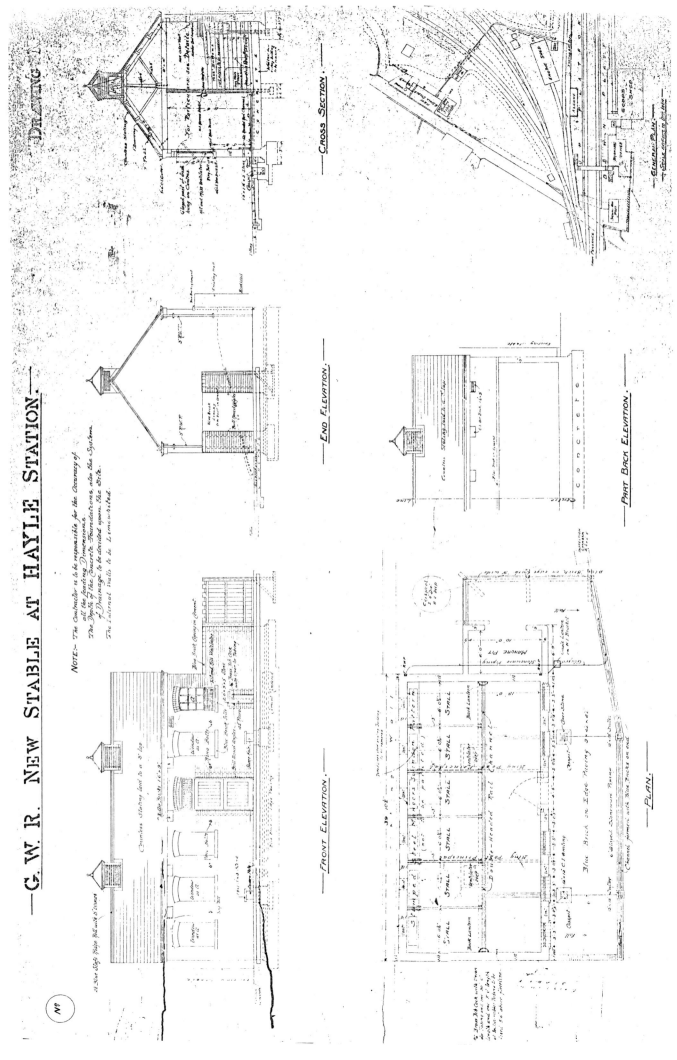

—G.W.R. NEW STABLE AT HAYLE STATION.—

Fig. 279

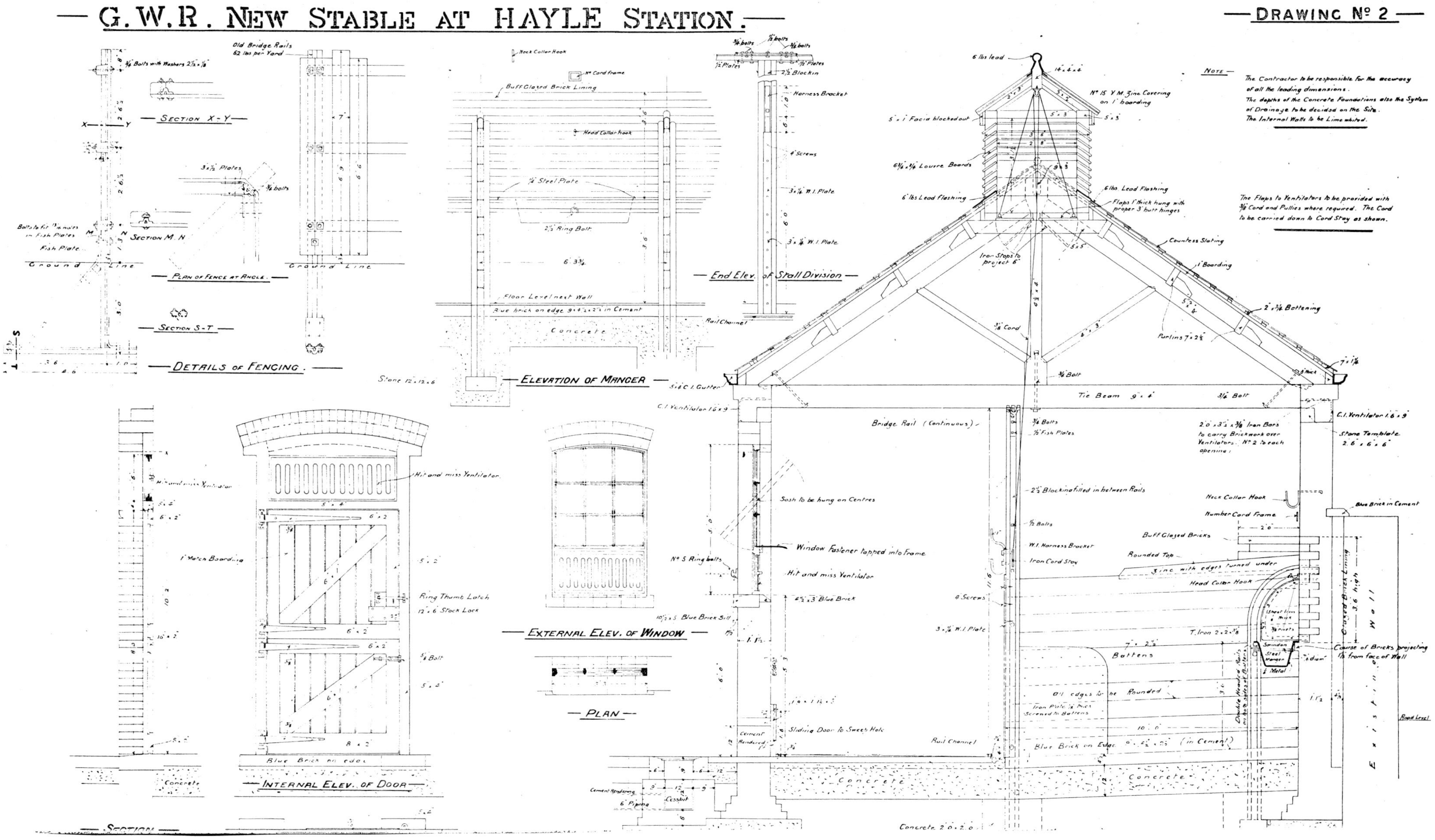
G.W.R. NEW STABLE AT HAYLE STATION.
DRAWING Nº 2
NOTE
The Contractor to be responsible for the accuracy of all the leading dimensions.
The depths of the Concrete Foundations also the System of Drainage to be decided on the Site.
The Internal Walls to be Lime whited.
The Flaps to Ventilators to be provided with 3/8 Cord and Pullies where required. The Cord to be carried down to Cord Stay as shown.
SECTION X-Y
SECTION M. N
PLAN OF FENCE AT ANGLE
SECTION S-T
DETAILS OF FENCING
ELEVATION OF MANGER
End Elev. of Stall Division
INTERNAL ELEV. OF DOOR
EXTERNAL ELEV. OF WINDOW
PLAN
SECTION
Old Bridge Rails 62 lbs per Yard
Ground Line
Buff Glazed Brick Lining
Head Collar Hook
Neck Collar Hook
Floor Level next Wall
Concrete
Rail Channel
Harness Bracket
Hit and miss Ventilator
Ring Thumb Latch
12 x 6 Stock Lock
1" Match Boarding
Blue Brick on edge
6 lbs lead
Nº 15 V.M. Zinc Covering on 1" boarding
5" x 1" Facia blocked out
6 lbs Lead Flashing
Countess Slating
1" Boarding
Purlins 7 x 2½
Tie Beam 9" x 4"
Bridge Rail (Continuous)
C.I. Ventilator 1.6 x 9
Stone Template 2.6 x 6 x 6
Sash to be hung on Centres
Window Fastener tapped into frame
Sliding Door to Sweep Hole
Buff Glazed Bricks
Rounded Top
Battens
Concrete 2.0 x 2.0
Existing Wall
Road Level

Fig. 280

—G. W. R. NEW STABLE AT HAYES STATION.—

DRAWING Nº 4.

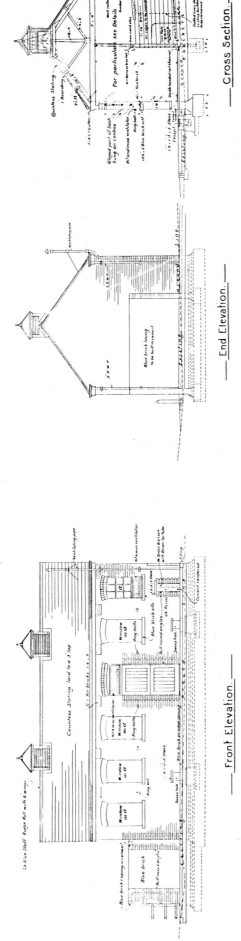

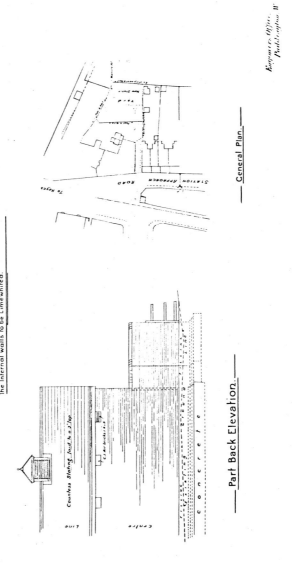

— Cross Section. —

— End Elevation. —

— General Plan. —

— Part Back Elevation. —

— Front Elevation. —

— Plan. —

NOTE:— The Contractor is to be responsible for the accuracy of all the leading dimensions. The depth of the concrete foundations, also the System of Drainage to be decided upon the Site. The Internal walls to be Limewhited.

Engineers Office.
Paddington W

Fig. 281

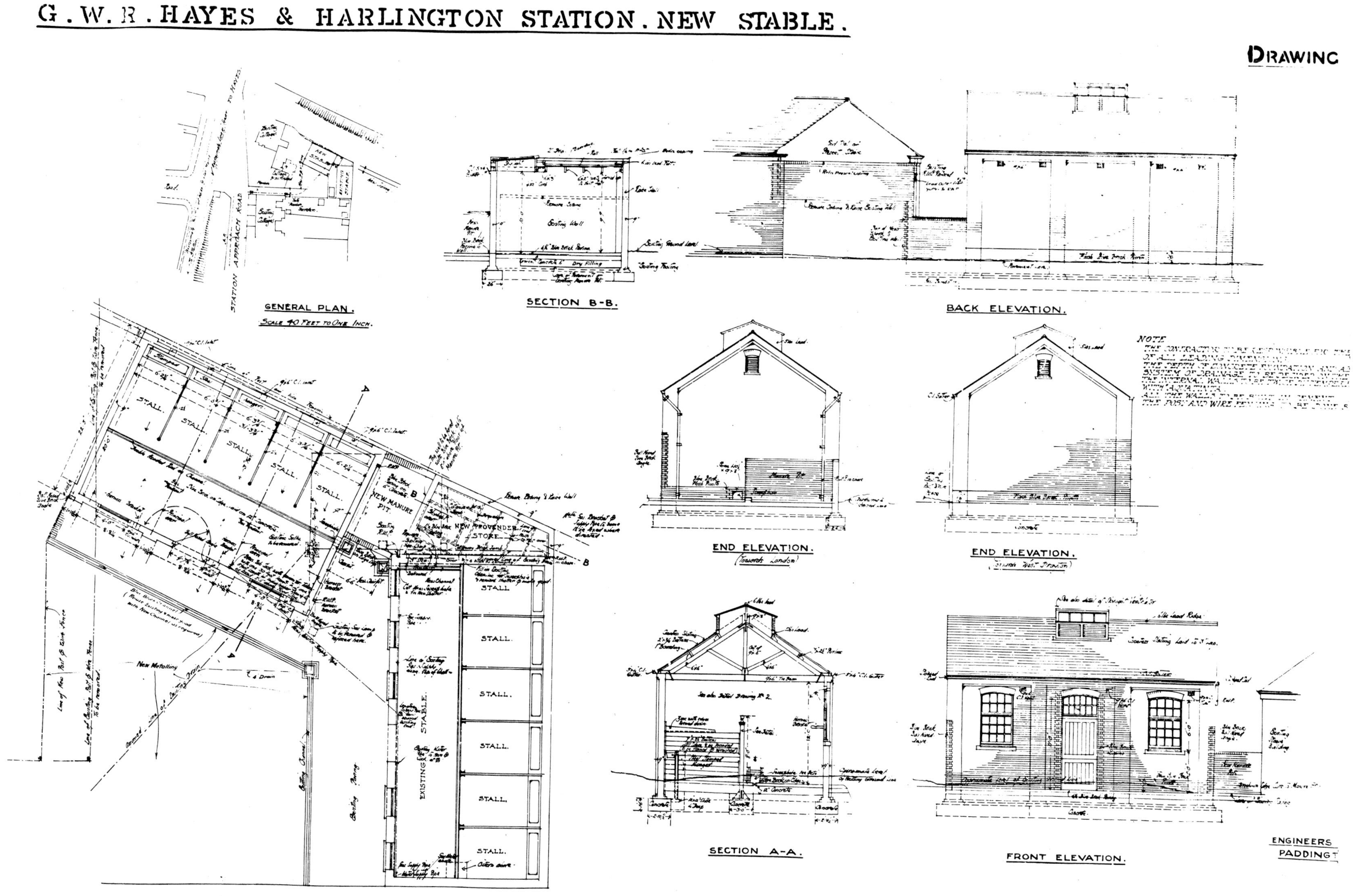

G.W.R. HAYES & HARLINGTON STATION. NEW STABLE.

BACK ELEVATION.

END ELEVATION.
(Towards South)

FRONT ELEVATION.

END ELEVATION.
(Towards North)

SECTION A-A.

SECTION B-B.

GENERAL PLAN.
Scale 40 Feet to One Inch.

STATION APPROACH ROAD.

PLAN.

STALL. STALL. STALL. STALL. STALL. STALL.

EXISTING STABLE.

NEW MANURE PIT.

NEW PROVENDER STORE.

STALL. STALL. STALL.

ENGINEERS
PADDINGT

Fig. 282

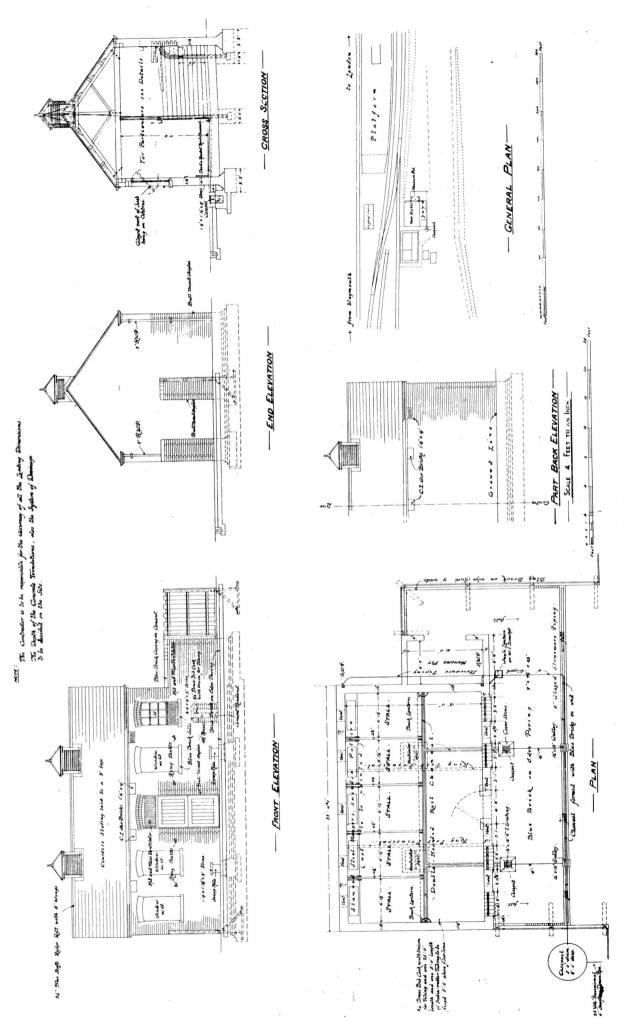

Fig. 283

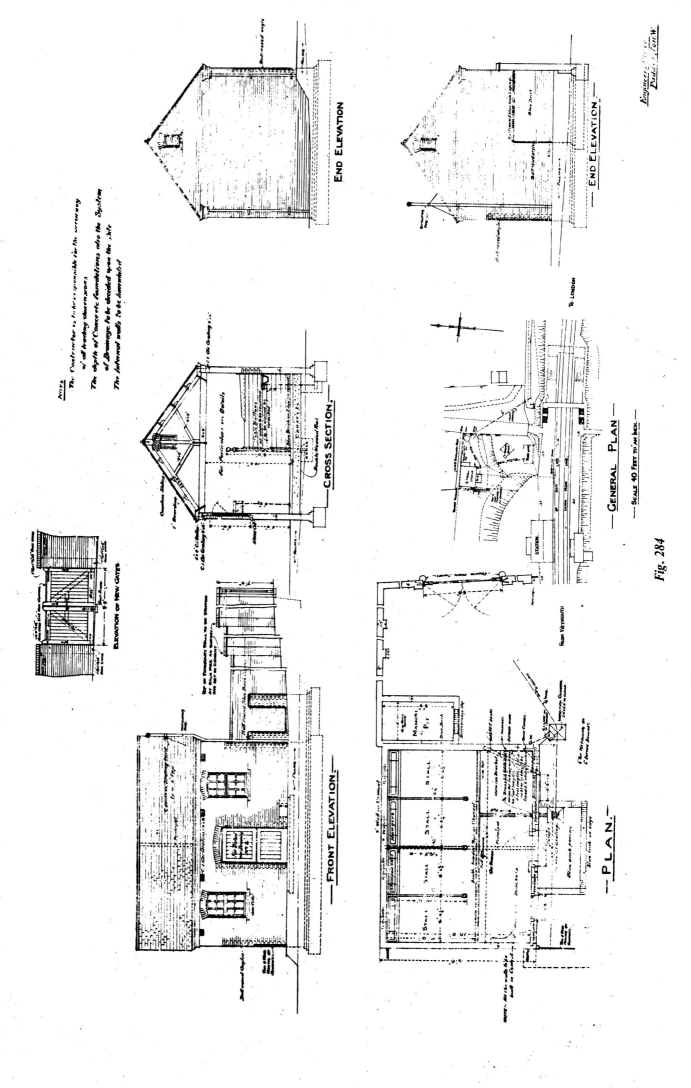

— G.W.R. NEW STABLE AT CASTLE CARY —

END ELEVATION

END ELEVATION

ELEVATION OF NEW GATES

CROSS SECTION.

FRONT ELEVATION.

GENERAL PLAN

SCALE 40 FEET TO AN INCH.

PLAN.

Fig. 284

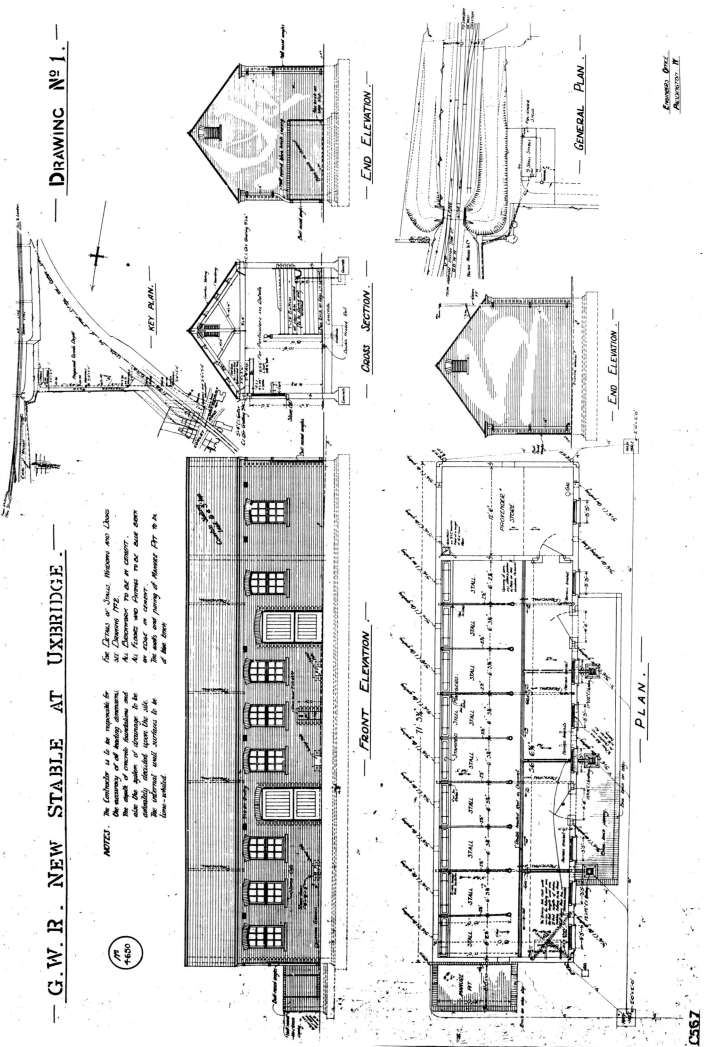

Fig. 285

Hayes the five-stall stable at **Henley** had swinging bails instead of stall partitions. The stables were built in 1895 and the bails were replaced within ten years according to reports made to the Horse Committee. No mention is made of the specific duties of the horses kept at this stable but they were probably used for local goods and parcel delivery work.

Westbury station also had a five-stall stable block built somewhat later than the previous example at Hayes. Again the drawing is undated, *Fig. 283*, and there is no record of any specific work that the horses were required to do, apart from goods and parcel delivery traffic. The pillar rein hooks can be seen on the outside of the stall uprights. These were used to secure a harnessed horse which had been turned round ready for work, but not yet put to. The horses could not rub their harness or move their heads more than a few inches, so pillar reins were only used when there were not enough staff to harness the horses and put them to in one operation.

Castle Cary stables were built a short distance from the station to accommodate four goods horses. Constructed to the usual high standard of Great Western buildings, the blue brick is again much in evidence. The vehicles were probably kept in the yard which would be sheltered from the worst of the weather by the 7 ft high wall topped with blue brick coping. From the style of printing the plans were probably drawn up just prior to the turn of the twentieth century. (*Fig. 284.*)

Uxbridge stables, *Fig. 285*, were built parallel to the lines, facing Eastwards. Accommodation for nine horses in stalls measuring 6 ft $2\frac{1}{4}$ in to 6 ft $3\frac{3}{4}$ in wide, each with its own ventilator, together with a harness hook on the opposite wall was provided in this neat block. A provender store capable of holding at least one week's supply of fodder and straw increased the overall length of the building to 71 ft $3\frac{3}{4}$ in with a sizeable manure pit at the opposite end. In the general plan a coal wharf can be seen and this may have provided the bulk of the work for the horses stabled at Uxbridge.

Although **Compton** station used a shunting horse which was provided by a local contractor, Ernie Stroud, there was no stable for it. The mare was kept in the station master's garden and was always in excellent condition despite the fact that the only rations she received were the sweepings from the horsebox mangers used by the racehorses loaded at the station. The mare moved many of these boxes around to make up the train as required and was a popular mascot of the many trainers who used to load their more exotic equine charges at the station.

The Great Western Railway provided a resident farrier at **Newbury** station in case his services were required for the racehorses, but there do not appear to have been any Company-owned stables or horses at the station.

Originally part of the West Midland Railway, **Colwell** station was absorbed into the Great Western Railway in 1863 and had stables for 15 horses adjacent to the coal store behind the main station buildings. No indication of the type of work that was carried out by these horses is recorded.

Helston was another station added to the GWR system in 1898. The stables at this station were situated next to the slaughter house which must have been very unpleasant for the horses in residence.

Newton Abbot stables and cart shed provided stalls for six horses. From the size of the cart shed there must have been a considerable choice of vehicles kept at this station to suit every need.

Inside the stable there was an additional fastening point by the mangers. A ring is bolted to the front of the manger for use with a halter rope fitted with a weighted ball at the end. As the horse lowered his head, so the ball dropped down, taking most of the rope out of the way. The horse may even have been able to lie down which was not possible when the halter rope was attached to either of the hooks above the stable.

Larger than the Park Royal stables was the 20-stall stable at **Weston-super-Mare**, a holiday resort of considerable popularity in the early 1900s. Unlike many of the other stables built at this time, there was a harness room/messroom for the staff and a loose box of unusually large proportions, which could be used for a sick or resting horse.

Figs 286 and *287.* Two photographs of a Great West-

Fig. 286

Fig. 287

ern stable in the process of construction. There would have been a row of ten stalls in each wing while the building at the rear, joining the two wings, may have been for the provender store and a messroom. A cart shed on the left of the second picture would have sheltered all the vehicles belonging to the stable which it has not been possible to identify.

Fig. 288. One of the smallest stables is this single horse loosebox at the old station at **Henley-in-Arden**, which was converted into a ticket office after the horse had been taken away. The upper half of the door has been closed and the windows are broken, giving the building the appearance of being neglected.

Fig. 289. This photograph may be an upper storey of one of the Great Western horse hospitals. The horses are obviously in looseboxes, without headcollars, an unheard of luxury in the working horse's stalls. Note the Great Western water tank in the centre of the picture painted in the familiar cream and brown.

Norton Fitzwarren, near Taunton was on the Bristol & Exeter Railway until it was absorbed by the Great Western Railway in 1878. It is recorded that the horses stabled here were used primarily for hauling wagons loaded with barrels of cider.

Rhayader on the Mid Wales Railway until 1922 had a stable behind the granary and goods shed, but no mention is made of how many horses were stabled or the type of work carried out.

Steventon near Reading, one of the early Great Western stations had its own goods and parcel horses in a stable near the corn store.

Fig. 290. **Park Royal** stables had twelve stalls and a provender store to hold a supply for one week. Harness brackets were positioned on the wall opposite each stall, but there does not appear to be a harnessroom/ messroom or a forge on the premises. Harness repairs from here were taken to the harness makers at Paddington and it is quite probable that a farrier from that stud called regularly at this North London station.

Fig. 288

Fig. 289

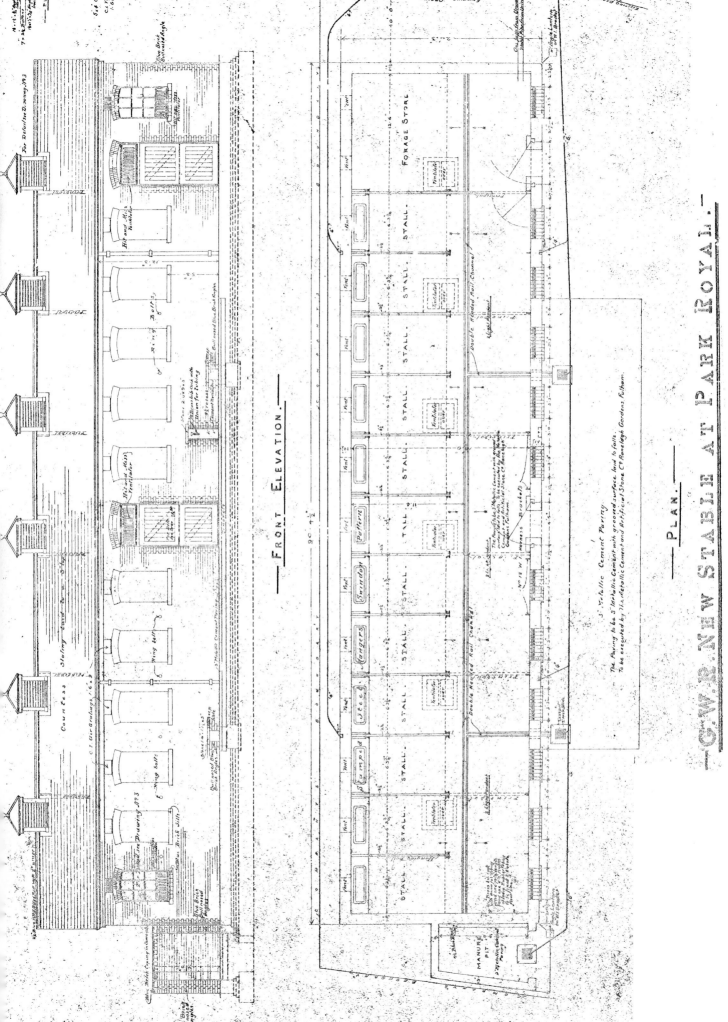

FRONT ELEVATION.

PLAN.

G.W.R. NEW STABLE AT PARK ROYAL.

Fig. 290

Construction of a Vehicle by Craftsmen

Many skilled craftsmen were employed by the Great Western Railway to construct the various vehicles required for the horse-drawn goods and parcel traffic. Bearing in mind that whole tree trunks arrived at one end of Swindon Works, and left the other in such diverse forms as finished vehicles right down to the diminutive pencil, and that similarly ingots of metal ore were also processed to produce locomotives, metal frames and the lowly nut and bolt, the factory was divided into departments or 'shops', each having a specific function.

The majority of the scale drawings give detailed measurements of the constituent parts of the vehicle body which will be of use to modellers. Oak was preferred for its durability, but instructions are frequently found as to other types of wood to be used for particular parts.

Fig. 291. This photograph of the sawmill shows the start of the manufacturing process. Roughly sawn 'posts'

of wood can be seen on the left, while planks are stacked on the right of the central rails.

In 1915 the Great Western Railway owned more than 3,600 horse-drawn road vehicles, the majority of which had been made at Swindon Road Wagon shops. Most of the vehicles however, in *Fig. 292* (this picture taken that year), were intended for use by the Army rather than the railway. Production of railway vehicles for its own horses was almost completely halted in order to help with the war effort. These carts were pulled by one horse and were of a very basic design, as indeed was the driver's seat.

The metal underframing was forged by a smith, known as a 'fireman', assisted by a hammerman and a viceman, working to detailed plans provided by the draughtsman. Another team of smiths made the iron tyres or hoops which were shrunk onto the rim or felloe of the wheel. With the introduction of new designs for springs, a specialist in this skill hardened and shaped the

Fig. 291

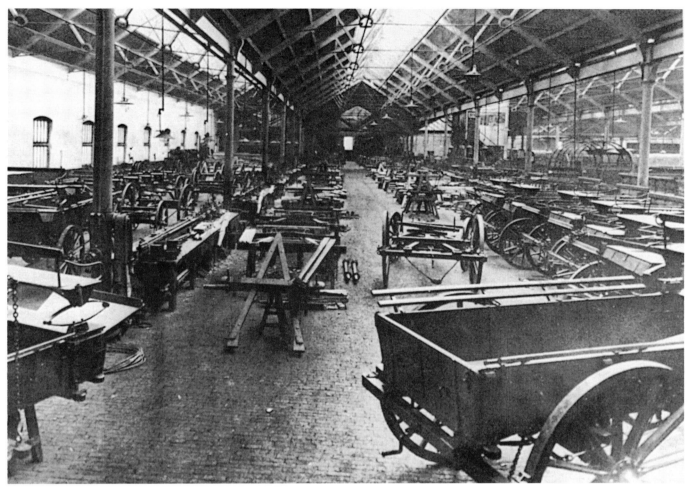

Fig. 292

iron and bolted several thicknesses together according to a preformed pattern required for each type of cart or wagon. The addition of a mechanical brake to four-wheeled vehicles called for precision engineering by the smiths, as did the advances which evolved with the development of the axle, the metal axis on which the wheels of the vehicle turned.

Fig. 293. This wartime photograph shows all the metal parts required for a military vehicle, one of 1,100 built at Swindon for the First World War. Fifty water carts were also produced, together with a vast number of posts and pegs for picketing the horses. In this particular case the underframe has been made from wood, probably for economical reasons, but many later Great Western vehicles had underframes either strengthened with metal or constructed so that load bearing areas were entirely metal.

Joiners cut the timbers to the required lengths and

Fig. 293

screwed or bolted them to the prepared underframe of the vehicle. Items such as screws, bolts, hinges and washers were all made by the metal workers within the system.

Wheelwrights prepared wheels to a set pattern or size according to the type of vehicle they were to fit. In this picture, *Fig. 294*, wheels are stacked in the yard according to size and appear to be new wheels. There is no evidence of broken tyres or broken spokes which would be evident if the wheels were ready to be scrapped.

Fig. 295. Another picture taken during the war effort is of the wheelshop where hundreds of 'artillery pattern' wheels were made to fit the army vehicles. Sections of felloe and spokes can be seen lying on the ground immediately behind the wheel in the foreground. The personnel have obviously been asked to leave the shop while the photographs were taken. Normally, during daylight hours the building would have been a hive of activity.

As the carman's seat was upgraded from plain plank wood to an upholstered, padded seat, so the trimmer or upholsterer was required to provide the cushion on the seat of a goods or parcel vehicle. His work had formerly been mainly on the interior of company omnibuses, and of course inside railway carriages where leather fittings were used before the introduction of hard-wearing fabrics.

Fig. 296. In the foreground of this busy scene are stacks of roughly sawn shafts after the wood has been steamed to the correct shape. The wood will be turned to produce the smooth finish that was needed next to the horse's flanks. Apart from the shafts, many other items are being processed for use in road vehicles and railway carriages.

The making of the pole for a pair horse vehicle was a much simpler operation. Notes contained on some of the detailed scale drawings show the position of the various metal attachments to be found on such a pole. The end

Fig. 294

Fig. 295

Fig. 296

which is attached to the vehicle was often plated with metal to strengthen it. A pin secured the pole to the futchells or pieces of wood which protruded centrally from the drawbar. At the other end or 'head' of the pole, was a metal cone protecting the wood. On either side a ring was welded to which the pole chains could be secured. These enabled the horses to hold the vehicle back when travelling downhill, or to slow the vehicle down when required. The height of the pole was most important and this may explain the unorthodox position of attachment on some vehicles with low floor levels. For horses standing about 16 hands, the head of the pole needs to be about 3 ft off the ground and be about 9 ft in length from the drawbar or splinter bar to the pole head. If the pole was much lower it was not beyond the capabilities of a young horse to actually get his leg over it, with catastrophic results! A pole that was too long or short resulted in adverse pressure on the collar.

Teams of four horses driven in a pole vehicle were arranged so that the 'wheelers' or pair nearest the vehicle were harnessed in the normal way before two additional horses, the 'leaders' were harnessed to bars suspended from a hook or 'crab' on the end of the pole. The 'crab' was made by the smiths and could be bolted on to the metal sheath of the polehead. A leather strap closed the gap between the tip of the hook and the pole. When buckled, the strap prevented the bars from jumping out of place when the vehicle was moving.

Leader bars were made from narrow staves of wood, turned and tapered at the ends and attached to each other by chain links. The main bar was nearly 3 ft 6 in long and was attached to the pole head by the crab. The two small bars were suspended from either end of this main bar. The traces of the leading horses were attached to the end of these smaller bars by hooks or slips and their drawing power transferred back to the vehicle down the pole to which the main leader bar was attached. It was thought that the two smaller bars were an unnecessary refinement, but it was quickly proved that if one horse pulled harder, a single bar tilted forward on that side resulting in one horse with sore shoulders and one lazy horse!

The traces were attached to the vehicle by various means. Heavy working horses used traces made of chain which had a hook at the end. The chain passed round a bar attached to the front of the vehicle and then hooked back onto a link when the correct tension had been measured. Slightly more sophisticated traces were made of leather which was much more comfortable against the flanks of the horse, with only a few links of chain and a hook at the end to afford adjustability. Later traces were made entirely of leather which had a keyhole slot cut into the leather a few inches from the end. 'Pigtails' or corkscrew-shaped hooks were fashioned by the smiths and bolted to the drawbar of the vehicle. The trace was then twisted slightly before being hooked onto the pigtail, counteracted by the twist of the hook so that the trace lay flat against the side of the horse.

Throughout the construction the various stages had been inspected and approved before it was moved into the painters' shop. Lettering was added acccording to the style selected by the manager of the Road Vehicles Department. The reader will no doubt have noticed the many types of lettering on the sides and rear of vehicles. A number was painted on the vehicle, together with its weight and recommended maximum load. The vehicle number was then branded onto the shafts or pole before it finally entered service.

Harness

Harness for Great Western Railway horses was initially made by commercial harness-makers at a cost of approximately £6 per set in 1850. By the late 1880s, the Midland Railway had not only taken the lead with harness-making at their Derby Works, but also had the largest number of working horses in their employ.

The GWR employed harness makers at Hockley and later at the Mint, but these men, frequently ex-army saddlers, mainly carried out repairs and renovations to the larger items such as collars. These men also made artificial limbs for wounded servicemen when they were not working on repairs.

Each horse required a set of harness, according to the type of work and the type of vehicle that would be involved. Most important was the collar. This was a stuffed leather pad which fitted snugly round the horse's neck, resting on the front part of the shoulders when the animal is pulling forwards or 'in draught'. The straw was pushed into the collar with an iron tool called a collar fork, 'plugging' it to the correct shape. A groove in the collar holds the hames in position, and it is to these metal pieces that the traces are attached. The curve of the

Fig. 297

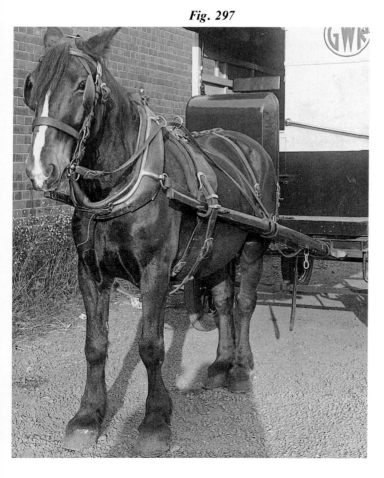

hames must fit the collar exactly otherwise they will alter the shape of the collar causing the shoulders to become sore and may even slip out of the groove completely. Most of the GWR collars were intended for use on large, well muscled animals and were wide, 'straight' collars, lined with serge or woollen material in order to absorb the sweat. Lighter collars were made for parcel ponies and these were slightly more shaped or 'bent' in style. Two brass rings attached to the hames guided the reins towards each side of the bit.

In the late 19th Century a Birmingham company introduced a hollow steel collar which was supposed to fit all sizes and shapes of horses, adjusted by means of springs which also absorbed sudden jolts. The surface next to the horse's skin was galvanized with zinc which has medicinal properties. A spring at the bottom or throat of the collar undid to allow the collar to be placed round the neck of the horse before being re-secured in position. These collars were not popular and after a short period, all new GWR horses were once again fitted with standard leather collars.

When a collar had been fitted to a particular horse, his number was stamped onto the leather at the top so that he would always wear and work in the same collar. This reduced the risk of galls and sore shoulders.

Fig. 297. A horse which is to be driven between shafts wears a leather saddle which is a flat pad through which the broad back strap passes, buckled on each side to a narrower belly band and girth. Small chains or leather straps shaped into a loop hang from either side of the back pad and support the shafts. On the upper surface of the pad there are two rings or terrets through which the reins pass.

A horse which was required to pull a heavy vehicle, wore a saddle which was larger and generally more robustly built. If the load was unbalanced a considerable weight could be transferred to the horse's back via the shafts. The heavier saddle was therefore built in a slightly arched shape to avoid pressure on the backbone. Across the centre of the saddle a wooden groove accommodated a chain back band instead of the lighter leather strap used for vehicles such as the lighter parcel carts, which had the tugs attached for taking the weight of the shafts. Short chains to the collar prevented the saddle slipping forward when eating from a nose bag.

The breeching gear is made up of four leather pieces. A strap attached to the rear edge of the saddle passes down the centre of the horse's back and divided into two just above the tail. A crupper or leather loop passed round the tail, thereby preventing the saddle from moving forwards. A narrow strap crosses the quarters, passing through a guide on the upper surface of the back strap. This is called the quarter strap and can be split into two when used with pole vehicles. A wide leather strap passes round the bottom or quarters of the horse and is attached to the ends of the quarter straps before being attached to the metal dee on the shafts. The breeching gear prevents the cart from running forward when going down hills. The horse is trained to take the weight and pressure of the vehicle on its rear end in this situation.

Traces are broad leather bands clipped, hooked or sewn to a ring on the side of the hames. They pass back to the drawbar of the vehicle. Many commercial traces, while being mainly made of leather which is more comfortable along the side of the horse's flank, had a section of chain at the end to make adjustment easier. In several photographs however, it can be seen that the entire trace is chain, particularly when a pole vehicle is being pulled by a team of horses.

Most important, the bridle. Made up of at least seven pieces of leather, adjusted to fit by means of buckles, the majority of driving bridles have blinkers attached to the cheek straps. The bit is suspended at the bottom of these straps and has rings to which the reins are attached after passing through the terrets on the back pad or saddle and those on the hames fastened round the collar.

Lastly, the reins are usually $\frac{7}{8}$ in or 1 in wide strips of leather, spliced to extend to approximately 12 ft in length.

When harnessed to a pole vehicle some different harness is required. The back pad or saddle still has two terrets for the reins but there are no tugs for shafts. The traces hook on to the hame rings as for a single horse, but instead of passing directly back to the vehicle, they are interrupted by being attached to a ring on the back strap. This ring acts as a communal anchoring point for the belly band, the two parts of the trace, the back band, and the breeching gear which cannot be attached to the pole on the outer side.

Short pole chains or pole straps attached to rings on the end of the pole and to the throat of the collar prevent the vehicle from runnng too far forward when going down hill. In some cases, breeching gear is not worn and this is the only method of holding the vehicle back.

Pair reins would be rather complicated if two single horse sets were used. The reins are therefore 'coupled', or joined so that the driver only has two lengths in his hand. A draught rein passes through the terrets to the outside of the horses' bits, and a coupling rein to the inside. Thus the left hand rein on both horses are joined above the horses' quarters as are the right hand reins. The buckle can be seen in the photograph, *Fig. 298*, about three feet in front of the driver's hands, well away from any point where the buckle could catch on any other piece of harness or terret. Many pairs of horses were skilfully matched and worked together for many years.

Although the vehicle in this photograph is similar, the load must have been increased to require a third horse to be added in front of the pair harnessed to this pole vehicle. Very simple harness has been used, with no breeching gear. A light saddle fitted snugly, with its own girth and the same anchorpoint for the backband, belly band and trace can be seen clearly. Note that the leaders traces are attached to a bar suspended from the crab on the end of the pole. The leader's effort is therefore transmitted directly down the pole to the vehicle, not to the two horses behind him.

The rein is attached to the leader's bit and passes through the terrets on his own harness in the normal way before passing through an additional pair of terrets on the outside of the wheelers' bridles. From there it goes through a centre terret in the middle of the backpads and up to the driver's hands, together with the coupled reins of the team. It is not coupled to the team's reins because there are occasions when the leader turns before the wheelers in order to pull the vehicle round a sharp corner.

Fig. 299. Note the pair in this photograph are wearing bridles without blinkers and that a crab, a curl of metal attached to the leading point of the pole, is available should a further pair of horses be added to this team.

Fig. 298

Fig. 300. A team of four horses are harnessed with two sets of reins coupled over the quarters of each pair so that the driver has four reins in his hands, two from the leaders and two from the wheelers. This vehicle has a pair of double shafts with a chain passing over the groove of the wheelers' heavy saddles. The chain traces of the leaders are attached to a 'D' fixture on the shafts with large hooks. The quarter straps are modified and split into two in order to give more support to the traces and so prevent sagging when the vehicle is stationary.

Additional horses placed in front of a team of four transferred their effort to the vehicle via bars suspended beneath the collars of the horses behind them. These lead bars, similar to the one used in the team of three (***Fig. 298***) kept the traces the correct distance apart and prevented undue sagging.

Fig. 299

Fig. 300

Harness and Putting To

The same principles apply whether the horse is to be driven by itself or with other horses.

The collar is put on first so that the widest part passes over the sensitive skin around the horse's eyes. The hames are also fastened in the groove while the collar is still upside-down. It is then turned round, in the direction that the mane falls, and placed in the correct position. Next the pad, backstrap and crupper, which are often left as one unit, are placed centrally down the back of the horse. The backband is usually left threaded through the back pad and one end of the belly band is also attached, so that there can be rather a complicated bundle of harness to be laid on the horse's back. Not forgetting that many drivers also leave the breeching gear threaded through the guide on the backstrap. Having put all the straps in their relevant places, checking that the hair beneath them is laying in the correct direction, the bridle can be put on and the traces buckled to the hames and laid carefully over all the other harness on the horse's back. The reins were threaded through the terrets, attached to the rings of the bit and the excess reins bundled neatly under the backstrap. This method or variations of it have been used since horses were first used commercially and is still used today.

As most of the Great Western vehicles were too heavy for them to be pulled up to the horse, the horse was backed carefully between the shafts. The carman or driver was responsible for both the harnessing and putting to of his horse, but was assisted by the van lad. As the horse backed between the raised shafts, they were guided through the tugs. The straps of the breeching gear were then fastened to the 'D' on the shafts and the belly band was tightened sufficiently to prevent the shafts rising if the load became unbalanced.

The traces were taken down from the horse's back and threaded between the belly band and the girth, parallel to the shafts, through trace carriers if they were used on the quarterstraps and so to the vehicle where they were attached after checking that the leather or chain was as flat as possible against the horse's sides. The carman then gathered up the reins and mounted while the van lad held the horse's head.

Training of a Driving Horse

The Great Western Railway Company purchased most of its horses from reputable breeders and only occasionally from horse fairs.

Those concerned with the training of the horses used several methods to achieve the end product – a biddable power source. Horses are intelligent animals and respond to patience and kindness. Preliminary training usually began when the horse was between two and three years old, before it had realised is full potential strength.

Having been taught to walk and trot beside the trainer while wearing a headcollar, the youngster progressed to wearing a roller to simulate a backpad or saddle. A long rein was attached to the headcollar and the horse driven round the trainer in a big circle in order to teach it the basic commands of 'walk on', 'trot on' and 'halt' or 'whoa there'.

It is at this point that all similarity with the modern patient methods of training cease. When the horse was more or less fully grown, possibly at four years old, it was forcibly harnessed alongside an older, steady horse in a cart with extra long shafts. The pupil horse was dragged along or pulled back by the other horse obeying the driver's commands. Gradually, all but the most stubborn horses learnt how to pull a cart!

Eventually the pupil horse was harnessed to a standard cart on its own and its performance checked until it worked satisfactorily.

The GWR Horse Inspector bought horses that were five or six years old, already broken to harness. They were taken by rail to Hockley where they were stabled separately from the regular working horses until they had been checked, both for health and efficiency. Any animal proved unsatisfactory on either count, was returned to the vendor.

When the horse had passed all the necessary tests it was allocated and sent to its new home, carrying its Great Western number firmly branded on one front hoof. Records were kept as to the loads carried and ailments suffered by each horse on the system. When a horse was past its best working years it was sent to a sale and the cycle began all over again with a new horse.

Van Lad to Carman in 20 Years!

A van lad could start work in the Goods Department under the Cartage Manager when he was 14 years old. He worked approximately twelve hours a day for a wage of 8s (40p) per week. It was his job to hold the horse's head during putting to, assist with checking the load at the station loading bay, clean the harness, and generally do what the carman asked him to do.

Before the majority of London horses were stabled at the Mint, it was also the van lad's job to collect the horse from its rented stable and take it to Paddington in time to begin work. They were not allowed to ride the horses and could be dismissed for doing so. The reader should bear in mind that while the horses used by the GWR were broken to harness, very few of them were broken to be ridden! By the time the lad reached 16 years old, he could earn 10s (50p) a week. It was to this age that the starting age for a van lad or guard was raised, as by 1883 it had become clear that many of the youngsters could not cope with the work. Parcel van guards were supposed to be of smart appearance with pressed jackets and trousers and well-shined shoes. A cap donated by the Company, completed his outfit but by the time he had finished cleaning the harness before starting work, his clothes were no longer neat and he feared relegation to the ranks of the goods van guards whose appearance was of less concern. Eventually the Board employed harness cleaners to overcome the problem. At the Mint stable, two men and a foreman, cleaned 25 sets each every day.

Van guards stood, perched or sat on the rear of the vehicle, primarily to prevent theft. Although set routes were recommended for crossing London from one station to another, or from Paddington to the docks, there were times when the vans were driven down less salubrious streets where theft was more commonplace.

As the van guard neared 20 years of age he was initiated into the art of driving a single horse, starting on the quieter roads or even within the station precincts. It took several years to progress to driving a pair and eventually a team around the streets of the town. Although normally attached to a particular depot, the van could be transferred to other local stations on a temporary basis and his training interrupted.

When the vehicle was out on the road, it was the van guard's job to jump down from the rear and unload the freight or parcel into the customer's premises, obtaining a signature for the same. Large items were manhandled down a pair of skids, boards slanting down from the back of the vehicle. When not in use the skids were stored in carriers on the side of the wagon, or just stacked on the floor of the wagon, or slung underneath.

The route back to the station passed collection points and items for onward conveyance were picked up and taken to the Goods Inwards bay. Several such trips were made during a working day, sometimes using a fresh horse in the afternoon. A bonus was paid to drivers who moved more than the minimum daily requirement of traffic, although the amount that each of his horses moved was carefully noted on record cards kept at the horse keeper's office.

It was also the van lad's job to get fresh water for a horse that needed a drink while out on duty. In the evening he assisted with the removal of the horse from the cart and handed it over to the stableman to be taken to its stable.

As the lad grew more experienced and older, he would be offered the occasional relief work if a carman was off sick. Whether he was entitled to the same pay as a carman is not recorded! Gradually, the senior carmen either died or left the Company to be replaced by the oldest and most experienced van guards, but it was rare to find a fully fledged carman under the age of 40. Most drivers supplied their own whips as a mark of their seniority and comparatively high wages. A quote from Underhill's *Driving for Pleasure* published in 1896 states that, "The town coachman must be a man of experience, and reasonable wages paid to such a man will often save a large expenditure in paint and repairs. The thorough coachman can be distinguished at a glance, and it is unfortunate that they are so few and far between".

However, the Great Western carman or driver was a man of considerable importance and standing in the staff hierarchy. As seen in many of the photographs in this book, he is standing or sitting somewhat aloof while his van guard or the goods porters rush round performing the menial tasks.

Great Western Horses at Shows

Inter-stable competitions to find the best horse had been part of the Great Western Board's method of encouraging the care of their horses. This undated photograph, *Fig. 301*, is of a gelding which won the Best Great Western Horse competition. Standing at over 16 hands, this well muscled cross-bred horse has been lavishly prepared to have his photograph taken. Notice especially the GWR boss at the end of the browband of the bridle and the braiding of the mane and tail.

Fig. 302. This well-matched pair were photographed outside Queen Victoria's waiting room at Windsor station in 1948. The turnout was on its way to the Windsor Horse Show having earlier arrived by horsebox and carriage truck. The pair were probably entered in the Trade Turnout (Heavy) section. Although the Great Western Railway had been absorbed into British Railways on Nationalisation, many of the individual railway companies still showed turnouts in their original liveries.

Fig. 303. This photograph of entry No. 48 on the left of the picture, shows the horse brasses on the brow. Unusually, two wheeler terrets are shown protruding from the bridle. Normally only present on bridles used by the wheelers of a team of four horses, the coupled rein of the leading horses passing back through a wheeler terret on the outside of the bridle before passing back to the centre terret on the same horse's saddle, and thence to the driver's hands.

No. 47 in single harness, may be a mare. Leather traces have been used, but apart from them, the harness is more or less ordinary working harness. Notice how the mare's forelock has been passed through a triangular gap between the browband and the narrow reinforced leather bands which keep the blinkers at the correct angle. The mare's number, '234', can be seen clearly, branded onto her front offside hoof.

Fig. 301

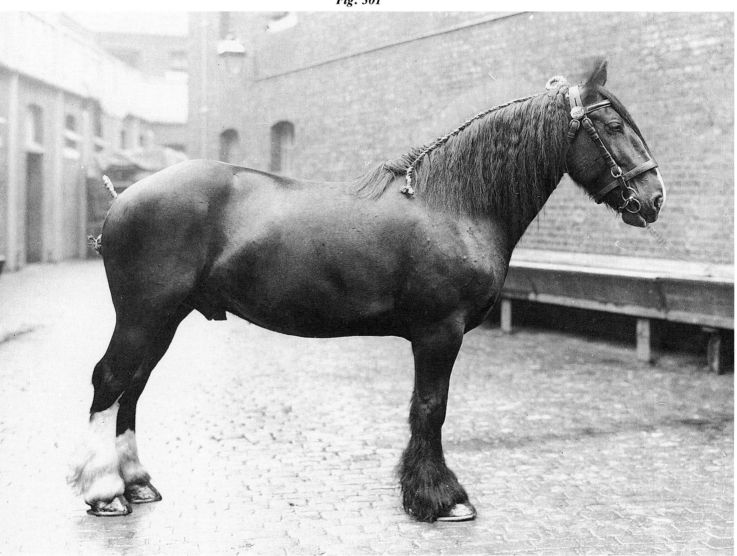

Fig. 302

Fig. 303

Fig. 304

Fig. 305

Fig. 306

Figs 304 and *305.* Two views of turnouts in British Railways Western Region colours after Nationalisation of the constituent railway companies. The venue is once again Windsor Horse Show. The van lad, a venerable gentleman of mature years, holds the horses' heads while the judges and the driver pose for the photograph. Note the feed bags on the rear of the wagon.

Other shows were conducted in London. The annual Van Horse Parade was run by the Van Horse Society to stimulate interest in the care and condition of the 6,000 or so horses used on the streets of London. The RSPCA awarded prizes for horses with undocked tails.

Fig 306. In 1949 the Royal Agricultural Society of England Show was held at Shrewsbury. The front of the station has been decorated, leaving the reader in no doubt as to the importance of the occasion. Notice that two horse-drawn vehicles are still in evidence outside the parcels office. Despite the introduction of the pneumatic tyre, both vehicles have earlier wood and metal wheels.